To know the world around you is to see the beauty of it.

- AMG

Our mission is to educate the public about mushrooms, their identification, various uses, and scientific, culinary and environmental value, whilst prioritizing safety; and to promote advancement in the science of mycology.

Moreso, our goal is to ignite enthusiasm about the fungal kingdom of life and engender a deep appreciation for its role in the web of life on our planet.

This book is designed to be a comprehensive guide to the new or experienced forager, as an aid in foraging, identification and harvesting the edible wild mushrooms found in the state of Alabama.

We believe Alabama and the neighboring states of the American Southeast present the most biologically diverse tapestry of flora and fungi in the whole of the United States. We lament the inability to present a comprehensive publication on all edible species of fungi in this region. But that book would be a colossus which would require several dissertations' worth of testing and documentation. Therefore, this book is limited to the list of approved species of edible mushrooms for the state (as of the date of this writing).

Alabama is one of the most underrepresented regions of fungal documentation. Several organizations are working together to correct this by leveraging social media, mobile phone apps, and citizen science to provide the framework necessary to document, store, and genetically sequence fungi to create comprehensive taxonomic studies. If you are interested in contributing to these processes, please reach out to the Alabama Mushroom Society.

Please be aware that the species' names in this book may change over time as mushrooms are re-classified taxonomically. These name changes will in no way alter the actual mushrooms or their general descriptions as we identify them here. In some cases, we will even describe mushrooms as groups (typically species groups within a given genus) to prepare for those inevitable re-classifications. For example, the genus *Cantharellus* is ripe for these taxonomic changes, though we may have to wait some time to see them.

Importantly, the approved mushroom list maintained by the state (Pg. 25) is somewhat open to interpretation insomuch as some species' names are no longer taxonomically correct (i.e., *Hydnum repandum*), or individual species have even been shifted from one genus to another (i.e., *Cantharellus ignicolor* > *Craterellus ignicolor*). The goal is to give you the most recent information possible in the hopes that the commercial picker will pass on this knowledge to their clients/consumers.

This book will rely heavily on mycological jargon. This may seem intimidating, but the reliance on these terms is to provide a common precise language. However, common names and terms will be utilized whenever possible.

Our goal is to provide a highly visual guide to the relevant features of those edible fungi which are approved for buying and selling in the state of Alabama, as well as their look-alikes such that the average forager can confidently identify each. For these purposes, a picture is worth more than a thousand words – but finding these mushrooms, handling them, and comparing to keys is worth far more. Therefore, we encourage use of this book as an authoritative component for education but encourage readers to gain skills and confidence by practical application. In other words: get out into nature and explore!

Notes.
While this book is designed to aid in the Alabama Wild Mushroom Sales certification course, it will only cover the portion relevant to foraging, identifying and harvesting the edible wild mushrooms on the list of approved species.

Since this book and related course work was commissioned by the Alabama Mushroom society the term "*we*" will be used frequently to delineate those views held by the society and "*I*" will be used to describe those opinions or experiences held by the author which may also be held by the society.

How to use this Book

This book is a written and pictorial guide to the edible mushrooms of Alabama. It is designed to be an easily accessible reference book and thorough introduction to easily identifiable edible mushrooms. This book is an adjunct to the Alabama Mushroom Society's certification course for the commercial harvest and sales of wild harvested mushrooms. For the purpose of learning we encourage you to read through the introduction and then work through the individual mushroom descriptions to follow. Each major mushroom group will have a detailed description as well as a summary preface for easy reference. It is intended to be the first book of many to cover an ever-expanding list of mushroom groups. The writing of this book will be a combination of casual but excitedly explained facts and will include more exact language used to explain wonderful features and fabulous phenomena.

The book will begin with a crash course, to be considered a "fungi and mushrooms 101" type of offering. Next the book discusses which of those features is relevant and how to know when. Included are easy to understand figures and simplified material. Features and figures will be first used for sample identifications using toxic mushrooms every forager should become familiar with.

Finally, there is an extensive list of edible species or groups of mushrooms which are relevant for the commercial sales certification. These descriptions will be grouped into related mushrooms with similar features to enhance those characteristics which separate them. Each group will be followed by a list of look-alikes with clearly defined distinctions. The goal is for this approach to make identification of these major mushrooms groups intuitive and to provide an easy-to-use reference.

Of course, no book can cover such a large scope of information without becoming overwhelming. However, this book will provide the reader with the competence and confidence to find, identify and harvest these mushrooms. Additional resources are available and include the following online repositories:

https://mushroomobserver.org/
https://www.inaturalist.org/
Both websites are designed for the documentation of fungi or organisms, respectively, by anyone and everyone., and include expansive photographs and even maps of documented species. These resources are highly recommended and documented contributions are strongly encouraged.

References for general information or as secondary sources:

Extensive information was gathered using the website www.mushroomexpert.com, curated by Dr. Michael Kuo, especially for ecological descriptions such as host trees, descriptive terminology, and to compare to similar species. Extensive information was gathered using the website www.mushroomobserver.org, primarily as a means to determine ecological descriptions such as growth habits or global occurrence of taxa and their allies, as well as updated taxonomic nomenclature, common misidentifications, and to verify the occurrence of minute features.

Several books listed below were used as primary sources to verify general information or as secondary sources to find original/primary sources of information. While they are rarely cited directly in this work, I feel they must be given more credit than simply being listed in the reference section. Thus, they are listed here as additional sources of information with my highest recommendations for the interested reader.

By Thomas Læssøe and Jens H. Petersen – Fungi of Temperate Europe (volumes 1-2).
By David Aurora – Mushrooms Demystified
By Britt A. Bunyard and Jay Justice – Amanitas of North America
By Alan E. Bessette, Arleen R. Bessette, and David P. Lewis – Mushrooms of the Gulf Coast States
By Alan E. Bessette, David B. Harris, and Arleen R. Bessette – Milk Mushrooms of North America
By Alan E. Bessette, Arleen R. Bessette, and Michael W. Hopping – A Field Guide to Mush-

rooms of the Carolinas
By Alan E. Bessette, Dianna G. Smith, and Arleen R. Bessette – Polypores and Simialr Fingi of Eastern and Central North America

By Robert M. Hallock – A Mushroom Word Guide

Table of Contents

'**Fungi**' is a term used to describe an entire kingdom of life, alongside Plantae, Animalia, Protizoa, and Chromista which is situated in the *Empire* (or *superkingdom*) Eukaryota (separate from Prokaryota). While the geneticists may squabble over exactly the best way to divide life, even at these super-classifications, we're going to narrow our focus and use **taxa** (taxonomical classifications) at the levels below the fungal subkingdom *Dikarya* which include Division, Class, Order, Family, Genus, Species, and sometimes varieties/subspecies.

The diagram on the right contains almost every fungi (classified to genus) covered in this book as well as their taxanomical relationships. The further up the classification chain (from Genus to Family to Order, and so on) one must go to connect any two fungi, the more distantly they are related. These relationships are important since classifications are typically made based on morphological characteristics (though in modern times genetic sequencing is used to fine-tune these relationships). Shared morphological (relating to the structure or form of things) characteristics (see page 6) are sometimes obvious (ex. most of Order *Polyporales* are woody/corky in texture and have pores) and sometimes require specialty equipment to observe (ex. *Bondezarwia* has ornamented spores which can be observed under a microscope to closely resemble *Russula* spores, though the structure of the fruitbody is extremely different).

For the purposes of identifying the fungi in this book, some of these relationships will be much more useful than others. We will reference these relationships for you and you may find that turning to this diagram is helpful.

What exactly is a mushroom?

There is actually some debate over this particular definition but to keep these definitions simple, this book will define the spore-generating (sexual or asexual) fruitbody of a dikaryote (Basidiomycota and Ascomycota) fungus as a mushroom.

If you have not heard the term **fruitbody** before, it means the temporary reproductive structure that emerges from the actual organism - which is itself comprised of a mass of cellular threads referred to as the mycelium (hyphae are the cells, mycelium are the threads you can see by eye).

This book will emphasize the term fruitbody because it better paints the picture of the mushroom as a fruit of the organism - somewhat synonymous to a fruit on a tree. In most cases, the fruit can be removed from the tree (or the mycelial mass in this case) without damaging the organism.

A classic toadstool shaped mushroom

Introduction

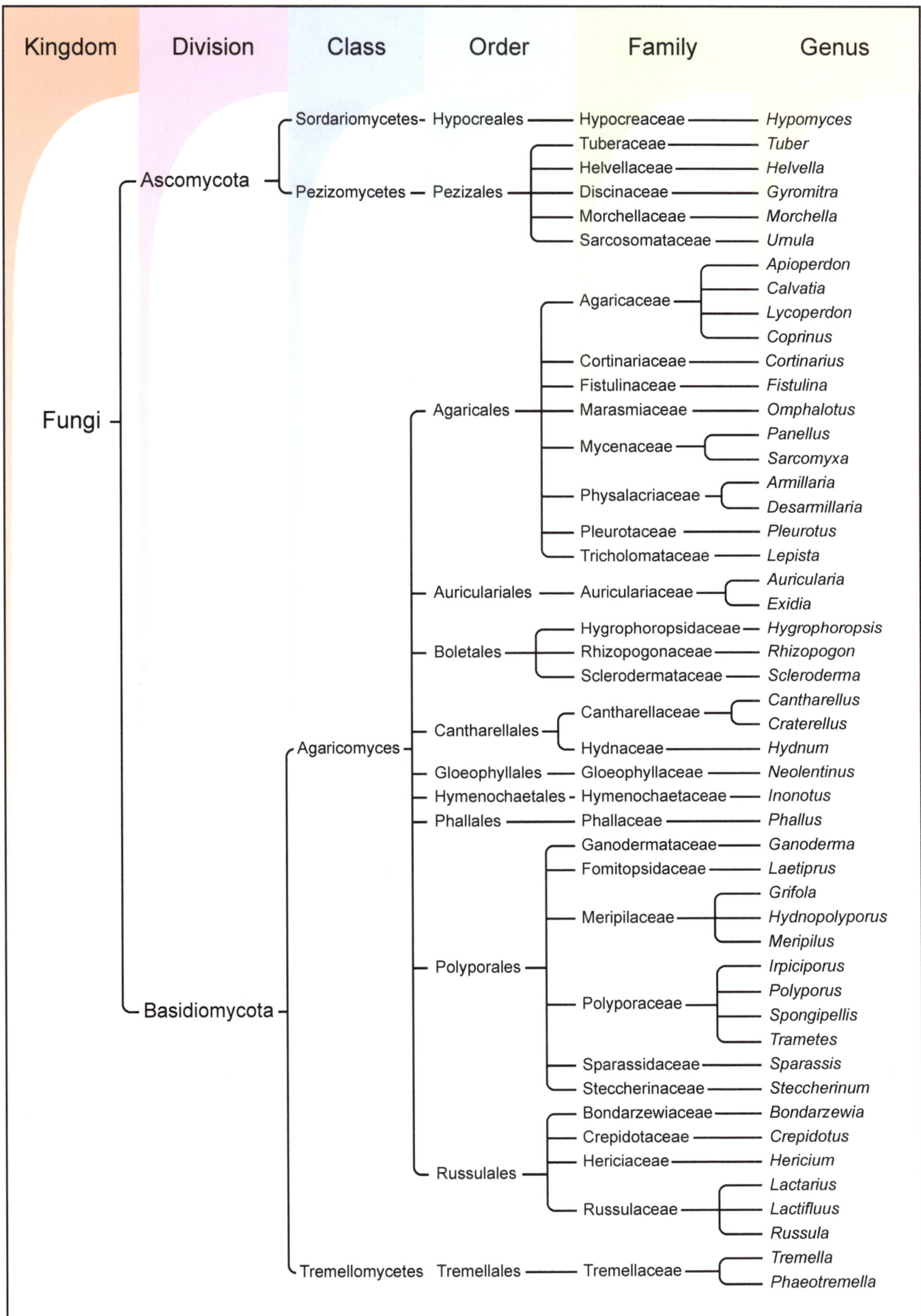

Kingdom	Division	Class	Order	Family	Genus
Fungi	Ascomycota	Sordariomycetes	Hypocreales	Hypocreaceae	*Hypomyces*
		Pezizomycetes	Pezizales	Tuberaceae	*Tuber*
				Helvellaceae	*Helvella*
				Discinaceae	*Gyromitra*
				Morchellaceae	*Morchella*
				Sarcosomataceae	*Urnula*
	Basidiomycota	Agaricomyces	Agaricales	Agaricaceae	*Apioperdon*
					Calvatia
					Lycoperdon
					Coprinus
				Cortinariaceae	*Cortinarius*
				Fistulinaceae	*Fistulina*
				Marasmiaceae	*Omphalotus*
				Mycenaceae	*Panellus*
					Sarcomyxa
				Physalacriaceae	*Armillaria*
					Desarmillaria
				Pleurotaceae	*Pleurotus*
				Tricholomataceae	*Lepista*
			Auriculariales	Auriculariaceae	*Auricularia*
					Exidia
			Boletales	Hygrophoropsidaceae	*Hygrophoropsis*
				Rhizopogonaceae	*Rhizopogon*
				Sclerodermataceae	*Scleroderma*
			Cantharellales	Cantharellaceae	*Cantharellus*
					Craterellus
				Hydnaceae	*Hydnum*
			Gloeophyllales	Gloeophyllaceae	*Neolentinus*
			Hymenochaetales	Hymenochaetaceae	*Inonotus*
			Phallales	Phallaceae	*Phallus*
			Polyporales	Ganodermataceae	*Ganoderma*
				Fomitopsidaceae	*Laetiprus*
				Meripilaceae	*Grifola*
					Hydnopolyporus
					Meripilus
				Polyporaceae	*Irpiciporus*
					Polyporus
					Spongipellis
					Trametes
				Sparassidaceae	*Sparassis*
				Steccherinaceae	*Steccherinum*
			Russulales	Bondarzewiaceae	*Bondarzewia*
				Crepidotaceae	*Crepidotus*
				Hericiaceae	*Hericium*
				Russulaceae	*Lactarius*
					Lactifluus
					Russula
		Tremellomycetes	Tremellales	Tremellaceae	*Tremella*
					Phaeotremella

Mycelium

The mycelium is the actual fungal organism. The size and shape of these mycelial mats ebbs and flows depending on nutrient contents, available water, and competition with other organisms.

You can find mycelium almost anywhere, but the large branching threads as pictured here will be most prominent under damp forest duff or bark on dead or dying trees. This is a sign of life, that conditions are great for fungi to be happily munching away and decaying the forest detritus into more basic components.

Fungi, as multicellular organisms, have individual cells which are more-or-less cylinders connecting to one another to form longer threads. The individual cells and the multicellular thread are both referred to as hyphae. Unlike animals (but like plants) they have both a cell membrane (lipid bilayer, common to all Eukaryotes)) AND a cell wall. The cell wall is not composed of cellulose as in plants, but of chitin – a primary protein that gives strength and rigidity to exoskeletons of crabs and insects. Masses or mats of these hyphae form the bulk of the fungal organism. The mycelium can take on a wide array of textures and appearances, most commonly as cobwebby white nets. The hyphal threads can also form larger cords (mycelial cords) called rhizomorphs (rhizome > root; morph > form = root form) which are apparent in some fungal groups such as the genus *Armillaria* (the honey mushrooms).

Importantly, fungi do not have 'true tissues' like plants and animals do. They do have some specialty cell types but lack clusters of those specialized cell types which are necessary for the survival of the organism as a whole. For example, without lungs, you wouldn't last very long nor would a tree which was removed from its roots. This means that almost any individual cell (or piece of tissue) can be removed from a fungus and be completely viable (able to survive and generate an entirely new organism) on its own. So, tromping through the woods, picking mushrooms indiscriminately, or the like will not damage the fungal organism. However, open wounds do introduce a pathway for pathogens to enter until crusted over - so maybe be gentle.

Mycelial relationships

If as fruitbody is found growing on wood, it is typically safe to assume the fungus is saprobic, meaning that it is decomposing dead or dying wood as the primary source of its nutrition. If you peel back the bark near the fruitbody, you can usually see the mycelium which is pumping water and nutrition into the fruitbody.

If a fruitbody is found growing on another fungus it is safe to assume that it is parasitizing the host mushroom. Though occasionally, it's due to a mutation in which a new fruitbody grows on an already developed one!

Fruitbodies growing from the ground, those of terrestrial origin can very easily be saprobic or mycorrhizal. Saprobic fungi decompose the detritus of the forest floor (or organic matter below the grass line) and some can even ensnare and consume nematodes (check out *Hohenbuehelia petaloides*).

Perhaps more interesting are the relationships which form between mycorrhizal fungi and plants. In these cases, the hyphal threads surround (ectomycorrhizal) or even penetrate (endomycorrhizal) the rootlets of plants. These connected organisms share resources, typically – the fungi provide massive amounts of water as well as odd nutrients and the plants provide sugars and carbohydrates. Since the hyphal threads are so small, the fungi have an exceptional surface area compared to their volume and can take up enormous amounts of water, much more than plant roots could accomplish alone due to their smaller surface area to volume. Conversely, plants produce sugars, a chemical fuel which the fungi desperately want. Plants can provide the sugars at a much cheaper energetic cost to the fungi than these fungi could generate from decomposition alone.

You can follow this relationship in real time by observing the massive flushes of mycorrhizal fungi following longer sunny days when plants begin to send large amounts of sugars to their root systems for storage rather that drawing from these reserves from their winter hibernations. That means in early spring and summer, before the leaves have matured, mycorrhizal fungi will be scarcer. In the late summer and through the fall, those sugars are pumped underground, and mycorrhizal fungi put that chemical energy into motion by fruiting prolifically.

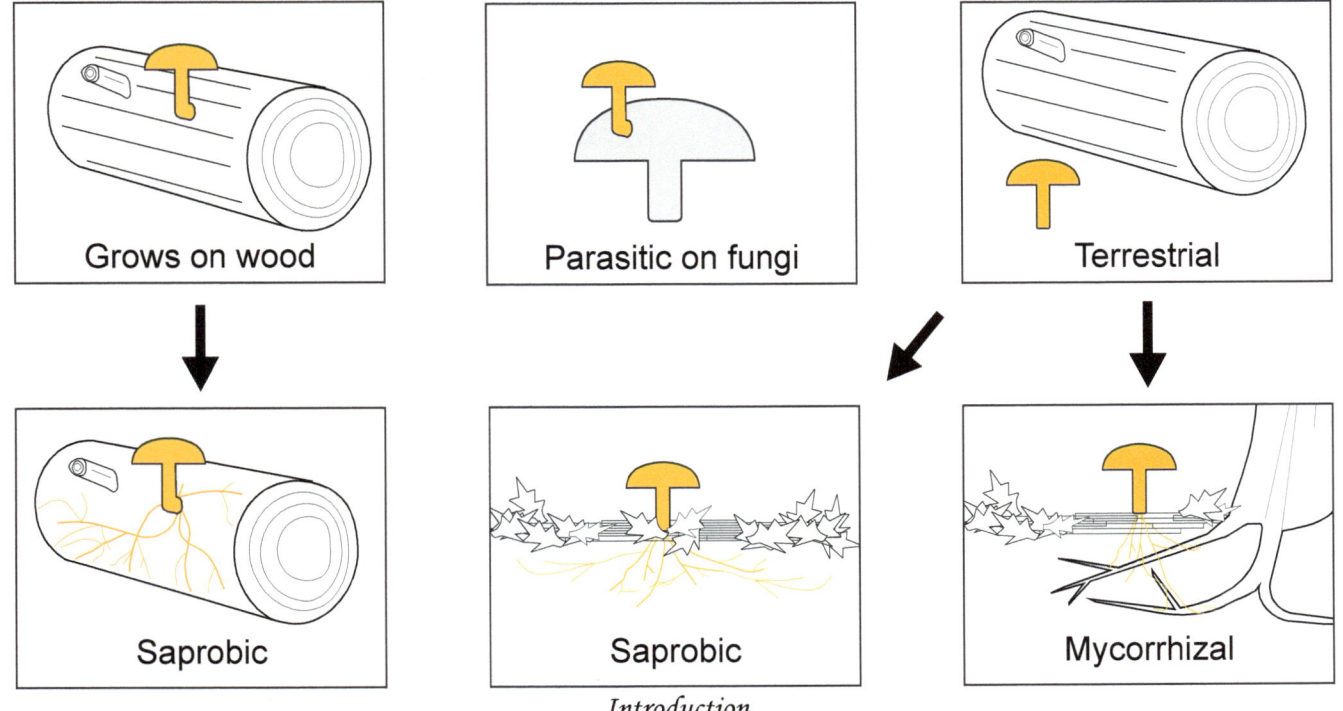

Grows on wood — Parasitic on fungi — Terrestrial

Saprobic — Saprobic — Mycorrhizal

Anatomy of a Mushroom

Mushrooms come in a massive array of shapes and sizes which we can use to identify them. The most familiar shape is that of the <u>toadstool</u>, the cap with a stem. We'll use this as our archetype and discuss variations later.

The mushroom or 'fruitbody' is a reproductive structure, designed to develop and release spores which may develop into offspring.

Gross Structure

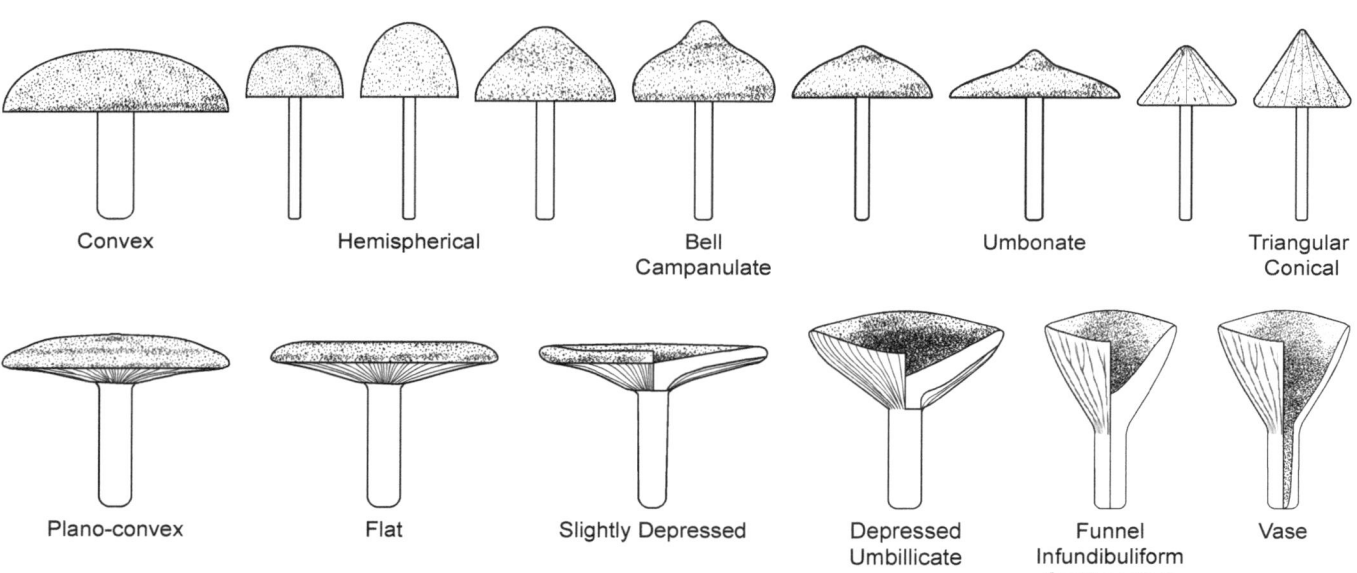

Convex   Hemispherical   Bell Campanulate   Umbonate   Triangular Conical

Plano-convex   Flat   Slightly Depressed   Depressed Umbillicate   Funnel Infundibuliform Cantharelloid   Vase

Cap shapes vary greatly though you may be most familiar with the convex shape typical of store-bought button mushrooms (*Agaricus bisporus*). When we describe a mushroom, we will describe the mature (but not old) specimen's shape. Sometimes the shape of the cap during development can also be helpful but those descriptions will be found with those specific mushrooms. Importantly, mushrooms of a given species often take on a small range of cap shapes. For example *Russula* (see page 170) species are typically described as convex, but you will surely find some that are closer to flat. The toxic *Galerina marginata* is similarly described as convex but may be found with bell-shaped caps - especially as the cap unfurls. In maturity, the umbonate center of *Galerina* is usually lost. In later pages, you will see one or two cap shapes for a given mushrooms but do know that there is some variability based on environmental factors or even small genetic shifts. That said if a mushroom is described as having a 'distinctly (insert feature here)' shape, be wary if your find doesn't match.

As illustrated above, the gross structure of 'toadstools' are typified by 9 primary shapes as seen in profile but many more fall between them. Conical shapes such as in *Conocybe apala* may have curved edges but are typified by the relatively sharp tip compared to hemispherical which have a much more rounded top. Umbonate and Bell shapes have a central 'umbo', the rounded knob or protuberance, and can go so far as to be *papillate* - Latin for nipple like. Typically, these umbonate features are very good identification characteristics. On the other side of convex are those mushrooms with depressions of the center of the cap. A small central depression, akin to a bellybutton is umbillicate while the entire upwards thrust of the cap margin (edge) is better described as a depressed cap. A more extreme depression which takes on a funnel like shape is infundibuliform, or we may use the term cantharelloid. If the central hole/pore goes through most or all of the stipe/stem, we might best describe the shape as a vase.

Structural components

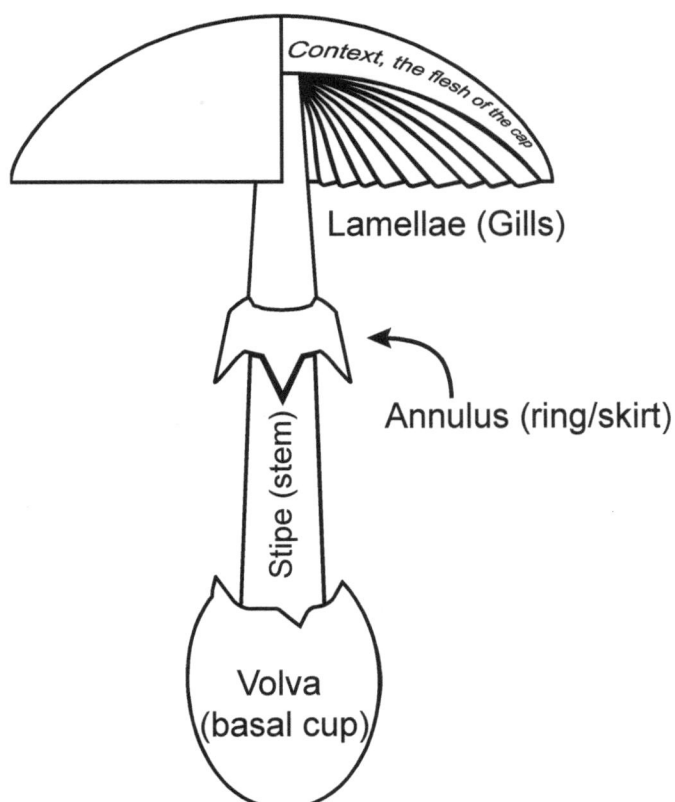

Context, the flesh of the cap

Lamellae (Gills)

Annulus (ring/skirt)

Stipe (stem)

Volva (basal cup)

Hymenium is the name given to the spore bearing surface. It comes in many shapes, but likely most familiar are the gills of a store-bought mushroom. The *Lamellae* (the scientific term for the gills) are a feature seen in the taxonomical Division Basidiomycota (though many other structures exist in this Division) and provide the microscopic *basidia* (the club-shaped cells upon which spores are developed and mature) a large surface areas from which to produce spores. The spaces between the gills also provide an ideal space from which these spores can be dropped, catching the air and hopefully floating to an ideal environment with which to propogate. **Context** is the term used to describe the inner flesh of the mushroom as seen by the naked eye. In other words, the flesh as a whole and not any particular microscopic structure. Specific textures and colors can be important for identification and will be discussed as relevant for each individual mushroom covered. You may also hear the context referred to as the sterile tissue. Like any other organism, fungi have their own immune responses which keep the inner flesh sterile from microorganisms. Though

we can't make any promises about insects. **Stipe** is the technical term for the stem or stalk. This structure supports the cap and provides distance from the growing media such that spores might better catch the currents. **Pileus** is the term used to describe the cap. This term encompases all of the structures which support the spore bearing surface (remember hymenium) above the stipe. Most typically, this includes the context and a superficial cuticle or membrane. **Veil** is a term used to describe two different structures, the *Universal Veil* and the *Partial Veil*. These structures are a membranous sheet of tissue which cover portions of the mushrooms during development. Specifically, the **Universal Veil** covers the entirety of the mushroom during its primordial development, hence the term 'universal'. This structure will only be seen with mushrooms following a determinant growth type of development (see page 8) and is common in the taxonomic family Amanitaceae. As the primordial mushroom is pumped full of water and expands upwards, it will tear through the universal veil. The shape and structure of the cells in this universal veil will determine how robust it is, and how much of it remains when the mushroom reaches maturity. Remaining universal veils are typically seen as a *Volva*, *Latin* for 'womb', which may form a cup or similar bulbous shape at the base of the stipe. These structures are especially important in determining sections in the family Amanitaceae. Much more commonly encountered is the **Partial Veil**, so named for only covering a part of the mushroom, the hymenium. The textures of these veils vary greatly and are typically flimsy or delicate. As the cap expands during the mushroom's development, the partial veil will eventually tear and leave remnants on the margin (edge) of the pileus and/or the connection point of the stipe. These broken partial veils are often referred to as an **Annulus**, *Latin* for 'ring' but also colloquially called a skirt or collar. These partial veil remnants, be they on the stipe or edge of the cap are often useful as an identification characteristic.

How they grow

Since you're unlikely to encounter every mushroom at its peak maturity, I think it prudent to have a general understanding of how mushrooms grow and develop so that you can recognize features and structures at several stages of development. With enough exposure, you can find small features in immature or even very old specimens that will key you into what they should look like in their prime.

There are two primary types of growth of fruitbodies, determinant and indeterminant – and like everything else, these have some overlap.

Determinate growth

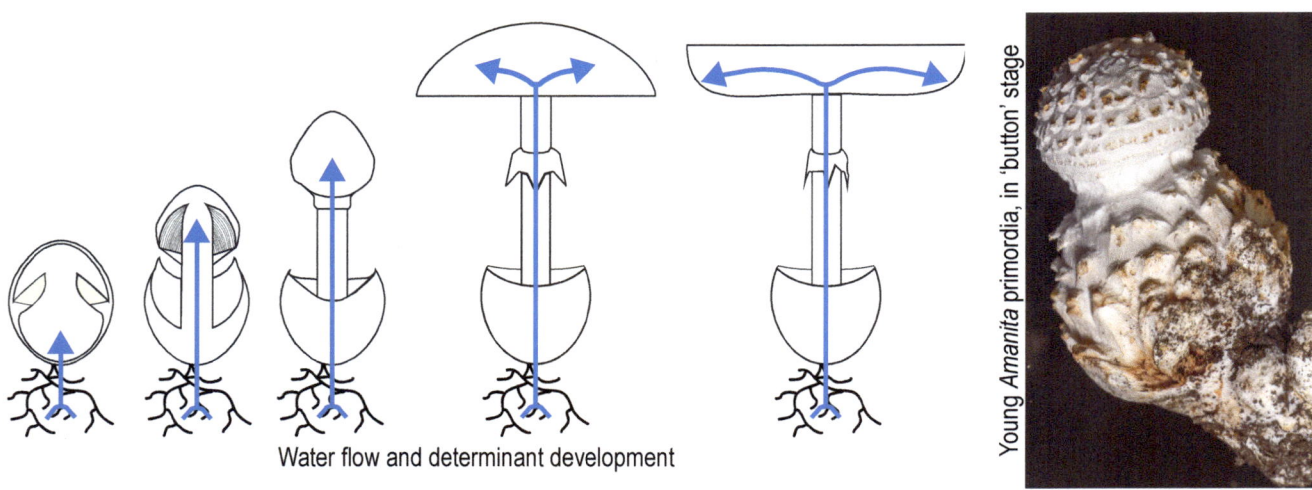

Water flow and determinant development

Young *Amanita* primordia, in 'button' stage

The 'typical toadstool' has a determinant growth pattern which means that most, if not all of the cells which will form the mature fruitbody are developed in the primordial phase and the mycelium simply pump water into the primordial mushroom to inflate it, not dissimilar to a balloon. The expansion of the tissues follows a logical order as water entering from the mycelial mat expands the cells of the stipe, projecting the cap upwards until the stipe is 'full'. If present, this step will tear the universal veil. Next the water can pass into the pileus (cap) expanding the cells of the cap and, if present tear the partial veil. Finally, the osmotic pressures (microscopic water pressures) expands the hymenium, sometimes uplifting the cap.

Why is this important for identification? I can't tell you how many times I (personally) ran into 'conflicting' information while trying to key out a mushroom until I realized that many, if not most of the shapes and features

being described were in some state of flux. The fluidity of these features (such as the shape of a cap) is largely due to genetics, developmental stage, and environmental factors. While genetic variations are largely unpredictable without extensive experience, both developmental stage and environmental factors can be predicted by anyone. If the stipe is short and the cap is rounded or unopened, the specimen is probably immature, whereas a short stipe and an open and depressed cap would indicate a more mature specimen and now the length of the stipe becomes a relevant feature. In these ways you can logic your way into determining which features are likely to match a guidebook and which are outside of those descriptions.

Indeterminate growth

Indeterminant growth is more common to polypores in which an external layer of tissue serves as a growth region in which cells actively proliferate (divide and expand, again and again). As this layer of proliferation expands outwards the fruitbody grows. These regions of growth will ebb and flow with precipitation and the weather and can typically be spotted as some form of zonate striation (rings emanating from the base or connection point of the fruitbody).

The evidence of these rings may be more of less prominent based on the speed at which the fruitbody is developed. For example, *Laetiporus sulfureus* (chicken of the woods, page 105) uses an indeterminant growth pattern but usually develops the bulk of its growth inside of a week and may not have obvious striations. Fruitbodies which better tolerate environmental exposure (especially those with woody or corky texture) may show seasonal or even annual growth as in the pictured Trametes versicolor (turkey tail, page 192).

Oftentimes rapid growth of this type can be observed as a fruitbody which has engulfed debris such as leaves and twigs on its growth path. This phenomenon is referred to as haptomorphosis and is exceedingly common. Though in nature the divide between determinant and indeterminant growth is a blurry line with several fungi utilizing components of both.

Mushrooms using determinant growth can push upwards to form 'shrumps' and in extreme cases rip upwards through asphalt streets!

Hymenial structures

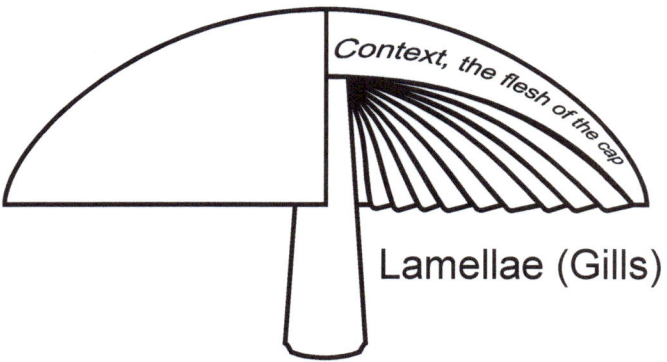
Lamellae (Gills)

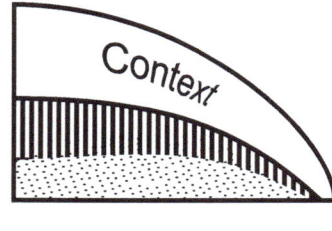
Pores/Tubes

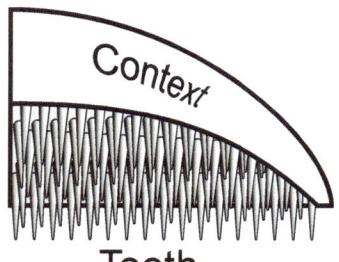
Teeth

The Hymenium is the most important part of a mushroom as it is where the spores are developed and distributed from - the rest of the mushroom is simply support for this critical component of reproduction. The hymenium is attached to the context (if present) with variable durability and may be easy or difficult to remove from the context (try using the flat side of your fingernail to gently push the layers apart). Important identification features of the hymenium are the **depth** of the layer (to the context), and the **attachment** to the stipe.

This structure comes in *many* forms, but I will focus on three main forms **Lamellae** (gills), **Pores** (tiny holes), and **Teeth** (spine-like projections). All of these structures provide a greatly expanded surface area upon which the spores can be developed (most typically found on Basidiomycota, so these structures house the basidia). Furthermore, the structures are protected from the elements by their shaded position under the cap context, yet open to the air so that spores can be dropped by the *trillion*.

You may be most familiar with lamellae as they are present on the store-bought button mushrooms and most mushrooms you may have encountered in your yard. Second most common are the pored mushrooms, those fungi which use holes (or in some cases fused tubes) to form an open sponge from which spores may be deposited. Most uncommon, but certainly not rare, are the toothed mushrooms which you might think of as having inverted tubes - still providing a massive surface area with all of the benefits of pores or gills.

Lamellae (gills)

Pores (tiny holes)

Teeth (spine-like projections)

10   *Anatomy of a Mushroom*

Hymenial characteristics

For the purpose of identification I will focus the discussion of hymenial characteristics to a minimum of those relevant features. However the following pages will focus on the most important characteristics broken down by these three primary hymenial forms. General features to take note of (beyond depth and attachement to stipe) include the precense of a partial veil (also discussed with the stipe), <u>bruising</u> upon contact (while many part of a mushroom may bruise, the hymenium is *often* the most striking), <u>guttation</u> (excretion of liquid without damage) and excretion of liquid (typically a milky-latex) upon damage to the structure.

Fibrous, cobweb-like annulus

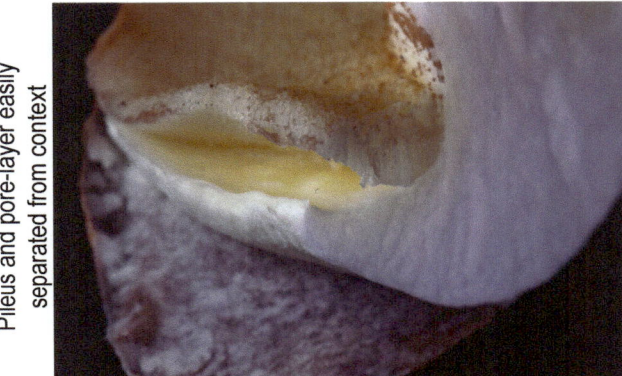

Pileus and pore-layer easily separated from context

Guttation

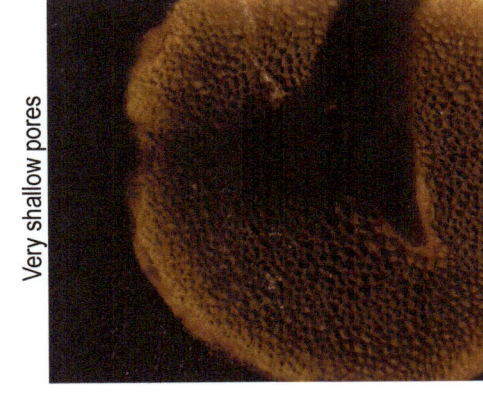

Very shallow pores

Exudation of latex on injury

Oblong, multi-pronged teeth

Hymenial attachments

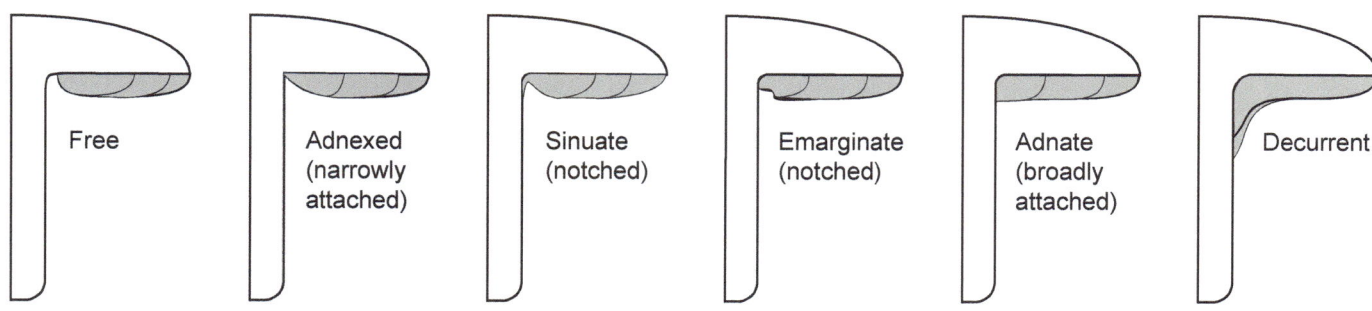

| Free | Adnexed (narrowly attached) | Sinuate (notched) | Emarginate (notched) | Adnate (broadly attached) | Decurrent |

The hymenium, particularly lamellae, have a variety of attachment types. Specifically, the attachment of the lamellae to the stipe is a critical identification feature for many gilled mushrooms. Some mushrooms will have strict lamellar attachment types and others will have a range which may be affected by genetic variability or environmental factors. For example, the genus *Pluteus* is known for having a free lamellar attachment while *Pleurotus* (the oysters) have dramatically decurrent gills. Oftentimes those mushrooms with the more intermediary attachment types may be easily confused with their morphological neighbor. This is especially likely in sub-prime or young specimens in which the attachment is obscured, underdeveloped, torn, or otherwise damaged. For example, an older specimen with emarginate gills may have a cap which over-extends, physically tearing the attachment point to look closer to adnexed or even free. Don't forget that other hymenial surfaces also follow these patterns, but some won't match up. For example, pored or toothed mushrooms will not have sinuate connections but can most certainly be decurrent, adnate, or free.

Hygrocybe with free gill attchament. Note the gap between the stipe and gill attachement.

Agaric with adnexed gill attachment. There is no gap between the stipe and gill attachment, nor is there a structure on the stipe.

Cystoderma with sinuate attachement. Note the notch in the gills which ends in a thin strip of lamellar tissue on the stipe.

Cortinarius with emarginate attachement. These gills are notched but still connect to the stipe.

Lactarius subplinthogalus with adnate attachment. These gills connect to the stipe in an approximately perpendicular angle.

Omphalotus illudens with decurrent gill attachment. These gills connect to and run down the stipe.

Lamellae descriptions

Lamellae (gills) have evolved to form a vast array of features, many of which we can use to identify the mushroom. To start out as simply as possible, the depth of the gill, from the bottom edge to the connection to the context/cap is an easily notable feature, with some fungi using extremely shallow gills and others with deep, luxurious gills.

Next is the spacing of the lamellae. Any given species is likely to use a range of spacing which is dependent on genetic variability or external factors. We will use the terms crowded, close, subdistant, and distant. This is best illustrated in the figure to the right, but for our mushroom description pages you will see the longer version (below) with a graph to illustrate the most likely range of lamellar spacing for that given mushroom/group.

Short gills are those lamellae which are shorter than the rest (not to be confused with shallow!). These gills are present at the cap margin (edge) but do not extend all the way to the stipe. This is a common feature but not all mushrooms have them.

Perhaps related to short gills are forked gills. Exactly what it sounds like, these gills fork or split as you follow them from the stipe/stem outwards towards the cap margin. This is an uncommon feature so if you see it, definitely take note.

Closely related to forked gills are those with anastomose features. These are often called cross veins and describe the

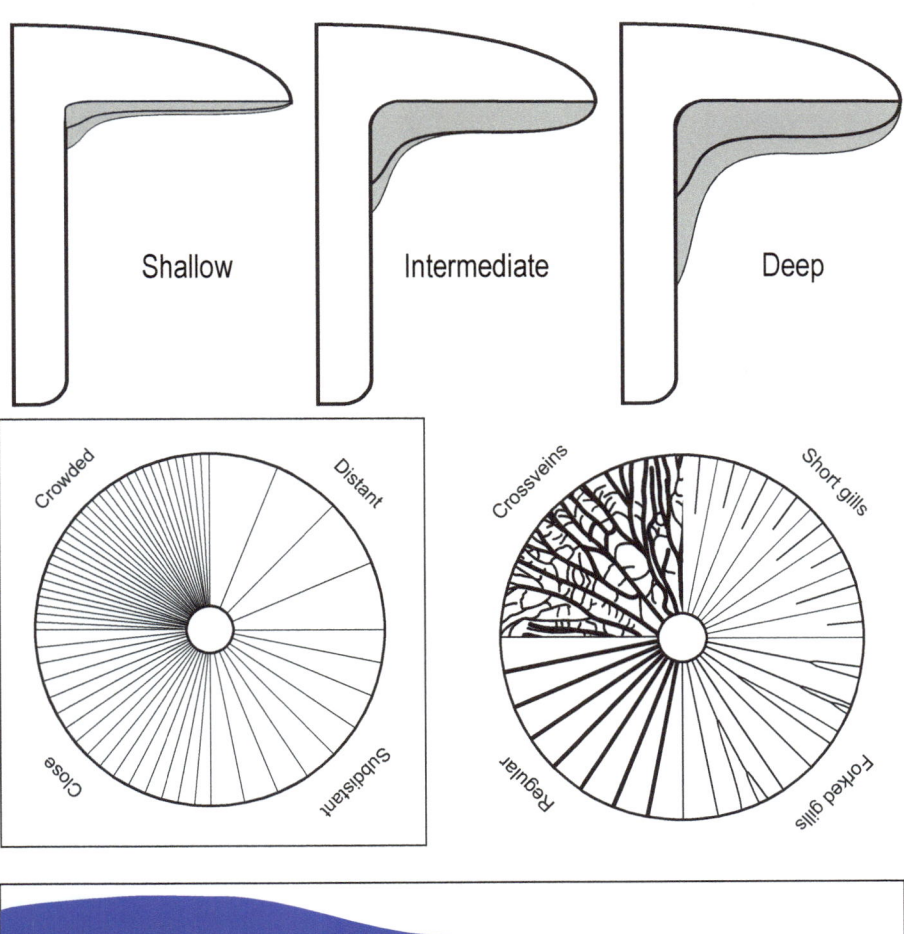

This graph will be used to show the probable distribution of gill spacing

This mushroom has an upturned or infundibular shape, subdistant to distant gill spacing, deep lamellar depth, and short gills.
Is this shape typical or is it overstreched? If overstreched, what is the true lamellae attachement type?

raised tissue which connect gills at odd angles. These cross veins can be bound to the bottom of the cap alone or can creep up onto the lamellae.

'False gills' is a term I prefer to avoid but should be discussed here. This term refers to ridge or wrinkle-like folds of the hymenial surface which form gill-like structures. These can be readily differentiated by their rounded/blunt ends (the bottom-most part) and their exclusively shallow depth. Normal lamellae are more akin to pages in a book – bound by the spine and with a sharp, clearly defined edge. While the terminology is useful for discriminating between the two types (see Cantharellus descriptions to see why this is useful) it isn't entirely correct since those folds or ridges do constitute lamellae.

Marginate gills, a very interesting feature which won't see much use in this book. These lamellae have a different colored edge (usually darker) than the rest of the gill. This is due to two major version of a single cell types which compose the outer portion of the gill; the cystidium (plural cystidia) form the bulk of the non-spore bearing cells (those are basidia) along the sides of the gills while those on the edge are called cheilocystidia and may take on different pigments.

Sawtooth gill edges are another un-

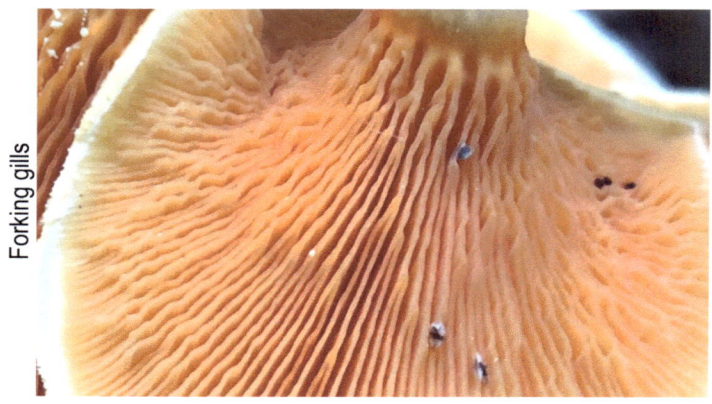

Forking gills

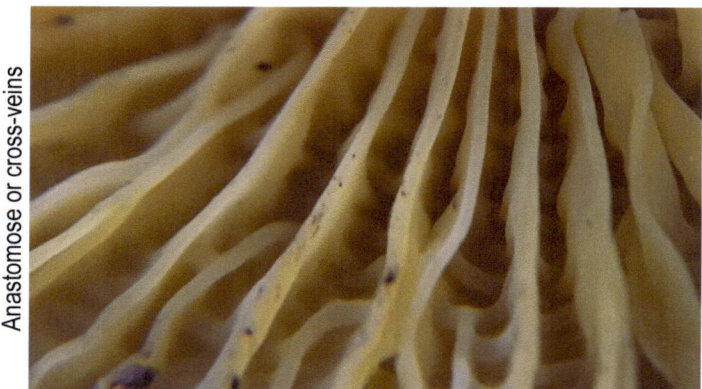

Anastomose or cross-veins

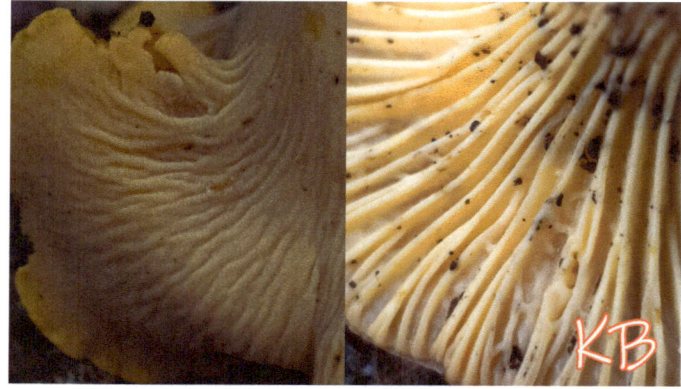

'False gills' of various depths. Note the rounded/blunt edges

Serrated/ saw-toothed gills

Marginate gills

common feature, but a fun one to find. The feature is exactly what it sounds like, the edges of the gills are serrated. The serrations are not perfectly even but are regular enough to not be confused with damaged lamellae. If you're unsure if the serrations are native features or environmental, consider how delicate or robust the lamellae are and if other tears are also present.

Lamellar variations

Of the three pictured mushrooms, only the first is actually decurrent. The other two have environmental or individual morphologies which make the lamellar attachment look decurrent. In fact, the second two photos are of fungi with adnate attachments. This is an example of how nature doesn't like to conform to our neat little structures and more importantly, an example of the non-ideal morphologies you are likely to encounter.

Spore prints

For some mushrooms, the color of the spores is an important identification feature. In my experience this is a feature which is too heavily relied upon or emphasized as critical. There are certainly instances where that is true, but I would like to stress the spore print color as a secondary identification feature which should follow macromorphology (big structural features you can see by eye).

Spore 'prints' are necessary because the individual spores are far too small to be seen by eye and the aggregate of millions will be sufficient to produce the colors we use as identification features. These prints can be acquired by placing the hymenial surface down onto a piece of glass or aluminum foil with a drop or two of water on the cap (or nearby) and covered with a bowl or Tupperware such that the humidity inside the chamber is high. Within an hour or five there should be a large enough amount of spores dropped for you to see. If you did the print on glass, move the glass over white and

dark backgrounds to see the actual color, if on aluminum foil, you should be able to determine the color without the movement.

The majority of the time, this process can be completely avoided by finding the spore print/drop in the field. Take a couple of extra seconds when you find the mushrooms to look at any surface directly below the caps to see if sufficient spores have already dropped for you to note the color. This is especially easy for clusters of mushrooms with overlapping caps and those with rings/partial membranes.

Chocolate brown spore print on the annulus

Stipe structures

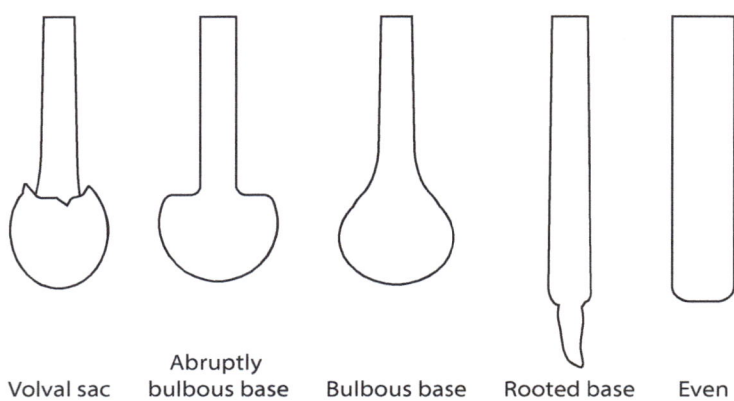

Volval sac | Abruptly bulbous base | Bulbous base | Rooted base | Even

Volval sacs

The stipe is next on the list of important features for identification of mushrooms. As a structure alone, its purpose is simple – to elevate the cap such that spores can be more easily caught on the air currents and distributed over a wider range. Functionally, it allows water and nutrients to be passed from the mycelial mat into the hymenophore such that spores can be produced. Luckily for us, the stipe has taken on several structures, shapes, ornamentation, and textures which we can use to further refine our identification of fungi. On the most simplistic side are tapering stipes in which the top or bottom of the stem is thinner than the rest. If this feature isn't dramatic or very consistent from specimen to specimen, it may go undescribed or at least unemphasized – so don't overthink this one.

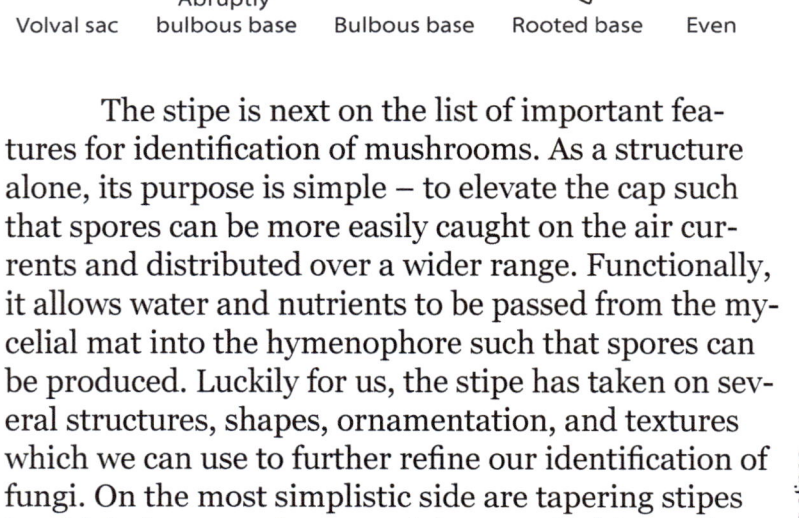

Rooting stipes

Before describing the next features, I think it prudent to discuss the removal of the mushroom from the substrate. You can pluck mushrooms indiscriminately – or you may cut them at the base to avoid dirt getting into your basket. Either are fine options and will have no bearing whatsoever on the fungal organism (think of plucking fruit from a tree). For those who would like to learn more about mushroom identification – I urge you to excavate the mushroom. Gently remove the detritus until the base of the stipe is evident, then go a bit deeper until the point at which the stipe connects to the mycelium is entirely out of the ground (you won't have this issue with wood-growing fungi) and remove the soil. You'll quickly learn which groups of mushrooms this is useful for and find many more features than you expected. Several fruitbodies of the Lepioids have tiny hidden volva, the Xeruloids have remarkable roots, and *Amanita* have wonderful

Bulbous base (left) and abrupt bulbous base (right)

16   *Anatomy of a Mushroom*

Stipe characteristics

and variable bulbs, bases, and volva.

Far less common than tapered stems are rooted stipes. 'Rooted' is really just a description of the underground portion of the stipe for fungal organisms which reside in or consume buried organic matter such as roots. These 'roots' can range from a small protuberance to several foot-long structures.

Somewhat common are bulbous bases. Rather than tapering to simply become wider, these stipe bases have distinctive bulbs. These are common features in the Family *Amanitaceae* and Genus *Cortinarius*. If taking notes, consider if the fruitbody has a tapering bulb or an abruptly bulbous base. Does the bulb have ornamentation or is it bare?

Most beautiful of these features (in my opinion) are the volval sacs, also called cups. These are the remnants of universal veils which were torn as the stipe began extension during the fruitbody's determinant growth. These volval sacs can be deep, shallow, wide, or narrow. In the Family *Amanitaceae*, the shape of the volval sac is also a critical identification feature – though this book will not rely on this highly specific feature range.

A related and similarly fantastic feature are the remnants of the partial veil – the ring, annulus, or skirt. These remains are most typically found on the stipe, but portions can be attached to the cap margins (so keep an eye out for dangly bits there which may indicate the fruitbody had a partial veil). Those portions remaining on the stipe vary in their thickness and robustness to environmental degradation, as well as composition and typical part of the stipe they are found on (high vs low).

Other notable features of the stipe are less structural and more ornamental. These include Scrobiculi (rounded pits in the stipe), reticulation (a net-like pattern), glandular dots, fibers of various densities, and scales.

Scrobiculi (scobiculum singular) are a feature unique to the genus *Lactarius* in which the outer layer of cells formed a gelatinous layer which has dried (Burdsall, 1980). These pits usually create a stunning set of colors with the hues of the stipe (and may also be present on the cap).

Reticulation just means net-like. This is a fea-

Annulus of *Amanita sp.*

Annulus pulled off by expanding cap

Robust and thick annulus on a scaled stipe

ture common to the *Boletaceae* in which some portion of the hymenial surface (pores in this case) have stretched out on the stipe (almost always at the top or apex). The color and depth of this reticulation can be an important feature for *Boletaceae* identification.

Glandular dots are small, slightly raised dots or bumps on the stipe surface. These dots may not be apparent until they darken upon handling. This is another feature important for *Boletaceae* identification.

Fibers as ornaments may not always be an apparent feature. Here, I'm describing large amounts or clumps of fibers which make a stipe furry, fuzzy, or woolly. Do be aware of cortinas as well. This structure is an especially fibrous partial veil most common to the genus *Cortinarius* which leaves remnants on the stipe and cap margins.

Related to fibers as ornaments are smaller tufts of usually much finer fibers which group to form various scales or other shapes. These features can be at the top (apex, apical) or bottom (basal) of the stem and can be somewhat variable from fruitbody to fruitbody within the same species.

Cortina remnants dusted in rust-colored spores

Soft fibers give this *Suillus* a wooly appearance

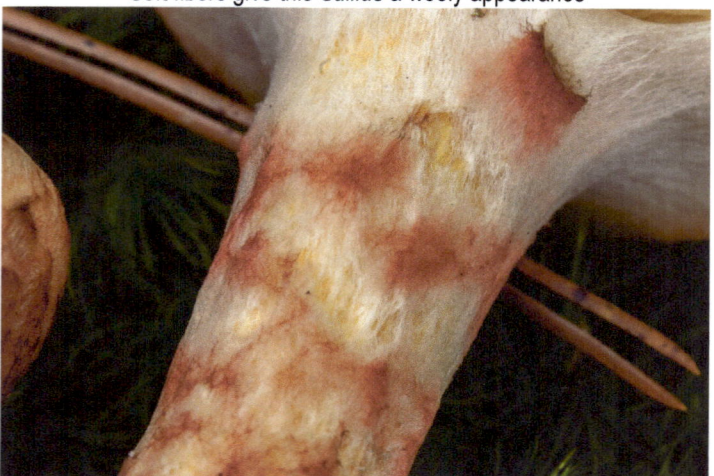

Scrobiculi

Reticulation

Glandular dots

Raised fibers make 'scales'

Raised fibers giving scurfy appearance

Anatomy of a Mushroom

Stipe textures

In my opinion and experience, the fine textures of the stipe are a highly underappreciated identification characteristic. This may be due to the overlapping nature of these textures or that dirty fingers or poor eyesight may obscure some of these finer details.

Beyond obvious ornamentation of the stipe, this structure is typically more robust than the cap and as such, the fibrous nature of the stipe may be helpful as an identification tool. In fact, in some taxa the cellular structure of the stipe is critical to creating notable features. In the genus *Russula*, the more spheroid cells allow the stipe to be snapped in half like a piece of chalk. Whereas in the genus *Cantharellus*, the longer fibrous cells allow it to be torn lengthwise like string cheese.

While cellular structure is outside of the scope of this book, the fine stipe textures typical of groups of mushrooms is not. Whenever possible, the texture of the stipe (and most structural components) will be described. Since the exact vernacular may not be as useful as desired for descriptions, we will provide as many images which highlight those relevant textures. See the captions of these images for more details.

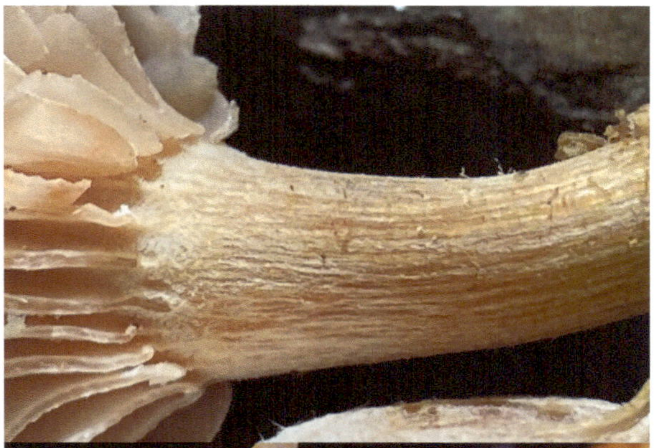

Laccaria stipe has distinctively wide fibers

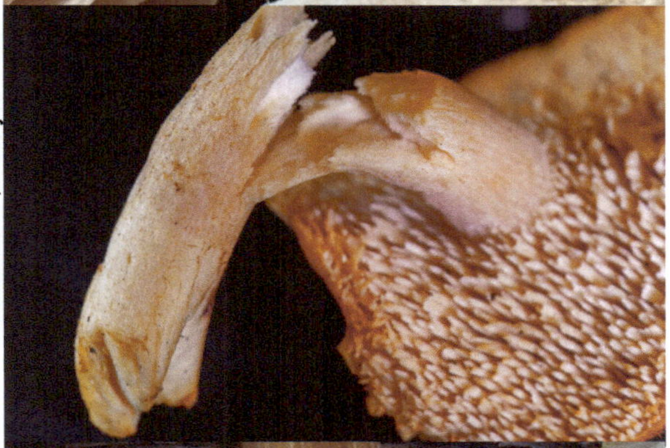

Hydnum stalk is similar to chanterelles, meaty

Xanthoconium stem is meaty

Cortinarius stalk is somewhat akin to plant pith

Russulaceae stalks are more crumbly or mealy

Tricholoma stipe is smooth but tears easily with the longer fibers of the stalk

Mushroom Edibility

This is a fickle subject because very few mushrooms are toxic. In fact, the percentage of toxic mushrooms is far fewer than that of plants. Yet we live in a mycophobic part of the world, and those ideas have worked their way into our culture and laws. Most toxicity reported to the North American Mycological Society (NAMA) come from a handful of especially common species, or those which were not cooked sufficiently. This book aims to take a directed approach to mycophagy (mushroom consumption) by categorizing mushrooms by either species, group, or genera into one of the eight pictured groupings. Some mushrooms may straddle a couple of categories or various species within a genus might have very different categories. Other times, the consensus of "how good" a mushroom is considered to be varies substantially. Therefore, many mushrooms in this book will be given multiple designations. It is your responsibility to read the text and even seek external resources to further understand why multiple – sometimes contradictory – categories are used.

Choice:

This category is reserved for those mushrooms considered the best for consumption. Often these are prized edibles which may only be found seasonally and are likely to fetch the greatest price on the market.

Edible and Good:

The name says it all, these mushrooms are well regarded for their flavor/texture by most people and are usually a good candidate for sales and personal consumption. The line between this category and 'Choice' may be based on personal preference or how easily obtained a mushroom type is.

Requires special preparation or Not as Good as SPAM:

A somewhat satirical catch-all group for those mushrooms which are often consumed but either not particularly well regarded (such as the congealed meat-product SPAM) OR those which require special preparation. For example, the jelly-ears (*Auricularia*) are eaten frequently in some parts of the world but are more of a textural additive than a main ingredient [Not as good as SPAM]. On the other side, some species of mushrooms (some Gyromitra and some Amanita) require careful detoxifying prior to being rendered safe for consumption. This book will not concern itself with methods of detoxification nor will it promote consumption of such mushrooms, but this category will be used to indicate EITHER a requirement for cautionary preparation OR mushrooms which do not garner much appreciation for flavor or texture.

Inedible:

Another catch-all group which implies the fruitbody is either insubstantial, not appropriate as foodstuff (woody, corky, leathery, acrid, bitter, etc.), of unknown edibility, or simply not worth eating for some other reason. An expansion to this group will be presented with *Trametes versicolor* and *Ganoderma* called "Teas and Tinctures" in which some otherwise inedible (but not toxic!) mushrooms can be used as the base of teas or tinctures.

Adverse Reactions Uncommon:

This is a categorization which will always be added to another as a warning that some portion of the population (greater than average) will have a mild reaction to eating this mushroom. Usually, these reactions are mild gastrointestinal distress and may include bloating, gas, diarrhea, or an upset stomach.

Adverse Reactions Common:

Another category added to others in which adverse reactions are more commonplace and more severe. These are reactions which are unlikely to lead to hospitalization, but more likely to lead to a night with the toilet.

Extreme Gastrointestinal Distress:

This category is for those mushrooms which, when eaten, cause extreme GI distress which may include a very uncomfortable day or two with the toilet or even hospitalization but unlikely to cause death in an otherwise healthy

Choice	Edible and Good	Requires special Prep or	Inedible

Adverse reactions uncommon	Adverse reactions common	Extreme G.I. Distress	Potentially Deadly

adult. Common species with this designation include *Chlorophyllum molybdites* and *Omphalotus spp.*.

Potentially Deadly:

This category is reserved for those mushrooms which are known to contain toxins which can lead to hospitalization and even death when consumed. While this is a very small group compared to the others, this book will point several out as part of the necessary education regarding mushroom education.

Due to the composition of most fungal fruitbodies, a large enough quantity of even the choicest mushrooms can cause some distress. This is thought to be a combination of some fungal-specific sugars and the chitin which composes the fungal cell wall. Heat breaks these compounds down (heat labile) into more manageable compositions which we can more readily digest – still some remains and may eventually lead to noticeable GI upset. Because of this, only a handful of wild-foraged mushrooms are recommended to be eaten raw (some boletes, *Fistulina hepatica*, *Auricularia*, & the edible *Amanita* included) and others must be cooked prior to consumption. This is especially true for species which contain heat labile toxins such as the morels (*Morchella*). As a rule, all but those specifically listed wild foraged mushrooms must be completely cooked (internal temperature 160°F/71.1°C) to be rendered safe and minimize any GI upset.

If you suspect a mushroom is toxic, do not eat it at all. However, even those mushrooms which are designated edible may cause allergic reactions in some people. Unfortunately, the only way to determine this is by consumption of the mushroom. The vast majority of these reactions are gastrointestinal distress with a rapid onset (~30 min to 2 hours). To minimize adverse reactions this book recommends that with the first consumption of any new-to-you species, a very small amount of the *cooked* mushroom is eaten, about a teaspoon in volume. If there is no adverse reaction 2-4 hours following consumption, the amount of cooked mushroom may be doubled. If this larger amount has also been well received after another 2-4 hours, a larger quantity may be consumed. Note that this method will not help with mycotoxins with a delayed effect such as amatoxins, only quick-acting irritants and most allergens.

Mushroom description page

The adjacent page is an example of the beginning of each major mushroom's section in this book. The page will contain variations of the same elements to provide an easy to interpret guide for you. The scientific name will appear at the very top, beneath which a common name(s) will be presented.

A **calendar** will follow with a graph above to illustrate the approximate time of year in which the mushroom(s) can be found. Please note that since coastal regions have a warmer climate, that the warm season should be considered expanded. Remember, this is just a rough guide - we can't control what the mushrooms are doing when we get a warm spell in December and end up seeing some chanterelles!

Below that is a **color** panel representing the typical range of colors that the particular mushroom can be found in. For some mushrooms this will be fairly monotone, and for others a veritable rainbow.

The **shape** of the mushroom will be described with labeled figures and will include the relevant portions of the fruitbody. I.e., a fungus without a stipe/stem will not have a description for it.

The **hymenial surface** will also have a labeled pictorial description. The lamellae wheel from "Anatomy of a Mushroom" will be present for gilled fruitbodies and will only contain those features which are possibly present on the given mushroom.

To the right will be another graph showing the **typical size range** of the fruitbodies as well as a ruler. For the behemoths which grow larger than the page, another pictorial guide will be presented.

The lower portion of the page will include pictorial descriptions of the **growth habits** of the mushrooms which includes a graph of the **growth types** from single to clustered as well as if the mushroom grows terrestrially or on wood. If the mushroom is mycorrhizal or parasitic with a particular plant or fungi, they will be listed.

Pages following this visual introduction will describe the fungus and its fruitbodies with as much detail as you need to confidently identify the mushroom(s) as well as comparisons with their look aikes.

Mushrooms are presented in groups based on identifying characteristics such that a major edible mushroom type will be followed by their look-alikes or close relatives.

Cantharellus
Chanterelles

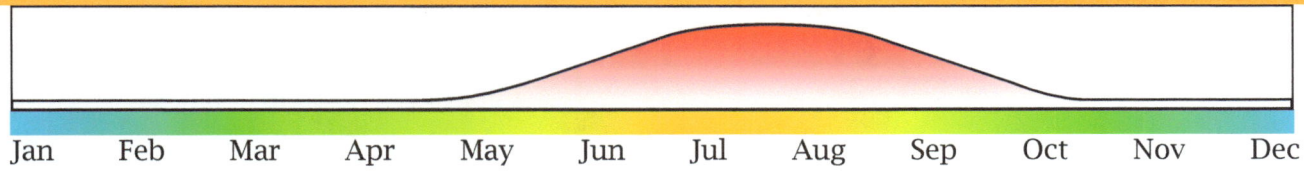

Jan Feb Mar Apr May Jun Jul Aug Sep Oct Nov Dec

Typical Color Palette

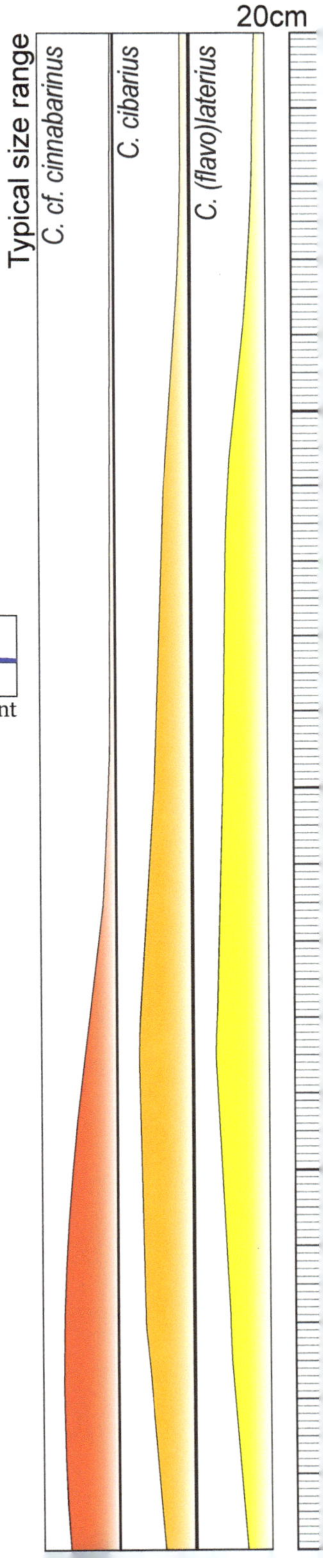

Shape

Funnel, Cantharelloid

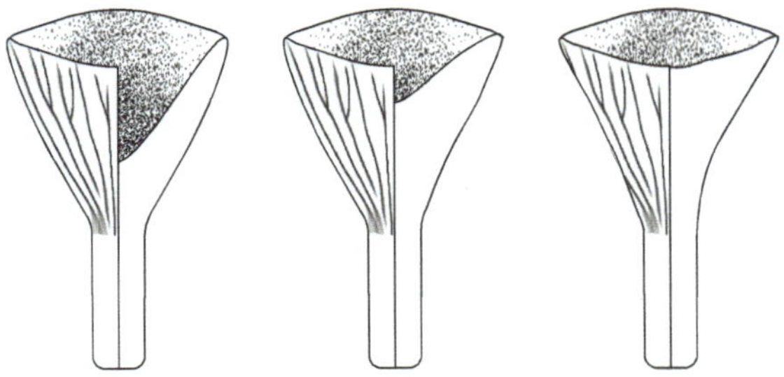

Hemenium: Lamellar ridges or folds

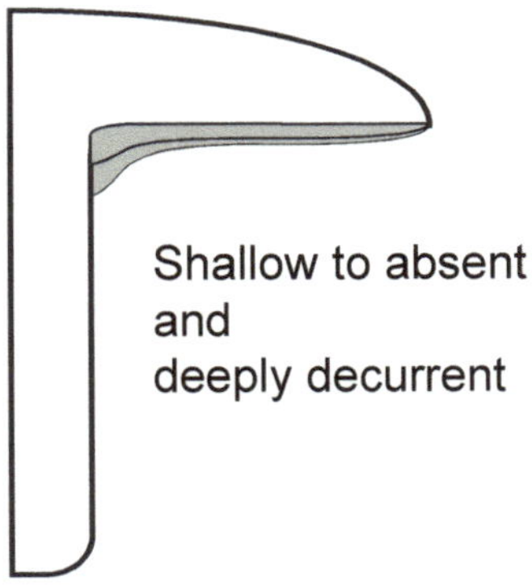

Shallow to absent
and
deeply decurrent

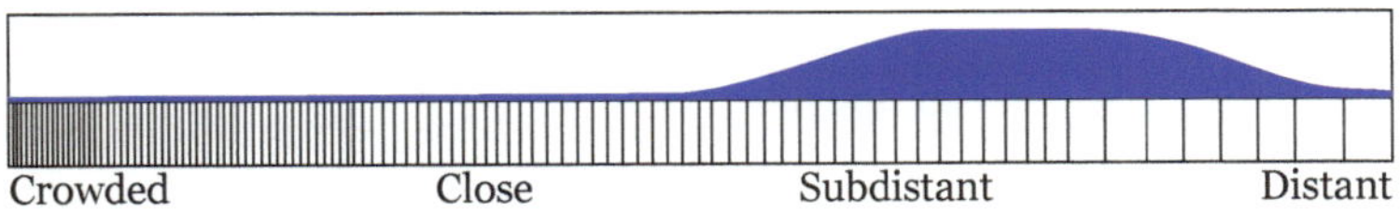

Crowded   Close   Subdistant   Distant

Growth

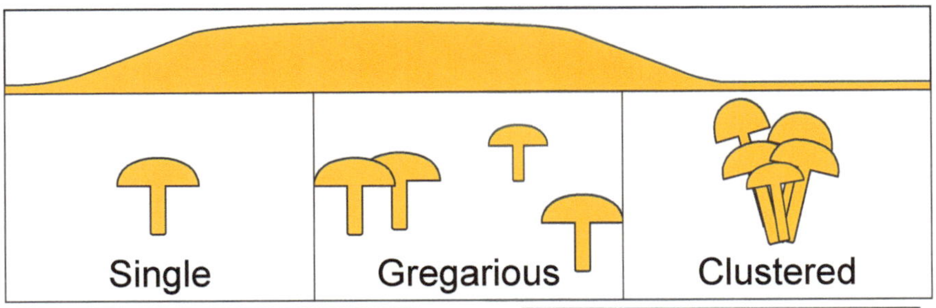

Single   Gregarious   Clustered

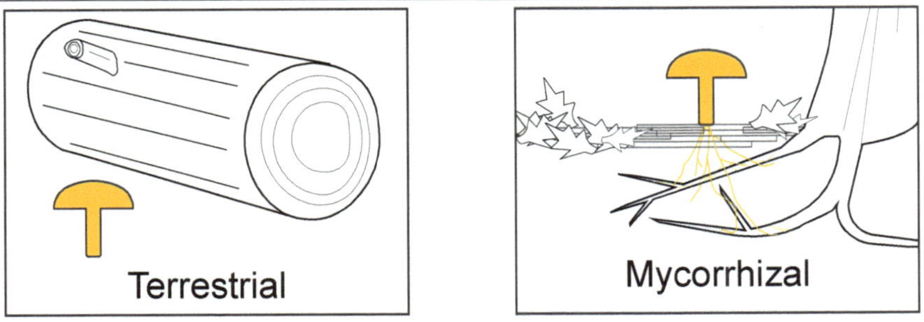

Terrestrial   Mycorrhizal

Cantharellus form mycorrhizal relationships with hardwoods such as
oak, beech, aspen, birch, and elm.
Cantharellus cinnabarinus prefer sandy soil such as in creek beds.

20cm

Typical size range

C. cf. cinnabarinus

C. cibarius

C. (flavo)laterius

Edible and Toxic Mushrooms of Alabama and Their Look-Alikes

Official list of approved wild harvested mushroom species

According to the ALABAMA DEPARTMENT OF AGRICULTURE AND INDUSTRIES FARMERS MARKET AUTHORITY ADMINISTRATIVE CODE CHAPTER 80-7-1- APPENDIX B:

Only the following wild harvested mushroom species may be offered for sale or service in a food service establishment:

Beefsteak (*Fistulina hepatica*)
Black Trumpet (*Craterellus fallax*)
Blewits (*Lepista nuda*)
Blue Milky (*Lactarius indigo*)
Cauliflower (*Sparassis spp.*)
Chanterelles (*Cantharellus spp.* Exception *C. persicinus*)
Chicken of the Woods (*Laetiporus spp.* Exception *L. persicinus*)
Golden and Burgundy Milkies (*Lactarius corrugis, L. volemus, L. hygrophoroides*)
Green Quilted Russula (*Russula virescens, R. parvovirescens, R. crustosa*)
Hedgehog (*Hydnum repandum, H. albomagnum*)
Honey mushrooms (*Armillaria mellea, A.tabescens*)
Lions Mane or Pom Pom or Bearded tooth or Bear's head (*Hericium spp.*)
Lobster (*Hypomyces lactifluorum*)
Maitake or Hen of the woods (*Grifola frondosa*)
Morels (*Morchella spp.*)
Oyster Mushroom (*Pleurotus spp.* Exception *Pleurotus levis, P. dryinus*)
Pecan Truffle (*Tuber spp.*)
Puffballs (*Lycoperdon spp., Calvatia spp.*)
Reishi mushrooms (*Ganoderma curtisii, G. tsugae, G. sessile*)
Shaggy mane (*Coprinus comatus*)
Turkey tail (*Trametes versicolor*)
Umbrella Polypore (*Cladomeris umbellata*)
Wood Ears (*Auricularia spp.*)

Interestingly, due to *recent* taxonomic work, several of these listed fungi are less exact than they were intended to be. For example *Hydnum repandum senso stricto* is not found in the United States, several *Cantharellus* species have been moved to *Craterellus*, *Apioperdon pyriforme* was moved from *Lycoperdon*, etc.. Unfortunately this leaves "interpretation" of this list in light of modern taxonomical descriptions to us. We will do our best to respect the intention of the list but need to provide you, the reader, with up to date and accurate information.

We strongly suggest that anyone harvesting wild mushrooms for sales purposes also base their interpretation of this list, and this book in the same light and consider the safety of their patrons a top priority.

Galerina marginata

Funeral Bells, Deadly Galerina

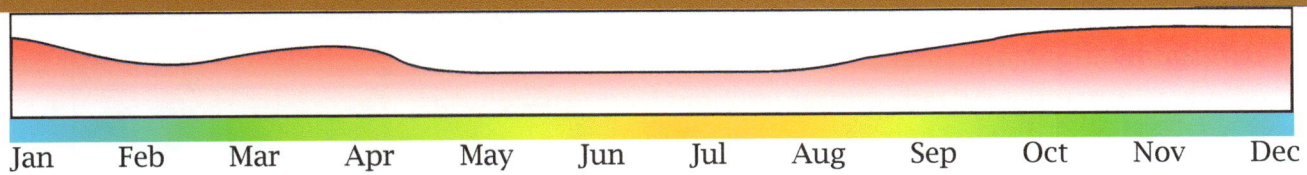

| Jan | Feb | Mar | Apr | May | Jun | Jul | Aug | Sep | Oct | Nov | Dec |

Typical Color Palette

Shape

Campanellate/umbonate when young.
Convex to flat to wavy when mature

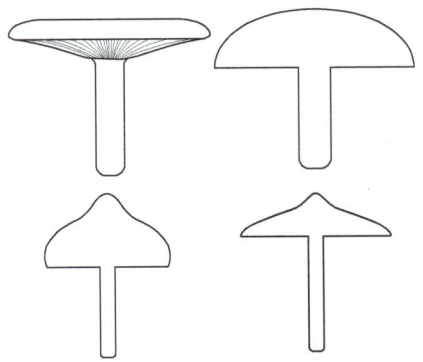

Hemenium: Lamellae

Adnate
medium depth

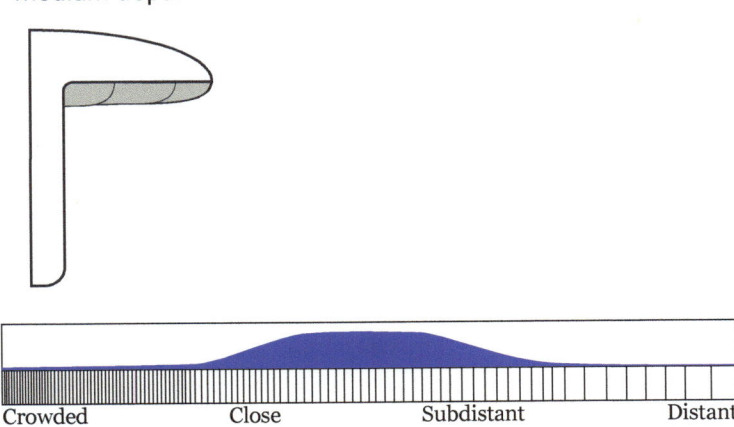

Crowded   Close   Subdistant   Distant

Typical size range

Galerina marginata

20cm

Growth

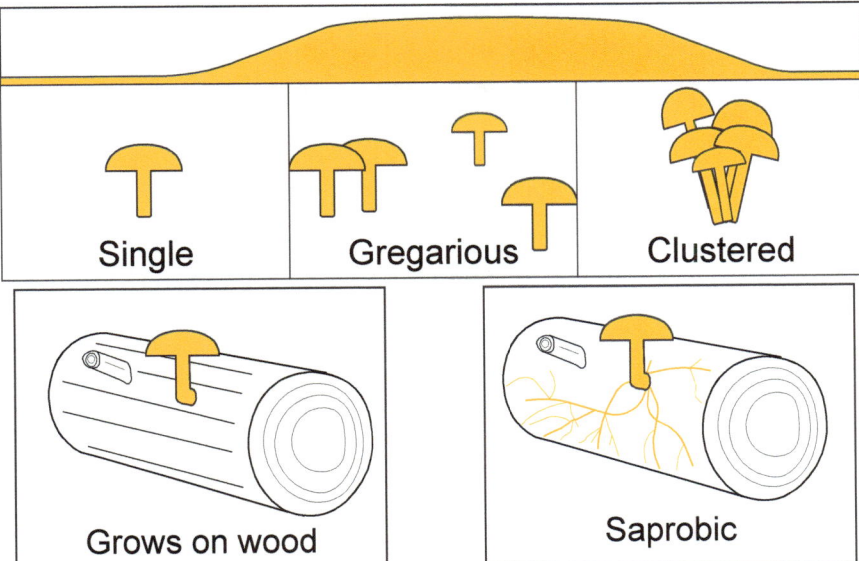

Single   Gregarious   Clustered

Grows on wood   Saprobic

Galerina grow in multiple fruitbodies from decaying wood. They can
be found year-round but develop in significant number following early
winter rains.

General Desciption

Description:

Galerina marginata is one of many in the genus *Galerina*, but it common enough to warrant consideration and a striking common name. Called "funeral bells" due to their campenellate shape (though those pictured and most documented are decidedly more convex) and potentially deadly nature. *G. marginata* contain amatoxins, similar to those common in the section Phalloideae of family *Amanitaceae*, and in great enough quantity to be potentially deadly.

Ecology:

A common sight on the sides of hardwood and coniferous wood alike during the early winter and spring. *Galerina marginata* is a ubiquitous saprobe often appearing in loose, or dense clusters in the week or so following cool rains. The reddish-brown and yellowish-brown margins appear as a more brightly colored patch amongst the muted browns of the decaying leaves and logs.

Pileus:

The cap takes on warm brown shades, typically darker towards the center of the cap and lightening towards the margin. The margin may appear striate when the cap is moist. The caps begin as tight balls which slowly unfurl to campenellate, umbonate, or convex and become flat or even wavy in maturity. In maturity some of the saturation of the pileal membrane may dull revealing multi-toned caps.

Hymenium:

Galerina sport lamellae with close to subdistant spacing and frequent short gills. The gills attach broadly (adnexed) and may slightly run down the stipe. The gills are a dull ochre to tan and darken with spore development becoming mottled with darker patches or completely darkened with brown to reddish-brown spores. The **Spore print** is a rusty or slightly reddish-brown and may often be found deposited on the adjacent caps or the partial veil remnants.

Stipe:

The stipe is softly fibrous, even, and some shade (or mix thereof) of white, ochre, rusty, vermillion, to dark brown, or even grey. The color of the stipe is highly dependent on the maturity of the fruitbody and the moisture content. Depressing or compressing the soft fibrils by plucking a fruitbody may darken the stipe.

The stipe will typically have a small ring, close to the apex. The partial veil is weak and breaks early in development leaving a feeble annulus which is an important characteristic for quickly differentiating these *Galerina marginata* from the edible *Flammulina velutipes*. This anulus is commonly eroded, but the slight remnants often catch much of the initial spore drop, painting it a rusty brown and bringing it back into focus.

Galerina marginata

Amanita sect Phalloideae

The Destroying Angel, Death Cap

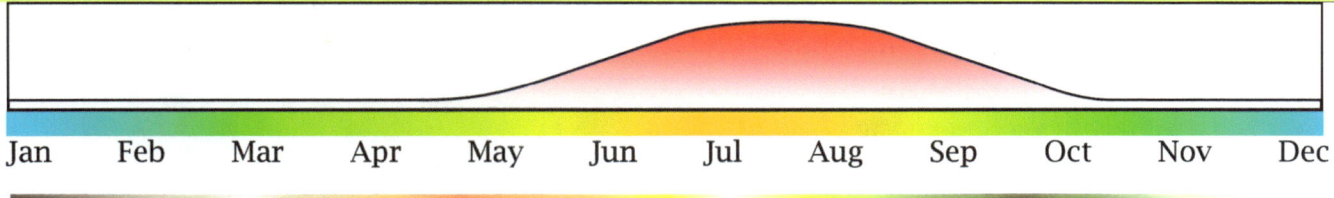

Jan Feb Mar Apr May Jun Jul Aug Sep Oct Nov Dec

Typical Color Palette

Shape

Opening convex and often becoming flat in age

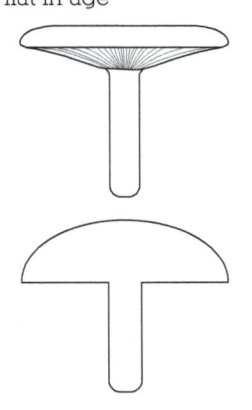

Hemenium: Lamellae

Bulbous base inside of saccate volva. Prominent annulus at apex

Free or Adnexed medium depth

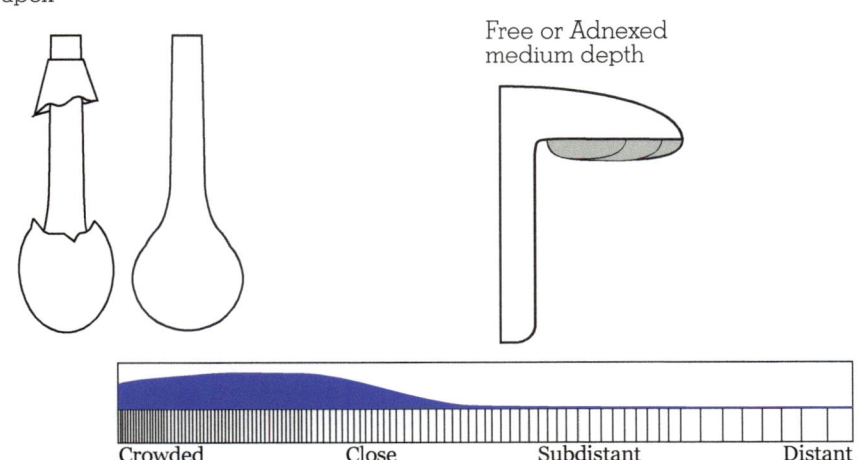

Crowded   Close   Subdistant   Distant

Growth

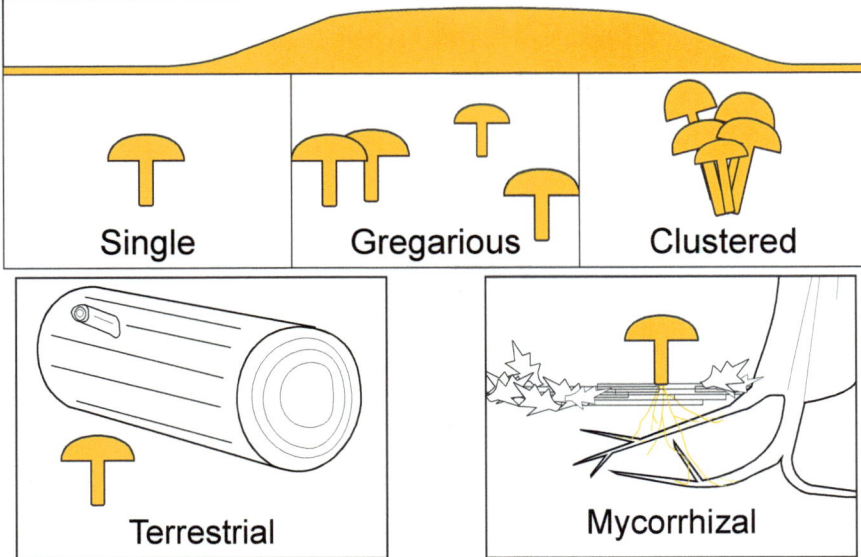

Single

Gregarious

Clustered

Terrestrial

Mycorrhizal

Amanita sect Phalloideae is known to be ectomycorrhizal forming relationships with several broad-leaved trees including oaks and some pine-trees such as hemlock and cypress.

Typical size range

20cm

Amanita sect Phalloideae

General Desciption

Description:

    Amanita section Phalloideae is a taxonomical division beneath subgenus *Lepidella* within the genus *Amanita*. The family *Amanitaceae* is extremely branched giving rise to the need for far more taxonomical subdivisions than most other fungal families. For a detailed review of these divisions see the well curated webpage amanitaceae.org. This section contains around 70-90 species worldwide which account for most of the deadly Amanita. These mushrooms (generally speaking) contain two families of toxins, the amatoxins (comprising about 8 related toxins) and phallotoxins (comprising about 7 related toxins). The amatoxins are a particularly brutal group which interfere with the generation of proteins within individual cells causing multiple organ failure very similar to extreme radiation poisoning. Importantly, the symptoms of these toxins are not apparent until 24-48 hours following consumption and may not present the gastro-intestinal distress typical of other mushroom poisonings. These toxins are not heat liable and cannot be cooked out or otherwise removed from the mushroom. There is a good reason this section has names like, "death cap" and "destroying angel". Death and destruction aside, these mushrooms are stunningly beautiful and safe to touch, the toxins must be ingested to have effect.

    Importantly, this taxonomical section is far too large to address properly in this context. The eight species known (or well suspected) to occur in the Southeast United States according to Bunyard and Justice (2020) include Amanitas *phalloides, arocheae, bisporigera, suballiacea, sturgeonii, ocreata, elliptosperma,* and *magnivelaris*. The following descriptions will apply to these species.

Ecology:

    Amanita section Phalloideae forms a wide range of ectomycorrhizal relationships and will almost always be found in association with a tree. Because this section of genus *Amanita*, subgenus *Amanitina* contains near 70 species (only some of which occur in the Southeast United States)

exact tree species cannot be provided. Regardless, the status of ectomycorrhizal relationships implies that these fungi will not be found in open fields.

Pileus:

The cap of the discussed species is most typically white, off-white/cream, to shades of yellow-green-grey in *A. phaloides*, and shades of brown in *A. arocheae*. The more highly colored species typically have deeper saturation towards the center of their cap which fades towards the margin. The margin will rarely have the striate patterns which are common to other sections of *Amanita*.

Cap shape is rounded to oval, often egg-shaped when developing which quickly expands to become convex and eventually flat in maturity with no umbonation. Cap size is typically 2-7 inches or 5-18 centimeters in diameter. Saccate volva remnants may be present on the cap, typically dried on and soft before drying out completely. These volval remnants will not be wart-like, but typically take on a single or small number of wide patches.

Hymenium:

Amanita all have lamellae, gills which are medium to deep in depth and section *Phalloideae* have gills white to cream in color. All Amanita will deposit a white to cream spore-print so spore-prints will rarely help in identification within the family *Amanitaceae*. The lamellae are free of the stipe but may attach close enough to the stipe to seem adnexed or even have a slight stipe-bound 'tooth' providing a sinuate appearance. Gills are crowded to close with common short gills. **Spore print** wil be white to cream as is common in most Amanitaceae.

Stipe:

The most important features for identification of Amanita are stipe-bound. Section Phalloideae have prominent saccate volva. This means that the cellular structure making up the universal veil are robust (for Amanita), pillowy, and membranous enough to not shred into small fragments during determinant growth. The volva is prominent and is either torn to have flaps (limbate), or remains a robust cup-shape. Within the volva, the stipe is bulbous.

The stipe is often adorned with some (usually white) fibrilose pattern such as uneven

chevrons, but this may not be a pronounced feature. The stipe shape is even to tapering with the base being globose (bulbous or round). There may be some coloration towards the base of the stipe (yellows in *A. phalloides*, and some greys in *A. arocheae*).

The partial veil will form a white flowing annulus which is connected somewhere near the apex of the stipe. The robustness of this stipe varies between the species, but some partial veil remnants should be present in all but the most decayed/weathered specimens.

Additional Notes:

While none of the edible species covered in this text are typically considered to be a look-a-like for Amanita, these majestic fungi draw enough attention to warrant discussion and education. *Amanita section Phalloideae* is responsible for many deaths, and as such should be recognized by anyone foraging for edible mushrooms.

The extreme nature of the toxins contained within these fruitbodies gives rise not only to the terrifying colloquial names, but rampant mycophobia. However, these fruitbodies are safe to touch, handle, smell, and in all technicality - to taste and spit. **Be Warned** we explicitly <u>do not recommend tasting</u> Amanita in this section (or this subgenus). Taste will almost never aid in identification of Amanita. Publications by Bunyard and Justice, 2020; and McNight et al., 2010, suggest that Amanita spores passively deposited from these fruitbodies onto other mushrooms in your basket are not sufficient to cause toxicity. However, for the commercial picker - edible and toxic mushrooms should *not* be stored or transported such that they come into contact.

Amanita sect Phalloideae

Auricularia
Wood Ears

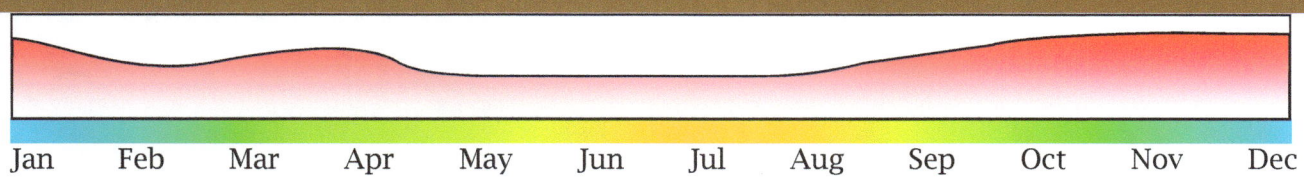

Typical Color Palette

Typical size range

Auricularia spp.

20cm

Shape

Ear to cup shaped, sometimes disk shaped, concave.

Hemenium: Smooth

Pseudostipe or none at all

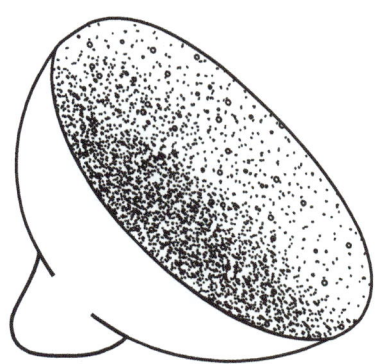

Growth

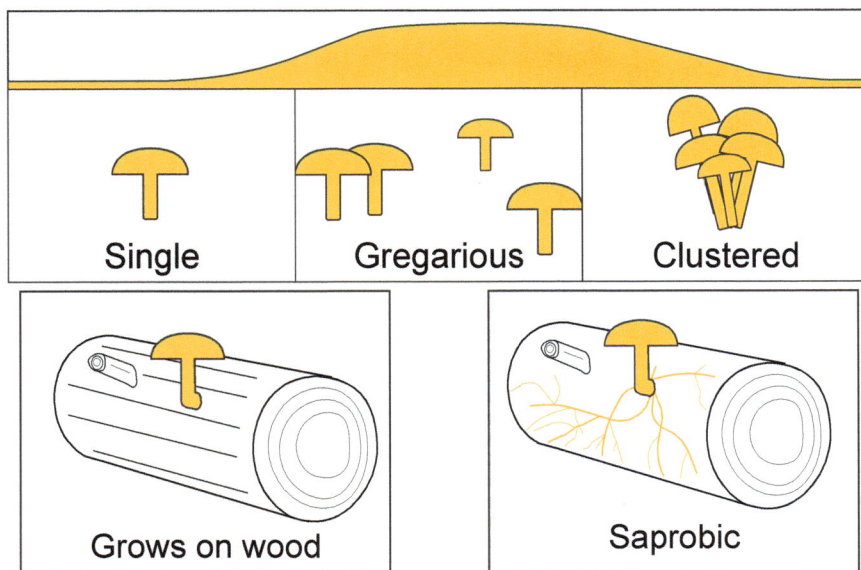

Single

Gregarious

Clustered

Grows on wood

Saprobic

Auricularia grows on several types of wood. In fact the type of wood being hardwood or coniferous is usually diagnostic in the species level identification

General Desciption

Description:

The wood ear or jelly-ear is one of those mushrooms that lives up to its namesake being both ear shaped and gelatinous. In the Southeastern United States, we have five species of Auricularia which include *A. americana* (previously called *auricula-judae*), *fuscosuccinea*, *mesenterica*, *nigricans*, and *scissa* which we will consider together.

Ecology:

A. americana is considered to have two 'units' or subspecies one of which grows on hardwoods such as elm, oak, beech, hickory and other hardwoods. The second unit of *A. americana* is the 'coniferous unit' growing on coniferous wood. *A. fuscosuccinea* is found on gumball, citrus wood, and boxelder. *A. mesenterica* is found on Chinese elm, beech, oak, chestnut, birch, and potentially other hardwoods. *A. nigricans* is found on sweetgum, coffee, and similar hardwoods. *A. scissa* is only known from the Dominican Republic and Florida but is likely found in regions near the Gulf of Mexico where it grows on decaying logs or limbs. (Looney 2013)

Fruitbody:

Auricularia develop as a small oblong drop shape which forms a depression (akin to a squirrel's ear) that the fruitbody widens around to form a downwards-facing cup or ear-like shape. This shape can be almost disturbingly similar to a human ear, or anything in the range of a squirrel's ear to a basset-hound's droopy ears to a (smaller) veritable elephant's ear in shape. They range in size from 1 cm to near 30 cm in some whopping specimens, but most usually are found in the 4-8 cm range.

It is from the inside of the cup-shaped structure which the basidia develop and drop the white spores. This surface may be quite smooth, to gently bumpy, to down-right cratered depending on environmental factors. If you find a specimen with distinctly netted or ridge-like surface near the Gulf of Mexico, you may have found *A. scissa*. The top (we'll call it the pileus) will be either glabrous (smoothly bald) or minutely fuzzy. In fact, those fuzzy specimens are most likely to be *A. mesenterica* or *A. nigricans*. The fruitbodies (each lobe) are often found growing near one another but are not fused at the base and

Auricularia, glabrous/bald looking when wet

Auricularia, semi-transparent

Auricularia, overlapping yet distinct fruitbodies

Auricularia, macro-texture

are usually easily distinguishable from one another (when fresh).

Auricularia take on an interesting assortment of browns but are almost always diaphanous (allowing some light to pass through). The colors can be a yellow-ish tan to various browns with shades of red and purple (especially on the extra large and somewhat bloated specimens).

Auricularia look-alikes

Exidia crenata

Description:
Commonly called the jelly-roll or amber-roll jelly fungus. This fruitbody lives up to its name in both the dark-amber color and jelly-like texture. The individual fruitbodies can be found on twigs, branches, and (typically thin) woody bits from hardwoods and similar trees. The fruitbody is often confused with Auricularia due to the overlapping color profiles, individual (mostly non-fused) fruitbodies, gelatinous textures, and growth habitats. *Exidia recisa* was recently "renamed" *E. crenata* when it was discovered that *E. recisa* only grows on Willow (*Salix*) in North America. These fruitbodies have the same edibility as *Auricularia* but are not included in the list of sellable fungi for Alabama.

Ecology:
A saprobe which favors thinner diameter wood/twigs upon which to fruit, favoring those which are not already decomposed. *Exidia* is not very picky about its host and is commonly found in the cooler months following regular precipitation.

Fruitbody:
The fruitbody lacks discernable pileus/stipe/hymenium features and typically grows in a gelatinous oblong bubble with a slight crimp following the outermost edge when absolutely prime. The fruitbody is usually 0.5-3cm in length and 1-2cm tall. Most often, this fungus will be found just post prime when large cavities begin to sink into its surface making potholes with somewhat sharp-looking edges. While these features can also be found in older *Auricularia*, these edges are usually sharper in Exidia and the fruitbody lacks the stretched lobe-like structures which typify *Auricularia*. *E. crenata* may has a very short centrally located pseudostipe which connect the bulk of the fruitbody to its substrate.

The color ranges from yellow-ish amber to dark brown with touches of red (think of the range of colors honey can take).

Exidia crenata, plump

Exidia crenata, most commonly observed as pitted and prunyv - partially dehydrated

Exidia nigrans/glandulosa

Requires special Prep or *Not* as good as SPAM

Description:
    Exidia nigrans/glandulosa are far less likely to be confused with *Auricularia* but are jelly mushrooms which share some color and growth medium overlap. *Exidia nigrans/glandulosa* have the same edibility as *Auricularia* but are not included in the list of sellable fungi for Alabama.

Ecology:
    Growing on recently dead hardwoods in cooler months.

Fruitbody:
    E. nigrans/gladulosa are usually encountered growing as a mass of fused fruitbodies 0.5-1.5cm tall. The mass can become substantial in size and takes on a lobed, brain-like texture. The color profile is dark brown to black and dries quickly becoming a wrinkled

Tremella fuciformis

Requires special Prep or *Not* as good as SPAM

Description:
    Sometimes called the snow-jelly fungus on account of its white color.

Ecology:
    Like the other *Tremellae*, *T. fusciformis* is a mycoparasite and favors the mycelium of *Hypoxylon* (the black bulbous crusts)

Fruitbody:
    A mass of opaque white to transparent gelatinous lobes which may have a divided, finger like edge. The lobes branch from a central growth region.

Exidia nigrans, wide growth

Exidia nigrans, close

Tremella fuciformis

Tremella fuciformis

Phaeotremella

Requires special
Prep or

Not as good as
SPAM

Phaeotremella

Phaeotremella, more widely spaced, closely resembling Auricularia

Description:

A much more convincing look-a-like for *Auricularia* due to the extended lobe-like structure of the fruitbodies, the matching color profile, and the gelatinous texture. Phaeotremella are, however, mycoparasites and will almost always be found growing on or near *Stereum* species. If you're not sure if your find is *Auricularia* or *Phaeotremella*, look for the *Stereum*.

Ecology:

Phaeotremella will grow on hardwood where *Stereum* are found.

Fruitbody:

The individual fruitbody looks remarkably like *Auricularia* – ear shaped lobes of various brown shades, diaphanous (somewhat transparent), and gelatinous. However, *Phaeotremella* grow in tight clusters with semi-fused bases making it closer to a single mass with several overlapping lobes rather than *Auricularia*'s several lobes which happen to be close.

Typical *Phaeotremella*, clustered, long-lobed and resembling *Auricularia*. However these share a common base and are growing near *Stereum*

Auricularia look-alikes

43

Peziza

Description:

Peziza are a large group of ascomycetes (much more closely related to morels) which very typically form cups. Most *Peziza* fruit terrestrially, but some cups may be found on decayed wood and have been known to beguile nascent foragers into thinking they are *Auricularia*. The range of colors in this genus is vast, but are usually some earthy shades.

Ecology:

This genus may contain well over one hundred species which can be exceptionally difficult to identify without the aid of microscopy. These species typically occupy different ecological roles and as such can be found growing terrestrially, on wood, on dung, or even in burn scars. Similarly, the specific species each have their own favored growing season- but many prefer cooler months and appear in great number in the early Spring.

Hymenium:

Unlike *Auricularia*, the concave portion of Peziza typically face upwards. This is because the spore-bearing cells called asci can forcibly eject the spores in small clouds rather than passively dropping the spores like most basidia. When encountering cup fungi, if you gently blow across the surface, or tap it with a finger, you may start the chain reaction necessary for the fruitbody to sporulate, resulting in a small column of billions of spores being ejected!

Importantly, the texture of the flesh of most of the order *Pezizales* (including *Peziza*) is fairly recognizable due to its rather delicate nature. These fruitbodies have more limited flexibility (though they are not by any means hard) before they snap, crack, or crumble. Auricularia and the other jellies are much more forgiving to being bent without breaking. I would not call *Peziza* gelatinous.

Stipe:

Absent to very short. Long-stemmed ascocarps with cups at the top are more likely to belong to the genus *Helvella*.

Peziza sp., growth on decayed wood

Peziza sp., growth on decayed wood

Peziza sp., growth terrestrially

Peziza sp., with pseudostem

Tremella mesenterica and allies

Requires special
Prep or

Not as good as
SPAM

Description:

One of the "witche's butter"s along with Tremella aurantia, Dacrymyces capitatus, and Dacrymyces chrysospermus which form lobed, gelatinous fruitbodies. Typically these fruitbodies are not elongated enough to be ear shaped or easily confused with Auricularia. They are however, all considered edible (but rarely worth eating). Occasionally the lobes of T. mesenterica (more so than the rest of the listed allies) can become long enough and concave enough to be worth mentioning here.

Ecology:

Like the other Tremella, T. mesenterica and aurantia are both mycoparasites, feasting on the mycelium of Peniophora and Stereum, respectively. T. mesenterica is found growing on hardwoods and the host fungus, Peniophora may not be visible (Peniophora are crust fungi and may be present beneath the bark). T. aurantia can be found growing on any wood which is hosting Stereum hirsutum (more commonly hardwoods). Dacrymyces species are common to coniferous wood. All of these species are found most commonly fruiting in the cooler to cold months.

Fruitbody:

Tremella mesenterica and aurantia commonly arise growing from cracks in the bark as longer lobes (minute – 4 cm) which are clustered forming some individual lobes and some which are highly fused at the base. Their colors range from pale yellow to yellow oranges. Dacrymyces will also erupt from between cracks in bark, but are commonly found growing on the bark itself or regions of the wood which have decayed sufficiently to no longer have bark. The colors of Dacrymyces are similar to those of the listed Tremella but may appear as almost white globules or more intense orange, expanding the range of Tremella mesenterica's palette. The lobes of Dacrymyces are shorter, more rounded, and more condensed- perhaps akin to the surface of a brain.

Tremella mesenterica

Tremella aurantia, note the stereum

Dacrymyces chrysospermus on decayed conifer

Dacrymyces capitatus on conifer

Lycoperdon, Calvatia, &
The Puffballs

Apioperdon

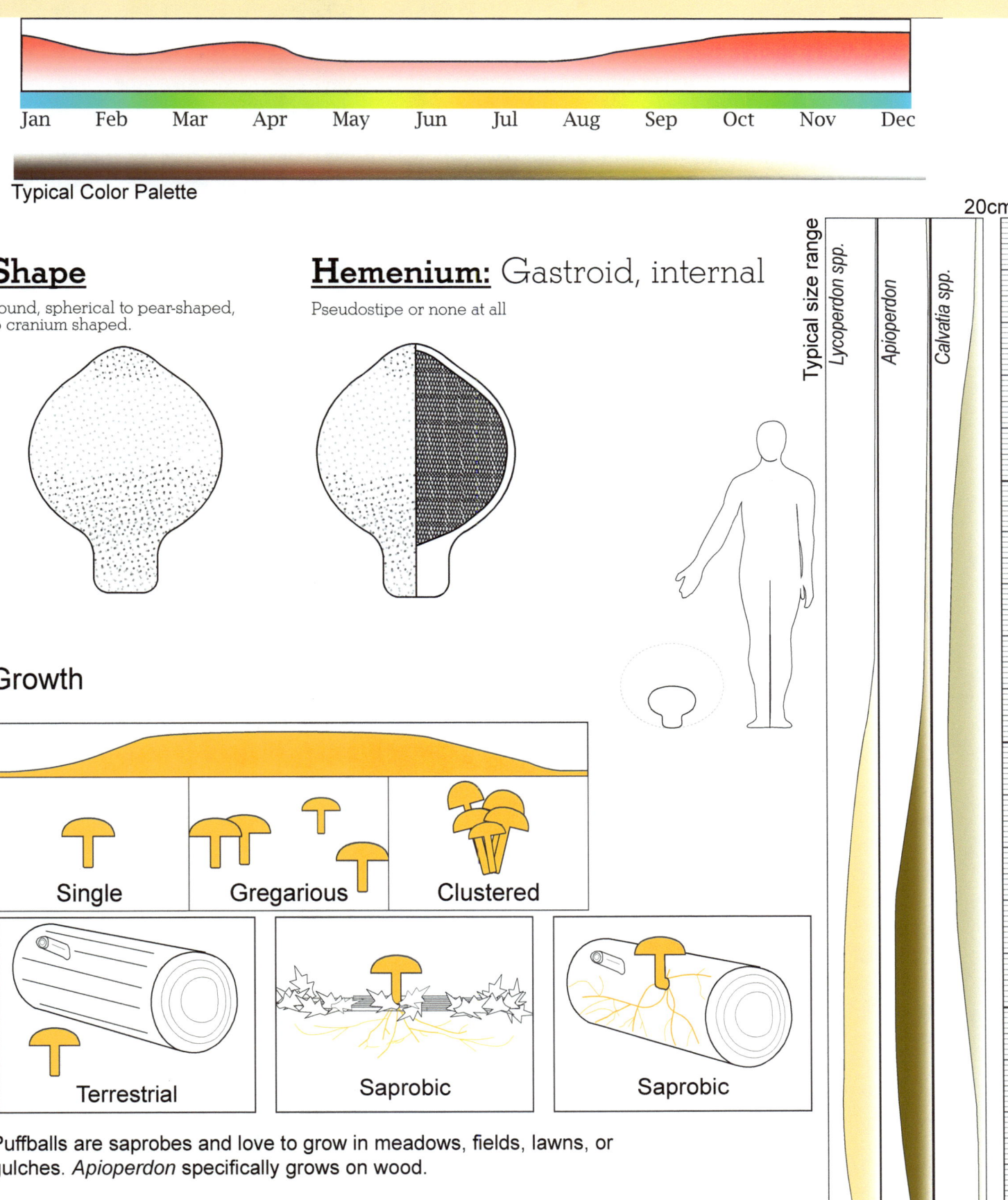

Jan　Feb　Mar　Apr　May　Jun　Jul　Aug　Sep　Oct　Nov　Dec

Typical Color Palette

Shape

Round, spherical to pear-shaped, to cranium shaped.

Hemenium: Gastroid, internal

Pseudostipe or none at all

Typical size range

Lycoperdon spp.

Apioperdon

Calvatia spp.

20cm

Growth

Single

Gregarious

Clustered

Terrestrial

Saprobic

Saprobic

Puffballs are saprobes and love to grow in meadows, fields, lawns, or gulches. *Apioperdon* specifically grows on wood.

The Puffballs

47

General Desciption

Description:

    'Puffball' is a colloquial used to describe most gastroid fungi which develop the spore mass internally that can then be ejected due to some external force (such as a good kick!). Gastroid is a term used to describe any 'stomach-like' (round) shaped fungus which produces the spores internally rather than on an external hymenial surface. However, we will use the colloquial 'puffball' to refer to the genera Lycoperdon, Apioperdon, and Calvatia – separating them from other gastroid fungi such as Scleroderma, Rhizopogon, Pisolithus, Geastrum, Zelleromyces, and true or false truffles (Tuber and Elaphomyces, respectively). One important distinction is that our puffballs will always be growing above ground (not half or completely buried) and may grow on well decayed wood. Several other fungi have gastroid forms- sometimes as a reproductive structure and sometimes as a structure designed to store nutrition.

Ecology:

    Puffballs grow worldwide and can be found in most any season (sans freezing weather). They are saprobes, decomposing organic matter which may include anything from fresh wood to layers of grass in a cultivated lawn.

Lycoperdon

Description:

    These are the prototypical puffballs which grow on the ground (not on wood) and are not gigantic in size. There are three primary species which are common to the Southeast US, Lycoperdons perlatum (previously gemmatum), pulcherrimum, and marginatum. All of these species are acceptable for harvest and sales.

Ecology:

    Fruitbodies of this genera are possible throughout the year but more common in Summer and Fall. They will grow just about anywhere there is something to decompose and may even be found growing in fairy rings in regions which allow for even growth of the mycelium (such as lawns). Found grow-

Calvatia cyathiformis, young

Lycoperdon perlatum interior, note the long pseudostipe

Lycoperdon perlatum

L. perlatum with cone-like ornaments

ing alone, scattered, gregariously, or even clustered. Lycoperdon perlatum is by far the most common of the listed species for our region. All of these *Lycoperdon* have a thin outer membrane (a skin or cuticle) which erodes in a central location at the top of the fruitbody when the spores have matured. This outer skin is otherwise robust to mild environmental damage, though is flexible like a fabric. Upon environmental disturbance (an animal stepping on them, a forager flicking them, or perhaps rain drops) the inner spores are ejected in a plume of smoke.

External Fruitbody:

The puffballs in this genus take on shapes ranging from almost perfect spheres to an inverted pear-shape which includes a stalk-like extension of the fruitbody. There is no clear delineation between this lower region and the upper, more bulbous region when young. During development the immature fruitbody may be more oblong and even peanut shaped. Size may range from less than 1 cm to 5-6 cm on the larger side. The color ranges from a stark-white to various shades of tan to light brown. There is rarely any adulteration of this color range with warm or cool pigments (i.e. no reds, yellows, blues, greens, or purples). However, the fruitbody may be slightly multitoned, especially those regions which are exposed to the environment (sun/reduced humidity) may have darker tones. Furthermore, the ornamentations may be different shades than the bulk of the fruitbody.

The gross shape of the fruitbody is more or less the same for the three species listed but differs most substantially in the ornamentation. L. perlatum is sometimes called the gem-studded puffball, an homage to the blunt, studded granules which can take an almost faceted appearance. Often these granules share real estate with cone-shaped spines (especially when young) which deteriorate with age. *L. pulcherrimum* and marginatum are both known for having elongated soft spines which are often fused at the tips into small clusters of 3-7 (or so). These spines are eroded or dropped in age. *L. marginatum* can be differentiated from *L. pulcherrimum* by the cracking of the peridium (cuticle) and loss of these spin-laden cuticles in large chunks.

Internal Fruitbody:

The fruitbody is little more than the outer membrane (peridium) wrapped around a soft marshmallow-like core. When appropriate for foodstuff, the inside will be pure white. As the spores begin to mature, the center of the fruitbody will take on a yellow

Lycoperdon perlatum with gem-like ornaments

L. pulcherrimum

L. pulcherrimum long fused spines

L. perlatum interior texture & thin cuticle

The Puffballs

hue which will spread outwards and darken to include a greenish yellow core. If the fruitbody has a basal region (the bottom, more oblong region) it will become apparent here that this region does not change colors as it is considered sterile tissue (meaning that it does not produce spores). Eventually the entire sterile tissue portion of the inside will become this green-tinted yellow until the spores are mature enough to turn brown and powdery. While color (other than pure white) on the inside of the fruitbody is not known to be toxic or dangerous- it is considered inedible and distasteful and should not be harvested in such a state for commercial sales.

Apioperdon pyriforme

Description:

The stump puffball or pear-shaped puffball are the colloquial names for Apioperdon pyriforme. Like *Lycoperdon*, the outer skin/membrane will disintegrate until a central pore is formed from which the mature spores may be released.

Ecology:

This fruitbody appears much more commonly in the cooler to cold months and is known for growing directly on wood – both hardwoods and coniferous woods. They may grow singly, gregariously, or densely clustered and range from 1-5 cm in diameter.

External fruitbody:

Similar to Lycoperdon perlatum, the young fruitbody is often ornamented with cone-shaped spines or granules which shed as the fruitbody expands to reach mature size. The color of *A. pyriforme* is always some shade of ochre to tan to brown usually with the ornamentation being slightly darker than the rest of the external membrane. This author considers the external peridium/cuticle to be slightly more robust than those of *Lycoperdon perlatum*, more akin to those of *L. pulcherrimum/marginatum*.

Internal fruitbody:

Similar to *Lycoperdon*, the inner context begins as a bright white and begins to show a yellow-tinged discoloration as the spore mass matures. This yellow discoloration spreads and the central portion darkens and takes on greenish and eventually olive-brown hues. Eventually the spore mass matures completely, becoming a fine brown powder. Only the completely white interior fruitbodies are considered

Apioperdon pyriforme scattered growth on wood

A. pyriforme clustered growth

A. pyriforme exterior texture, young

A. pyriforme mature, with open pore

prime or fit for consumption.

Calvatia

Description:
The giant Puffballs, some the size of a base-ball, some the size of a beachball, are very similar to the genus Lycoperdon. The genus *Calvatia* has four species which may occur in Alabama, *C.s craniiformis, cyathiformis, gigantea,* and *fragilis*. All of these species have the same edibility as *Lycoperdon* species, edible when completely white on the inside. Only *C.s craniiformis*, and *cyathiformis* are regularly reported to occur in Alabama.

Ecology:
The giant puffballs are saprobic, being found growing most commonly in fields, lawns, mulch, and ditches. They grow individually, gregariously, or in fairy rings. Typically found following regular, light precipitation in summer and fall.

External Fruitbody:
Calvatia take on two primary shapes, those with sterile bases, and those without. Those without large sterile bases, *C.s gigantea* and *fragilis* tend to be more spheroid. *C. gigantea* is known to take on many rounded, lumpy shapes including being oblong or with multiple large bulbous regions of the fruitbody. *C. gigantea* can be found as small as softballs and as large as beachballs, weighing in at over 50lbs in extreme cases. *C. fragilis* is unlikely to be found larger than a cantaloupe. These two *Calvatia* species can often be found with a mycelium like cord attaching it to the mycelial mat, almost like an upside-down pumpkin. *C. craniiformis* and *cyathiformis* both have a nota-ble pedestal of sterile tissue upon which the more bulbous portion sits. The pedestal is far thinner in *C. craniiformis*, whereas in *C. cyathiformis*, the pedestal is typically more oblong in width. These two species range from 6 cm to over 25 cm in diameter. Though both are more likely to take more oblong, cranial shapes (hence the name *craniiformis*).

The external skin (or peridium or cuticle) is thicker in early development of Calvatia and thins in maturity. It is extremely thin in *C. gigantea*, thicker in *C. fragilis*, and somewhere in the middle for both *C.s cyathiformis* and *craniiformis*. This outer layer is almost always a pure white for *C. gigantea*, but takes

C. fragilis with thick cuticle and no sterile base

C. cyathiformis with narrow sterile base

C. cyathiformis with mosaic-like texture

on more brown colors (tan, ochre, akin to a Russet potato) for *C.s cyathiformis* and *craniiformis*. *C. cyathiformis* can be distinguished by its patterned cuticle, typically forming a motley or patchwork of slightly darker colors (the size and distribution is fairly tight but may widen with large size).

Internal Fruitbody:

The fruitbody's interior consists of a dense and uniform white marshmallow-y texture which form the immature spore mass and supportive sterile tissue. This context is surrounded by a cuticle/peridium or external shell which is thicker when young and thins as the specimen matures. This external cuticle is more fibrous (though still not very fibrous) and tough (but still soft, flexible, and malleable) than the dense but extremely soft interior. The growth of *C.s gigantea* and *fragilis* is fairly uniform whereas the growth of *C.s craniiformis* and *cyathiformis* start more rounded and develop with a more pronounced pedestal. For all *Calvatia*, the central spore mass will discolor yellow in the center and this maturation will spread outwards. For *C.s gigantea* and *fragilis* the color will darken and typically take on olive tones. For C. *cyathiformis* the color will stay a more dingy yellow with brown undertones and the interior pedestal will become more cottony and tan. Unlike the rest, *C. craniiformis'* central spore mass and pedestal will shift from yellow-ish to dark purple. As the spore mass and outer cuticle disintegrate, the more robust (though still soft and cottony) pedestal remains, leaving a powdery purple bowl.

Tuber lyonii
The Pecan Truffle

General description

Description:

The Pecan truffle is one of our few well documented truffles and perhaps the only one worth collecting. This tuber is actually an ascomycete in the order *Pezizales*, more closely related to morels than other puff-like fungi. This fungus is subterranean and typically requires some excavation to find. This genus is thought to rely on small mammals unearthing them, consuming them and dispersing their spores as their main means of spreading.

Ecology:

Tuber lyonii forms mycorrhizal relationships with *Quercus* (oak), *Corylus* (hazelnut), and *Carya* (hickory) trees but may be most easily found in pecan (*Carya illinoinensis*) orchards where it derives its common name. Typical fruitbodies form in July and maturation of the fruitbodies occurs from August to September in the Southern US, but may in the right conditions, last until December. Gentle excavation of the topsoil in pecan orchards may yield the most fruitful results.

Fruitbody:

T. lyonii forms mostly round fruitbodies which are gastroid (form spores internally) which may be oblong, multi-lobed, peanut-shaped, or somewhat irregular in shape. They range from <1 cm to 6 cm in diameter. The exterior (peridium) is some shade of brown (Russet potato-brown to dark cinnamon) and glabrous (bald) but may be wrinkled or furrowed. The interior of the fruitbody is marbled (looking remarkably like a split pecan!) with a lighter (white/ochre) sterile tissue and a more colored (tan to peanut-butter) gleba or fertile tissue where the spores are formed. The fruitbody should be aromatic and generally pleasant to smell and taste.

T. lyonii in situ

Collection of *T. lyonii*

T. lyonii interior

Puffball and truffle

look-alikes

Scleroderma

Description:

Called earthballs or poison puffballs or pigskin puffballs, *Scleroderma* is a typically toxic genus of gastroid fungi with a similar morphology, color range, and habitat as the edible puffballs. There are several species of *Scleroderma* in the Southeast US so they will be described together here with only two species listed, *S. citrinum* and *polyrhizum* (previously *geaster*). While this book does not cover any of the Family *Boletaceae* (to include the genus *Boletus*), the Family *Sclerodermataceae* shares the same Order, *Boletales* despite their radically differing morphologies.

Ecology:

Like many taxa in the Order *Boletales, Scleroderma* are typically mycorrhizal. They form relationships with hardwoods or coniferous plants – though *S. citrinum* (the most commonly found species) may be comfortable fruiting in a saprobic setting such as on dead wood. *Scleroderma* can be found fruiting through most of the year but less in the winter and early spring outside of extremely warm locations. These fruitbodies are usually found partially submerged in the soil.

Fruitbody:

Scleroderma are rounded, gastroid fungi which take on a variety of oblong and multi-lobed shapes. When bisected, the external peridium (cuticle) is thicker and more rigid than those of the puffballs (*Lycoperdon*; see images), but usually somewhat compressible between your fingers (hard as a fresh potato when young). The external peridium may take on a variety of textures from scaled in a mosaic pattern in *S. citrinum* to completely bald, to scurfy from environmental battering. The size of *Scleroderma* ranges depending on the species but can easily be found <1 cm to 8 cm and all the way up to 20 cm in *S. polyrhizum*. The immature or developing *Scleroderma* will have a white interior which is denser than those of *Lycoperdon* but can easily be confused as such. Importantly, these young *Scleroderma* have a

Scleroderma citrinum, immature

Scleroderma citrinum, mature

Scleroderma polyrhizum

Scleroderma citrinum, mature with open peridium

much thicker peridium and this is a good discriminating feature. Even when young, most *Scleroderma* will quickly develop a purple-brown discoloration in the center of the gleba (internal spore mass) which will rapidly expand outwards to include the entire gleba while darkening to a purple-tinted brown or black color. The gleba will then become densely mealy, and eventually dry to a powdery texture. When mature, the peridium will not open a small central pore, but rather a massive central gap into which environmental disturbances may disturb the spore mass and send trillions of spores into the air.

Geastrum arms opening

Inedible

Geastrum

Description:

Also called earthstars due to their split peridium which forms a star-like shape and as a direct translation from the *Latin 'geo'* - earth and *'astrum'* – star. These inedible fungi share many visual features with the puffballs but have the star-like collar which is their most distinguishing feature.

Ecology:

Geatrum are saprobes, decomposing leaf litter on the forest floor found in either hardwood or coniferous woods. The fruitbody appears throughout the year except when freezing.

Fruitbody:

Geastrum are round gastroid fungi with three primary layers, the outermost cuticle, the innermost, thin peridium, and the gleba (spore mass). The fruitbodies begin as round to egg shape with a pointed tip which becomes more apparent as the fruitbody develops. Fruitbody size ranges from <1 cm (*Geastrum saccatum*) to 8 cm. The outer cuticle (far thicker than the innermost peridium) has a texture similar to *Scleroderma* and quickly splits into ~4-9 arms or rays which bend back towards the base. The bending of the outer cuticle exposes the inner peridium and may go so far as to lift the peridium and gleba or a stipe like structure may push this up (for an extreme example see *Geastrum pectinatum*). The inner peridium is a thin papery layer which typically sports a beak-like pore surrounded by a lighter ring. The gleba does begin white, but quickly matures to form a brown spore mass. As the spore mass has been ejected, the inner peridium loses internal support and is

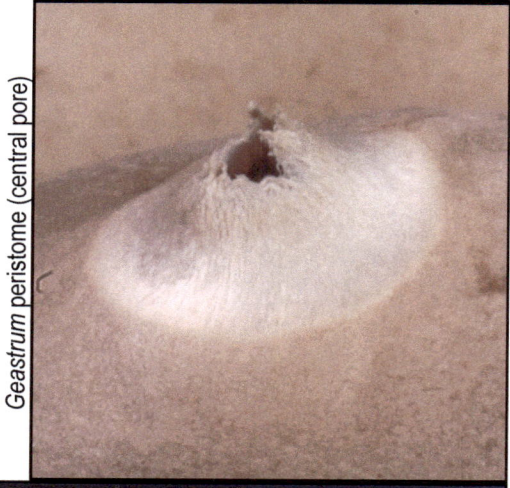

Geastrum with 7 arms

Geastrum peristome (central pore)

Immature *Geastrum* shape and interior

Puffball and truffle look-alikes

often found collapsed. The external color of Geastrum is a range of grey-tans and browns.

Pisolithus

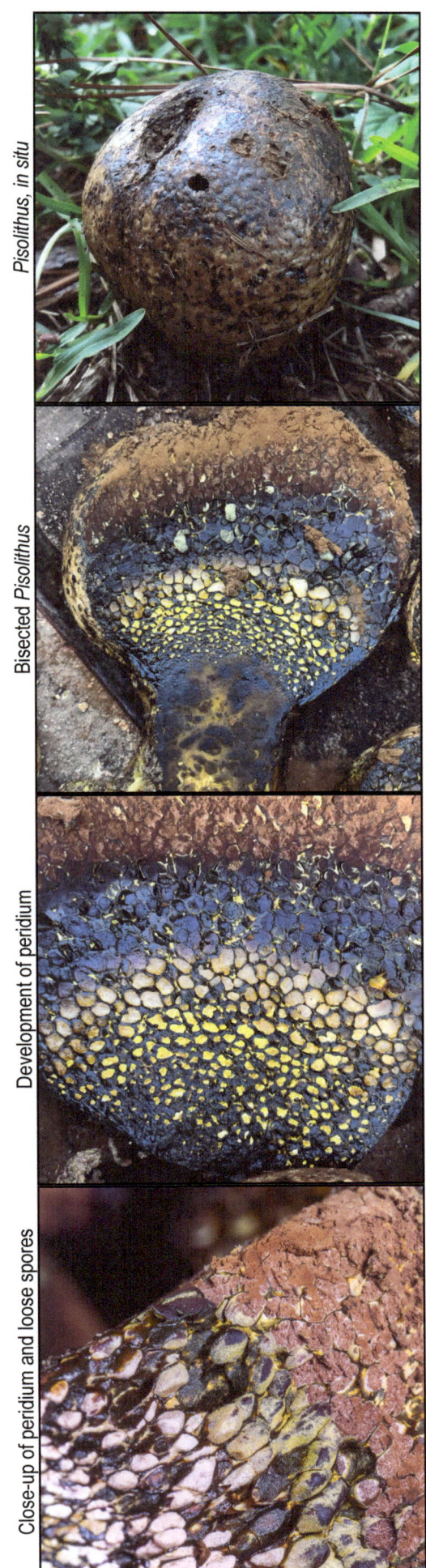

Pisolithus, in situ

Bisected Pisolithus

Development of peridium

Close-up of peridium and loose spores

Description:

Sometimes called the "dead man's foot" or "dye balls". These fruitbodies may look rather drab when first encountered, but when split open present a stunning mosaic of small peridium which mature from the top down. In this case, peridium refers to the individual ball-like structures which contain the maturing spores. This structure disintegrates when the spores are mature, seen as a purple-tinted brown mass which loses its compartmentalization.

Ecology:

Commonly found growing in lawns, mulch, or other manicured regions but unlike most other fungi with this distribution, Pisolithus are actually mycorrhizal with hardwoods, coniferous trees, and almost every other plant out there. In fact, their promiscuous relationship with rooting plants is an attractive feature for fertilizing new soil with their spores. These fungi are typically found growing in small groups (though not typically clustered). The fruitbodies appear most typically summer through fall.

Fruitbody:

The mushroom emerges from the ground as a round body from 3 cm – 14 cm which may be oblong or sphereoid but less commonly multi-lobed. The fruitbody sits atop a pedestal (not truly a stipe or stem) from which the internal peridium are generated and pushed upwards. The outer cuticle is thin and glabrous (bald) and may appear wrinkled or patterned, especially as the many small peridium push into it. The outer cuticle is easily split revealing the maturing gleba. The individual peridium are multiple shades of bright yellow to black and become a beaver to wood brown (sometimes with hints of red or purple) powdery spore mass. The external cuticle ranges from white (in the most immature base) through browns to black.

Extreme G.I. Distress   Adverse reactions common

Rhizopogon

Description:

While not known with any particular common name, the Greek roots, '*rhiz*' – root and '*pogon*' – beard describe the rhizomorphs (mycelial cords) which often adhere to the base of these fruitbodies. *Rhizopogon* are often mistaken for *Tuber* (truffles) due to their subterranean growth and are sometimes called false truffles. *Rhizopogon* are a member of the Order *Boletales* and closely related to the genus *Suillus* as they are in the suborder *Suillineae*. The edibility of this genus is disputed but typically considered to be inedible or poorly regarded.

Ecology:

These fruitbodies are gastroid and develop underground, though often break the soil surface when large or mature. *Rhizopogon* are mycorrhizal with conifers (again similar to *Suillus*) and can often be found growing at or near their bases, especially in disturbed or sandy soil. Fruitbodies develop from late Summer to early Winter.

Fruitbody:

Rhizopogon form round fruitbodies which are very often oblong, uneven, and take on the lumpy shape (and size range) of potatoes. The exterior peridium is thin and ranges in color from light tan to darker browns with various shades of yellow and red depending on the species. Some may have a lattice-like thread structure which darkens upon handling. The exterior texture is smooth, cracked, or slightly scurfy (but not fuzzy). The interior gleba takes on a dense matrix most similar to a foam mattress. The gaps (lacunae) are irregularly shaped (think of a warped *Suillus* pore layer) and tight. The gleba begins as white and fades into green, yellow, or olive-brown colors. The feeling of the gleba may range from a firm foam mattress to mealy, eventually drying to become crumbly.

Rhizopogon, in situ

Rhizopogon roseolus, bisected

Rhizopogon, interior texture

Rhizopogon, bruised exterior

Zelleromyces

Description:

Several species peppered throughout the Family *Russulaceae* will take on occasional gastroid forms. While those species are outside of the scope of this work – a unique genus in this taxonomic Family, *Zelleromyces*, takes on an exclusively gastroid form. Closely related to the genus *Lactarius*, these fruitbodies share a unique trait – they bleed latex upon damage.

Ecology:

Mycorrhizal with *Pinus* (pine) and *Quercus* (oak) developing fruitbodies in late Summer through non-freezing Winter. Found individually, scattered, gregarious, or clustered/fused at the base with white basal rhizomorphs. These fruitbodies appear as partially buried or erupted from the soil at the base of their favored trees.

Fruitbody:

Fruitbodies appear as rounded nodules which expand into lumpy, oblong, or spheroid shapes. *Zelleromyces* range from <1 cm to 6 cm with a thin peridium (external skin). This peridium is bald to slightly scurfy(use a hand lens). The external color ranges from creamy white to pale champagne pink but is more likely to appear in various shades of cinnabar (as seen in *Z. cinnabarinus*) to brick reds.

When the fruitbody is cut into, the inner flesh is akin to a more expanded foam (with wider lacunae [the gaps]) than in *Rhizopogon*, akin to densely packed egg noodles. This flesh will bleed a white, milky latex which becomes scarcer and waterier with age. In maturity the inner flesh will darken to shades of brown and shrink, expanding the size of the lacunae.

Z. cinnabarinus, top view

Z. cinnabarinus, bottom view

Z. cinnabarinus, interior with latex

Z. cinnabarinus, internal texture and lacunae

Amanita eggs

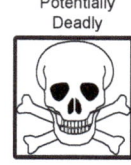

Description:

Amanita and a few similar agarics will erupt from an egg-like primordial structure. The 'shell' is the universal veil which expands with the growth of the primordial form and is eventually ruptured as the mycelial network pumps water and nutrients into the fruitbody causing it to expand. Prior to expansion, the egg may be confused with some puffballs as they are white, round, and often sit just above the soil. As you familiarize yourself with the mushrooms around you, bisect some puffballs to ensure you cannot detect the telltale shape of a primordial mushroom inside. While some *Amanita* sections or species may be determined based on the egg alone, for the purposes of wild mushroom harvesting for sales, this book suggests discarding or at least separating any *Amanita* from the sellable fruitbodies.

Stinkhorn eggs

Description:

The Family *Phallaceae* contains several genera which form foamy, lightweight fruitbodies which create spores externally suspended in a liquid called gleba. This liquid is dispersed by various insects, arthropods, and other bugs after being attracted to its malodorous scent. Colloquially, these genera are called the stinkhorns. The fruitbodies erupt from a gelatinous egg surrounded by a thin cottony to leathery outer membrane. These eggs range in size based on the species and individual specimen from < 1 cm to over 5 cm in diameter. When bisected, the primordial fruitbody can be seen, not yet inflated with water from the mycelial network. On occasion these eggs are eaten, but this book does not explore the individual genera or species with enough detail to consider any edible.

Amanita egg

Amanita egg, colorful cap

Stinkhorn (Phallaceae) egg

Various other stinkhorn eggs

Puffball and truffle look-alikes

Key to Gastroid Mushrooms

1a. Rounded cap growing on a distinctive stalk (longer than the cap is wide)................*Calostoma, Tulostoma,* or immature agaric
1b. Not as above...2

2a. Single fruitbody larger than 6 inches and not full of many small seed-like gleba .... *Calvatia*
2b. Single fruitbody from 2 to 6 inches with many small seed like gleba; yellow, black, and/or brown..*Pisolithus*
2c. Not as above 3

3a. Fruitbody with distinctive radial arms curving away from the central puff...............................
....*Geastrum/Astraeus*
3b. Lacking radial arms 4

4a. Inside texture marbled, gritty, patterned; or multicolored in a distinctive pattern, mushroom shape, or with a gelatinous layer 6
4b. Not as above, inside a single texture with either single color or darker center 5
.

5a. For prime specimens: "skin" (pellicle) is thin with an entirely white/cream interior with marshmallow-like consistency ....true puffball – *Lycoperdon, Bovista, or Apioperdon*
5b. For prime specimens: "skin" (pellicle) is thick, usually surrounding a dark colored interior which is soft but dense and not marshmallow-like, but more like a condensed powder..Scleroderma

6a. Interior has distinctive layers, maybe multicolored, and/or multitextured 7
6b. Interior texture is mostly consistent 8

7a. Interior layers are different in texture, often containing a condensed foam like layer and a gelatinous layer ....Stinkhorn egg
7b. Distinct 'mushroom' shape with or without different colors or textures ....*Amanita* egg
7c. Fruitbodies partially or fully subterranean, found near acorn or nut-bearing trees, marbled interior .... *Tuber lyonii*
7d. Not as above and containing curled, fused, or curly gill-like structures which forma donut-like shape around the stipe .... gastroid *Russulaeceae* or similar

8a. Fresh fruitbody containing latex (may be scant or not present in dry specimens), and many small chambers ....*Zelleromyces*
8b. Fresh fruitbody containing memory foam-like or grainy texture ....*Rhizopogon*

Cantharellus
Chanterelles

KB

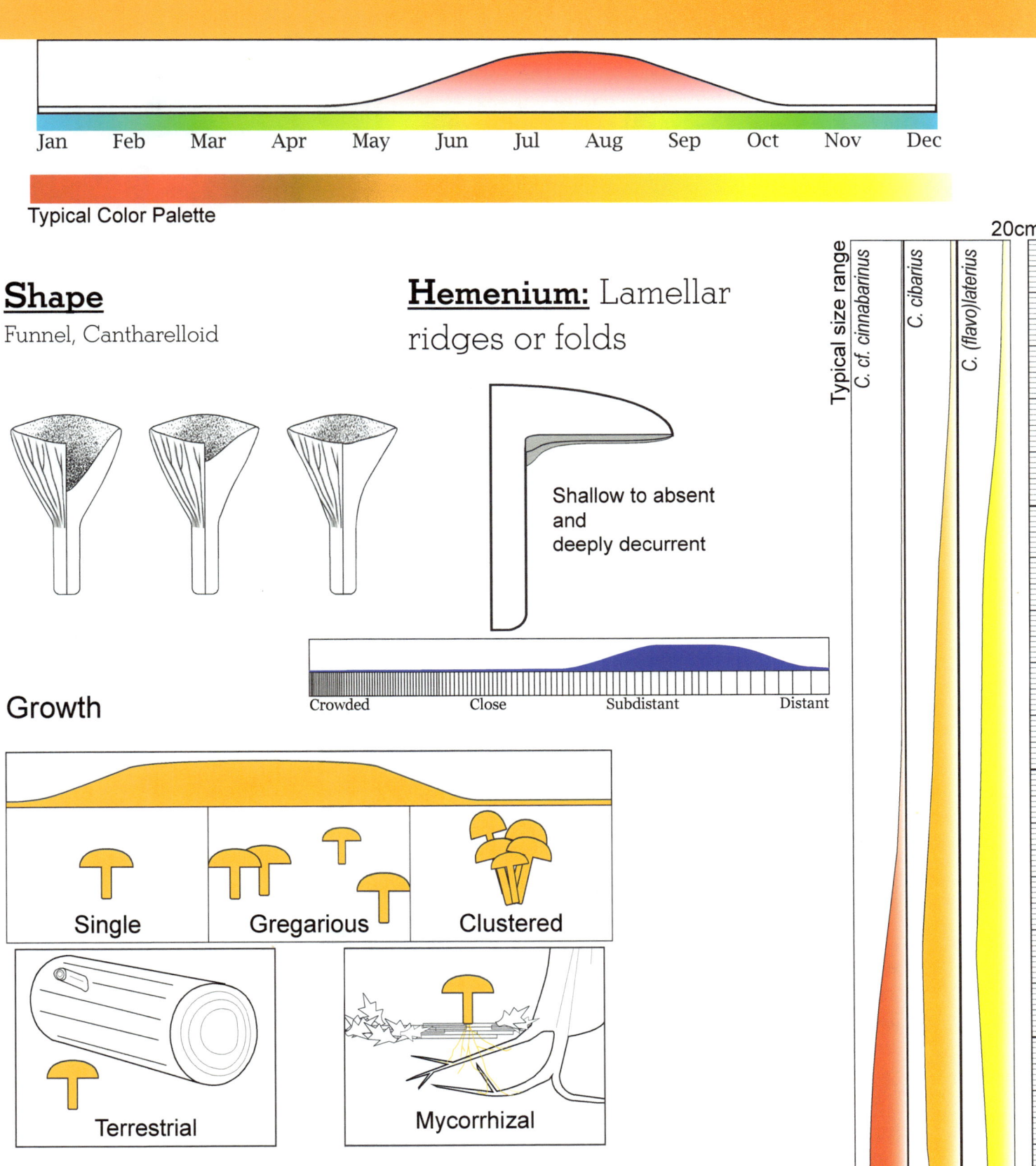

| Jan | Feb | Mar | Apr | May | Jun | Jul | Aug | Sep | Oct | Nov | Dec |

Typical Color Palette

Shape

Funnel, Cantharelloid

Hemenium: Lamellar ridges or folds

Shallow to absent and deeply decurrent

| Crowded | Close | Subdistant | Distant |

Growth

| Single | Gregarious | Clustered |

Terrestrial

Mycorrhizal

Cantharellus form mycorrhizal relationships with hardwoods such as oak, beech, aspen, birch, and elm.
Cantharellus cinnabarinus prefer sandy soil such as in creek beds.

Cantharellus

Typical size range

C. cf. cinnabarinus

C. cibarius

C. (flavo)laterius

20cm

63

General Desciption

Cantharellus is a genus in the family Cantharellaceae along with Craterellus. Cantharellus are often referred to as chanterelles (shan-ter-els) and the entire genus is known worldwide for being choice edibles. The entire genus forms mycorrhizal relationships with hardwoods and are therefore often found in forested areas. This work will discuss three groups of species within this genus, C.s cibarius, laterius, and cinnabarinum. Importantly, there are several species outside of these groupings including C.s appalachiensis and tabernensis which are not currently approved for sales in Alabama but are still good edibles and worth collecting. The following species groups are discussed as groups for two reasons, 1. Several of the included species or variations have overlapping features which are not readily discriminated from one another and 2. It is believed that Alabama (and the Southeast US in general) is home to many cryptid species (i.e. many as of yet undescribed species). As luck would have it, all of these cryptid species are still considered choice edibles and can be collected within the following species groups.

Fruitbody:

The exact features relevant for the species groups will be presented with them. However, Cantharellus share many features which help differentiate them from other genera. Fruitbodies are roughly vase or funnel shaped, sometimes flat, and often misshapen by environmental pressures. The variety of 'cantharelloid' shapes become easily recognized after a couple of exposures. Most Cantharellus are considered to have a light fruity aroma which is often only obvious with larger collections. The aroma is akin to apricots.

Pileus:

Cantharellus have variable thickness to the pileal region but are generally 'meaty' with thick contexts in cibarius and laterius groups. The pileal shape is typically flat or upturned and will not contain a central pore (outside of environmental damages). When cut into or torn apart, all Cantharellus will have a white interior. This feature is especially important for differentiating Cantharellus from the toxic look-a-like genus Omphalotus.

Hymenium:

Cantharellus appalachiensis in situ

Cantharellus cibarius in situ

Cantharellus lamellae

Cantharellus lamellae and stipe

A central identification characteristic for *Cantharellus* are the lamellae, which are unlike the deep, paper-like gills typical of store-bought button mushrooms and are better described as ridges. These ridges are technically a form of lamellae, so we'll stay away from the colloquial "false gills" description as this can be misleading. The depth of these ridges is both species and individually variable but will never be "deep". Importantly, *Cantharellus* will always have decurrent lamellae, often stopping together in a sort of ring (not akin to an annulus). The lamellar ridges can often be scraped from the fruitbody like a waterlogged skin with the back of your fingernail but will not peel off as a layer as in some boletes. Importantly, *Cantharellus* have forking lamellae which commonly contain cross-veins between them. *Cantharellus* drop white spores.

Stipe:

The stipe of *Cantharellus* is a continuation of the pileus, without the obvious changes in texture or structure that is present in many other mushrooms. This can be readily observed by tearing the fruitbody down the middle which should split as if tearing 'string cheese'. The longer fibrous (yet soft and pliable) structure is oriented vertically making tears in this direction substantially easier than horizontal tearing.

The overall shape of the stipe is typically even, but does enlarge near the hymenium to form the somewhat triangular (as seen from the profile) context region. The stipe may also be enlarged at the base, but not bulbous.

Cantharellus cibarius, interior is white

C.appalachiensis anastomeose cross veins

Cantharellus found in great abundance

Cantharellus cibarius group

Description:

    C. cibarius senso stricto (in the truest or most strict sense) is a European species. However, the epithet is used indiscriminately to describe the myriad of similar species in North America. The American Southeast is particularly ripe for genetic and morphological studies to begin to unearth our diversity of chanterelles, especially in this group. That being said, there is considerable morphological diversity within this species group which is commonly called the golden chanterelle. Fruitbodies are typically robust, meaty, and range from 3 cm - >15 cm in height.

Ecology:

    Occurring in the spring through early winter, this group is found most often and in greatest number/size from the mid-summer though early fall, strongly linked to our monsoon season. _C. cibarius_ group form mycorrhizal relationships with hardwoods such as oak, beech, aspen, birch, and elm. They also (though to a lesser degree) associate with coniferous trees such as pine, fir, spruce, Douglas-fir, and hemlock. This species group is best found in well-draining forest soils with low nitrogen content and slightly acidic soil (pH 4.0-5.5) (Danell 1994a, Jansen and van Dobben 1987). I often find them in greatest number on or around slopes (well-draining) and near exposed roots of associated trees. Growth occurs in small troupes to massive flushes with individual fruitbodies often (but not always) growing near one another. While very close growth (without a shared base) is common clustering with shared tissue is uncommon – but does occur.

Pileus:

    The cap of _C. cibarius_ ranges from flat to depressed to infundibular depending on the environmental conditions and growth conditions. The cap can become grossly malformed taking on irregular shapes such as petal-like growths of the margins, uneven development of the entire pileus, and even semi-scalloped margins. Regardless, the cap will take on yellow hues most akin to an egg yolk with a white interior (context). The context is thick, forming a triangular mass of tissue with highly variable thickness.

Hymenium:

    The lamellae are shallow to barely present (near, but not smooth) ridges, wrinkles, or folds of a delicate consistency. The lamellae have regular and

Cantharellus cibarius lamellae

Cantharellus cibarius in situ

C. cibarius lamellae forking and crossveins

C. cibarius, with thick stipe, decurrent gills

obvious forking, many short gills (lamellulae), and frequent cross veins. The lamellar structures are highly decurrent.

Stipe:

The stipe is robust, meaty, and shares the same context as the cap (there is no discernable division between the two). Lamellae can run down the stipe a considerable distance, even reaching the base, especially when the fruitbody is irregularly shaped.

Cantharellus (flavo)laterius group

Description:

Called the smooth chanterelle due to the propensity for the lamellae to be so short that they are actually smooth. While this feature may be especially useful for the novice forager to identify a chanterelle, this group is also known for being buggier. The cause of this is unknown, but it appears that some deterrent present in many other *Cantharellus* groups/species is either not present or is reduced in C. laterius. Fruitbodies are typically robust, meaty, and range from 3 cm - >15 cm in height.

Ecology:

Occurring in the spring through early winter, this group is found most often and in greatest number/size from the mid-summer though early fall, strongly linked to our monsoon season. I often find them in greatest number on or around slopes (well-draining) and near exposed roots of associated trees. Tree associations are similar to *C. cibarius*. Growth occurs in small troupes to massive flushes with individual fruitbodies often (but not always) growing near one another.

Pileus:

The cap of *C. (flavo)laterius* ranges from flat to depressed to infundibular depending on the environmental conditions and growth conditions. The cap can become grossly malformed taking on irregular shapes such as petal-like growths of the margins, uneven development of the entire pileus, and even semi-scalloped margins. Regardless, the cap will take on yellow hues most akin to an egg yolk with a white interior (context). The context is thick, forming a triangular mass of tissue with highly variable thickness.

Hymenium:

The lamellae are shallow to barely present, often completely smooth. The lamellae (if detectable)

Unknown species within *C. cibarius* group

Almost smooth wrinkled hymenium

More exagerated wrinkles

Almost completely smooth hymenium

Cantharellus

have regular and obvious forking, many short gills (lamellulae), and frequent cross veins. The lamellar structures are highly decurrent, and due to their near smooth depth, seem irregular. Like other Cantharellus, the hymenium, even when smooth is a soft and delicate layer.

Stipe:

The stipe is robust, meaty, and shares the same context as the cap (there is no discernable division between the two). Lamellae or a soft hymenial layer can run down the stipe a considerable distance, even reaching the base, especially when the fruitbody is irregularly shaped.

Cantharellus cinnabarinus group

Description:

Called the cinnabar chanterelle due to the cinnabar color of these fruitbodies. *C. cinnabarinus* is a specific species, but for the purposes of harvest and commercial sales we may consider it a complex with difficult to discriminate species *C. texensis, coccolobae*, and sometimes *minor*. Unlike the previous species groups of chanterelles discussed, *C. cinnabarinus* and allies are markedly smaller in stature and mass. Oftentimes collecting a couple is insufficient for addition to a meal, but they often occur in great numbers. In my experience, this group of chanterelles does not retain its texture as long as other more substantial chanterelles in storage and should be used sooner to the harvest date.

Ecology:

This group is mycorrhizal with oak, beech, hickory, and other hardwoods but has been noted in oak/pine regions. *C. coccolobae* associated with sea grapes in coastal regions (think sandy earth) and has not been reported from Alabama, but it very likely present in isolated regions. *C. cinnabarinus* fruits alone, scattered, or gregariously sometimes is truly massive numbers and sometimes with small clusters of semi-connected stipe bases. *C. cinnabarinus* and texensis are commonly found growing along the sides of streams, creeks, or flood plains and have a propensity to fruit in sandy areas and to accumulate sand between their lamellae. These two species grow in greatest abundance along with *C.s laterius* and *cibarius* groups in the mid to late summer following regular

C. laterius growing from moss

Bright cinnabar color

C. cinnabarinus en masse

C. cinnabarinum group in situ

KB

rains. *C. minor*, unlike the others, has a longer growing season and is almost always found growing out of moss on hillsides.

Pileus:

The general shape of the cap for this group ranges from convex (with slightly in rolled margin when young), flat, depressed, to infundibular/cantharelloid. The shape is round with irregularities being commonplace. *C. texensis* may be more likely to have a scalloped margin but most of these species sport wavy, wrinkled, or irregular margins. The diameter of the cap usually ranges from <1 cm to 5 cm with the volume of the context (that internal flesh) being just as variable.

As mentioned above the typical color of this group (especially *cinnabarinus* and *texensis*) is cinnabar (specifically this hex code #E34234) but the red/orange range is dependent on environmental effects and individual fruitbodies often becoming washed out or pallid with more orange left than red. *C. coccolobae* takes on some distinctive pink hues which can make an appearance in others of this group but is less common. *C. minor* are typically yellow with some underlying orange especially in the center of the cap.

Hymenium:

Like many of the other chanterelles, *Cantharellus cinnabarinus* group have false gills which are actually folds, wrinkles, or deep ridges of the hymenial surface which form lamellae. Compared to the size of the cap, these lamellae can look mush more like 'true gills' than in many other *Cantharellus* species but will still lack the sharp 'sheet of paper' like stature of normal gills. These lamellae are decurrent, forking, and often contain short gills and cross veins. The hymenial surface may be differently colored from that of the pileus to be more washed out, pink, or even more yellow.

Stipe:

The stem will be colored like the cap but may be pale, washed out, or pallid at the base where it connects to the substrate. Mycelial threads are typically scant but there may be some tufts of white mycelial mass at the base. The stipe is unornamented and glabrous (bald). Stipe thickness is variable but usually thin and insubstantial (>0.5 cm diameter) compared to the more robust chanterelles. Though the stipe of those in this group is sometimes found with surprising girth, usually when the cap context is also wide and more commonly in *C. texensis* and *coccolobae*. The stipe will not be hollow (outside of environmental damage) and the context will be white.

Cantharellus

C. cinnabarinus fruiting *en masse*

Wavy/scalloped margin of *C. cinnabarinus* group.

C. cinnabarinus, likely *texensis*

C. minor

Cantharellus look-alikes

Omphalotus (sub)illudens

Extreme G.I. Distress

Description:

Commonly called the "Jack-o-Lantern" mushroom due to its highly saturated orange pigmentation and the occasional bioluminescence from the gills of fresh specimens. We only have two species of this genus in the Southeast US, *Omphalotus illudens* and *subilludens*, which are for all intents and purposes, indistinguishable. This species is most common in the Autumn but will make some summer appearances, overlapping with *Cantharellus* season. Because of this and the bright yellow-orange colors, it is often mistaken for either *Cantharellus* or even *Laetiporus* by the novice. This is especially unfortunate since *Omphalotus* are <u>toxic</u>. The toxins "illudin S" and "illudin M" are unlikely to be deadly to an otherwise healthy person, but the ensuing gastro-intestinal symptoms cause many to wish they were dead.

Because *Cantharellus* is the mushroom most confused with *Omphalotus*, we'll use it to make our comparisons.

Ecology:

These species, *O. illudens* and *subilludens*, are present in Eastern North America where they grow as saprobes at the base of dead/dying hardwoods and seem to be particularly fond of oak. Growing most commonly in clumps/clusters with stipes attached at the base (but not all growing from the same stipe, i.e., not branched). They can also be found growing scattered, or alone, but most typically singles will be growing just feet from gregarious clusters. Fruitbodies can be found in the summer, but most will not fruit until autumn seasonally alongside *Grifola* and *Laetiporus*. When fruiting en masse, the forest almost looks like a pumpkin patch from afar- truly a sight to behold.

Pileus:

True to their name, *Omphalotus* are the color of jack-o-lanterns (well pumpkins at least), various shades of orange with yellow and sometimes reddish brown undertones depending on their maturity and

O. illudens single fruitbody

Older *O. illudens* cluster growth at oak base

O. illudens in situ showing threadlike fibrils

Cantharellus look-alikes

water content. The cap is bald/glabrous and may have a whitish central region. The texture, while glabrous does not describe the threadlike splitting, radiating from the center, which may be present and is substantially enhanced in very mature or dried specimens. The cap/pileus ranges from 2 cm to >15 cm in diameter and the shape is somewhat unique insomuch as it takes on an angular, boxy appearance just past its prime. The cap is usually short in height relative to its diameter. The cap begins convex with an inrolled margin, becoming flat at prime and then, depending on environmental conditions, either infundibular as the margins reach up, or boxy as the margins droop. When droopy, the cap looks much like a table with an overly large cover hanging over its sides. When dried, the fruitbody takes on redder hues and blackens.

Hymenium:

Bright orange lamellae are decurrent (running down the stem) just like in *Cantharellus*, however these are deep 'true gills' which are much more blade like (as opposed to the extended ridges of *Cantharellus*). *Omphalotus* sports frequent short gills but lacks the anastomose (cross veins) connections of *Cantharellus*. Perhaps most excitingly, the gills of young, fresh specimens glow in the dark! Though, not every specimen does, and most are extremely difficult to see. I have only observed it with a dark room and long exposure photography.

Stipe:

The stipe is also bald and pumpkin-orange though may be several shades lighter and more yellow than the cap sometimes almost white. The shape is even, with minimal tapering at the base and any bulbosity being restricted to the lower middle region of the stipe. Stems are often connected at the base to one another and feature white mycelial threads at the very base. While the stipe in unornamented, the fine fibrous nature of the tissue is easily observable and allows the fruitbody to be torn down the middle, like string cheese, and like *Cantharellus*. However, unlike *Cantharellus*, when bisected, the context (internal tissue) of both the cap and stem will have distinctive orange coloration (maybe completely or patchy).

O. illudens, mature pileus / cap

O. illudens decurrent lamellae

Older, dried O. illudens cluster

O. illudens stipe interior contains orange

Cantharellus look-alikes

Hygrophoropsis aurantiaca

Inedible

Description:

Hygrophoropsis [Hi-grow-fore-op-sis] *aurantiaca* [Ah-rahn-tee-aka] is commonly called the "False chanterelle" due to superficial similarities in color and the common forking gills. While anything not a chanterelle (especially those with similar superficial features) can be called a "false" chanterelle, this species is the one to truly hold that title. You are unlikely to run into many of these in the Gulf States, but they are present. While these are considered inedible, there have been reports of their consumption with no ill effects. Regardless, this document does not recommend eating them. This species is located in the Order *Boletales* and was previously considered to be a part of the *Paxillaceae* Family, making them more closely related to the Boletes than to *Cantharellus*.

Ecology:

These saprobes grow on forest detris especially under, around, or sometime on decaying logs of either hardwoods or coniferous wood. They are common to North America and Europe but their documentation in the Southeast United States is very low. *H. aurantiaca* is a cool-weather fruiter and most likely to appear in later Autumn.

Pileus:

The cap ranges from convex to flat and eventually infundibular. Convex and flat instances will likely have a central depression. The margin (cap edges) may be slightly in-rolled (especially when young) or concurrent with the cap shape. The color of the pilus ranges drastically from near white to yellows, ochres, oranges, and cinnabar-red. The pileal center will almost always be a darker color or shade than the margins of the cap which are usually pale in comparison. The pileal surface is covered in short, soft fibers with a somewhat velvety texture which can be easily damaged by the environment. The context of the cap is soft and easily damaged, nowhere near as robust and meaty as *Cantharellus*.

Hymenium:

The hymenial surface is composed of highly forked deep lamellae which run down the stipe (decurrent). The lamellae are soft and easily damaged. They range in color from pallid or bright yellows to oranges with undertones of red or pink and even cinnabar.

H. aurantiaca, growing under log

Grapefruit-to-orange colored hymenium with forking gills

Hymenial and pileal colors

H. aurantiaca, growing under log

Stipe:

Commonly off-center, the stipe is thin compared to the cap (the pictured specimens have thicker than usual stems) and bald/glabrous or finely textured (tiny scales/fibers). The color is similar to that of the middle of the cap (usually darker than most of the cap) and may darken further with handling.

Gerronema strombodes

Description:

Once you get to know *Gerronema strombodes* [Jer-on-ih-mah Strom-bode-es], you'll be able to identify it by eye from some distance. This is due to it's fairly distinctive growth habitat and large clusters. *Gerronema* is a genus in the family *Marasmiaceae* - meaning that it is a 'close' relative of the other marasmoids (*Marasmius*). If you've taken the time to get to know any of these - typically - small or even dainty mushrooms which grow prolifically on dead wood and sticks after a rain, you'll begin to notice some morphological similarities. Specifically, the texture of the flesh (including the entire cap [pileus, context, and hymenium]) is delicate and almost waxy (though less crumbly than the *Hygrophoraceae* [the wax caps]).

The color and summer growth sometimes confuses the amateur chanterelle forager, but *Gerronema strombodes* can be distinguished quite easily by their growth habitat, on wood. *G. strombodes* are not typically considered edible, but they are not known to be toxic. I've tried them and the flesh is insubstantial and degrades with heat becoming a less than palatable mush with no flavor. Regardless, these pale-yellow mushrooms are a delight to find because of their typically substantial number and quick growth following summer rains.

Ecology:

G. strombodes grows exclusively on dead/decaying wood as a saprobe and are found in the summer months. In fact, following a summer storm a log might explode with massive clusters of *G. strombodes*. They can be found growing alone, in small clusters, or covering a section of woods - erupting from almost every log.

Pileus:

Gerronema strombodes first develops with a convex cap with an umbilicate center (a depression)

Typical clusters of *G. strombodes* growing from the side of a log.

Young *G. strombodes* with grey/tan caps

Older waterlogged *G. strombodes*.

Cantharellus look-alikes

and quickly becomes flat and eventually infundibular with upturned cap edges, especially as the fruitbody matures. The cap color varies from shades of grey to deep or pale yellow and may appear fibrous but is waxy in texture. The fruitbody will become somewhat less opaque when wet. Diameter ranges from 2 cm to 13 cm.

Hymenium:

The lamellae (gills) are close to subdistant and broad, typically lighter (almost white) when young and yellowing with age. The gills are decurrent (running down the stem), and often forking. Short gills are common.

Stipe:

The stipe is long (2-8cm) and may widen when close to the cap. The bottom may be curved as it grows around debris. The stipes are not commonly connected at the base.

G. strombodes lamellae. Note the diaphenous cap.

Young, pale *G. strombodes* growing from coniferous wood. Note the fibrous striations on pileus and pale lamellea.

Choice

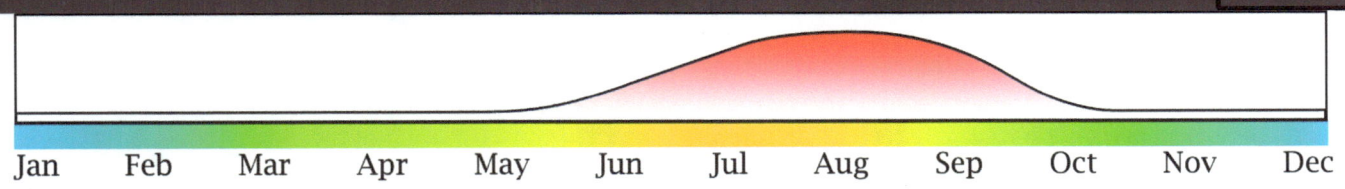

| Jan | Feb | Mar | Apr | May | Jun | Jul | Aug | Sep | Oct | Nov | Dec |

Typical Color Palette

Shape
Vase, Trumpet

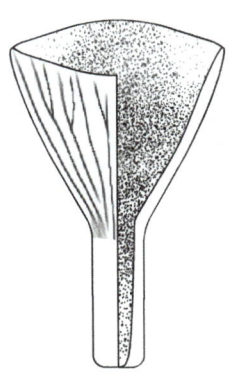

Growth

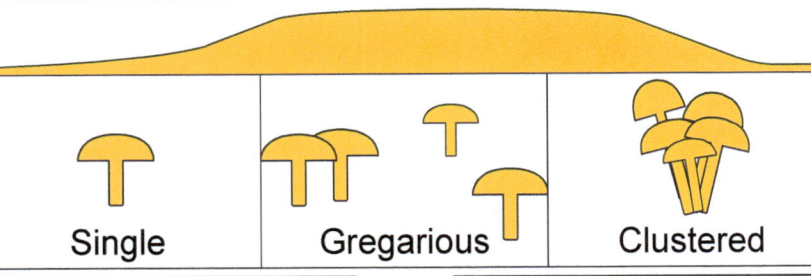

Single — Gregarious — Clustered

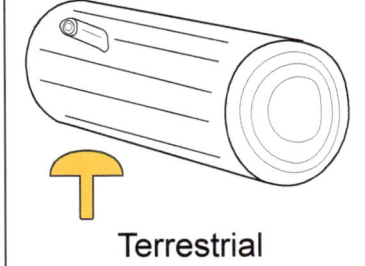

Terrestrial

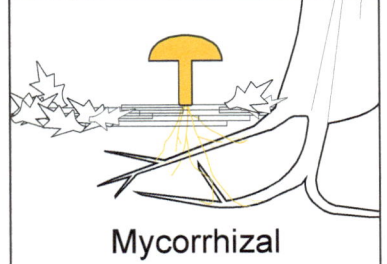

Mycorrhizal

Cantharellus form mycorrhizal relationships with hardwoods such as oak and beech but some prefer coniferous trees.

Craterellus

Hemenium: Lamellar ridges to smooth

Shallow to absent and deeply decurrent

Crowded — Close — Subdistant — Distant

20cm

Typical size range

C. odoratus

C. ignicolor / tubaeformis

C. fallax/foetidus

77

General description

Craterellus is another genus in the family *Cantharellaceae* along with *Cantharellus*. *Craterellus* [Krater-ell-us] are often referred to as black trumpets and the entire genus is known worldwide for being choice edibles. The entire genus forms mycorrhizal relationships with hardwoods and are therefore often found in forested areas. This work will discuss three groups of species within this genus grouped based on morphological overlap, *C.s fallax* and *foetidus*, *ignicolor* and *tubaeformis*, and *odoratus*. *Craterellus* is another genus which may be hiding cryptic species in the Southeast United states, especially those related to the *ignicolor* and *tubaeformis* taxa. Regardless, any similar species which have yet to be appropriately described from this genus are considered choice edible and may be collected as part of the *Craterellus* species groups.

The following species groups are discussed as groups because several of the included species or variations have overlapping features which are not readily discriminated from one another.

Fruitbody:

The exact features relevant for the species groups will be presented with them. However, *Craterellus* share many features which help differentiate them from other genera. Fruitbodies are roughly vase or funnel shaped, though the open top may be misshapen by environmental pressures. The variety of 'cantharelloid' or more like trumpet shapes become easily recognized after a couple of exposures. This shape is so extreme that the context of *Craterellus* is very thin, making the entire fruitbody far less substantial than most chanterelles. Most *Craterellus*, like *Cantharellus* are considered to have a fruity aroma which is often only obvious with larger collections. The aroma may be akin to sweet apricots but is deeper, more earthy, and somewhat reminiscent of truffles. This aroma intensifies upon drying, which is an excellent method of preservation for this genus.

Pileus:

Craterellus lack the typical cap-and-stem designation of a toadstool which *Cantharellus* still fits into. This is due in large part to the highly upfolded fruitbody which, when young is more akin to a tube with a small trumpeted lip, rolled outwards. The pileus is

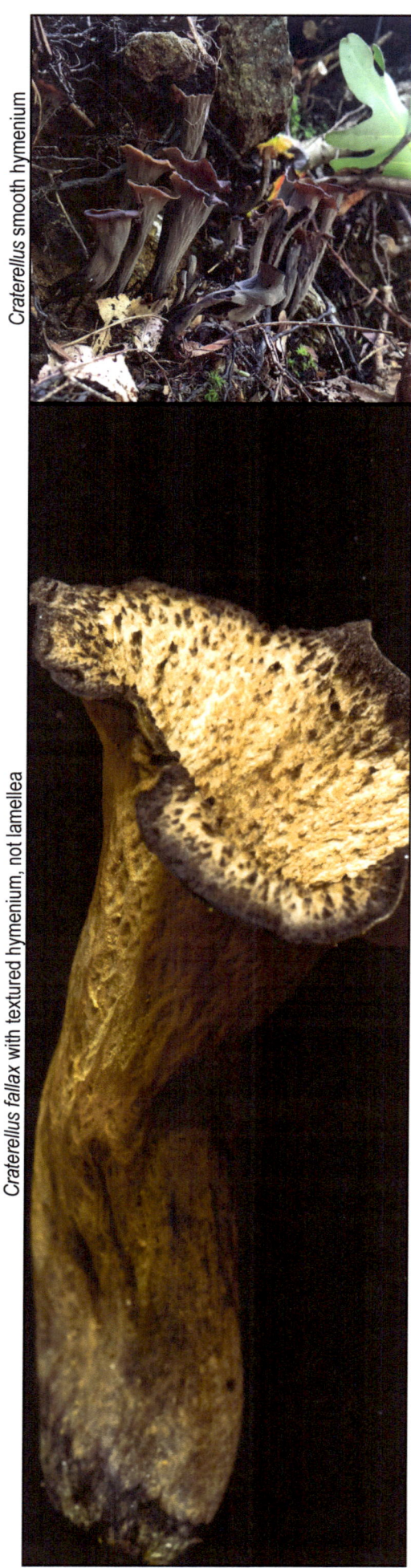

Craterellus smooth hymenium

Craterellus fallax with textured hymenium, not lamellea

best described here as this lip and the inner top portion of the fruitbody. The margins of this lip eventually grow outwards sometimes becoming flower-like with even or wavy portions. Critically, the defining morphological feature delineating *Craterellus* and the more insubstantial *Cantharellus* species is the central hole, sometimes only a pore – which reaches down through the stipe.

Hymenium:

The hymenium of *Craterellus* ranges from completely smooth to wrinkled, furrowed, and even displaying the same "false gills" as in *Cantharellus* (folds, wrinkles, or deep ridges). The depth of these ridges is both species and individually variable but will never be "deep" and will always be decurrent. The lamellar ridges can often be scraped from the fruitbody like a waterlogged skin with the back of your fingernail but will not peel off as a layer as in some boletes. *Craterellus* drop a white spore print.

Stipe:

The stipe of *Craterellus* is a continuation of the pileus upon the top of which the hymenial layer forms. The stem is hollow and the flesh is far less substantial than most chanterelles.

Craterellus fallax and foetidus

Description:

This group contain the prototypical black trumpets for Eastern North America. *Craterellus* in this group have a similar shape, are highly fragrant, are dark or otherwise low saturation in color, and especially easy to identify. *C. fallax* is the thinner fleshed and more common of these two named species in this group whereas *C. foetidus* has more substantial flesh for its stature. These species can grow from minute (1 cm) to well over 15 cm in height and take on more variations of stature than a drunken trumpet maker could ever muster.

Ecology:

Mycorrhizal with oaks and other hardwoods, the *Craterellus fallax* group is typically found in mid to late Summer and through the early Fall. This group has a propensity to grow out of moss beds or regions where moss is common, and the soil layer is thin and well-draining (such as between rocks or roots). A well-draining and thin soil layer usually means slopes,

C. fallax profile *in situ*, growth from moss in oak woods

C. fallax pileus and central pore.

C. foetidus from above

so if you spot one *Craterellus*, take the time to look up and down that adjacent hill where moss is growing and under root balls. Until you have stumbled upon good spots, these can be devilishly difficult to find. *Craterellus* can be found growing alone, scattered, gregariously, and oftentimes in gregarious clusters with fused bases.

Pileus:

The pileus – in this case – includes the inner portion of the vase-like structure and the top of the protruding lips or petals that form the opening of the 'trumpet' shape. The wavy, petal-like lips can take on several shades of black, grey, brown, and even white-grey. The margin is often darker than the inner regions even prior to drying out. The pileus is scaled with minute clumps of fibers which darken at the tips, especially as they dry or are closer to the margin. These scales can give the upper surface a spotted appearance.

Hymenium:

The fertile surface (the spore bearing hymenium) is a layer of tissue which often lacks the defined textures of other mushrooms in this book. In fact, for *Craterellus fallax*, the hymenium can be entirely smooth and glabrous (bald) to minutely ridged in irregular patterns. However, the hymenial surface is the best defining feature for *Craterellus foetidus* which has much more pronounced ridges, wrinkles, or folds which are highly anastomose (cross-veined) and more akin to a cross between *Cantharellus cibarius* and *Gomphus clavatus*.

Stipe:

The stipe for this group is less a definite structure and more an extension of the pilus and hymenium such that the immature specimens often appear as irregular grey tubes with small dark lips.

Prime *C. foetidus*

Extreme anastromose hymenium of *C. foetidus*

Young, irregular growth of *C. fallax*

Common growth pattern of C. fallax under roots

Craterellus ignicolor and tubaeformis

Description:

    Craterellus are not always the ideally shaped cornucopia or horn of plenty – in fact, many take on a more familiar shape such as the funnel-shaped *Cantharellus* shape. This shouldn't be too surprising since these close cousins of genera have repeatedly swapped some species until genetic testing more reliably placed species within specific genera. Two of these species housed firmly in *Craterellus* are *C.'s ignicolor* and *tubaeformis* colloquially called the 'flame-colored chanterelle' and the 'winter or yellowfoot chanterelle', respectively. These species take on a far wider variety of color than *C. fallax* group, as described below. The fruitbodies range in size from 1 cm to 10 cm

Ecology:

    Like other *Craterellus*, these can be found growing singly, gregariously, or in small clusters gently attached at the base. They are mycorrhizal but their favored hosts trees differ such that *C. ignicolor* is found with hardwoods such as oak and beech while *C. tubaeformis* favors conifers and more acidic soils. Both prefer damper soils than the *C. fallax* group and can be found in bogs around moss, and near disturbed soil (near trails). Both of these species are cool-weather lovers and begin to fruit in later summer and can continue fruiting until early winter.

Pileus:

    Craterellus ignicolor is usually some shade of yellow, gold, or orange and stands out along the forest floor. This species has a finely fibrous cap along the margin and a central pore which becomes concurrent with the stipe as a hollow entity. *C. tubaeformis* has a more modest pileal color range of darker grey, brown, and sometimes tan-tinted blacks. Again, a central depression will inflow into a pore which becomes concurrent with the hollow stipe. The outermost margin of *C. tubaeformis* may be slightly scaled or cracks in the finely fibrous tissue may show lighter streaks or make the outermost margin appear lighter in color.

Hymenium:

    Both of these species have variable lamellae (that's the gills) depth from the more pronounced anastomosing typical of *Cantharellus* to completely smooth as in *Craterellus fallax*. *C. ignicolor* has brightly colored lamellae ranging from yellow, gold,

C. ignicolor with central pore and finely fuzzy margin

bright yellow lamellae of C. ignicolor

C. tubaeformis with lamellae and yellow stipe

C. tubaeformis with smooth hymenium

orange, to pink (think grapefruit flesh for the pink). *C. tubaeformis* has a wider range of hymenial surfaces from smooth to distinctly ridged, wrinkled, or folded with irregular anastomose (cross-vein)-like structures. These lamellae are off-white, grey, tan, and may contain lilac or pink undertones. The hymenial structures (lamellae or not) are decurrent.

Stipe:

Like other *Craterellus*, the stipe is hollow, and this feature may be apparent without bisecting the fruitbody by the long grooves which run up and down the stem where it has partially collapsed. The more-or-less central stipe is substantially thinner than the cap/pilus more akin to the typical toadstool proportions. The color of *C. ignicolor*'s stipe is concurrent with the rest of the fruitbody as a range of yellow, gold, and oranges. *C. tubaeformis* has a yellow stipe which is brightest (or most saturated) at the base and some shade of brown or yellow-brown at the apex. This difference in color from stipe to cap can be striking and gives this mushroom its colloquial name (yellow-foot).

Craterellus odoratus

Description:

Colloquially called the fragrant chanterelle, this species of *Craterellus* is known for its intense sweet and fruity aroma. They are morphologically distinct from the others in the genus and from *Cantharellus*, appearing as a amorphous cluster of variously sized trumpets or tubes fused at irregular intervals. Almost coral-like but with the individual appendages each a hollow tube or trumpet. This is an unmistakable species and well worth including in your foraging basket.

Ecology:

Mycorrhizal with hardwoods and fruiting throughout the warm months of late Spring through early Autumn (think chanterelle season). I have found this species to grow away from the bases of trees and in more open regions, often trailside amongst short greenery and forest debris. Individual trumpets may be found, but most commonly gregarious or scattered clusters of many, many fused trumpets are found.

Pileus:

Like the *C. fallax* group, we can consider the pileus to be the top-most inner portions of the tubes and trumpet shapes of the individual fruits within the

C. tubaeformis with conjoined stipes

C. ignicolor

Older, dried C. odoratus

Moldy C. odoratus showing the individual trumpets

greater bouquet. The pileus is golden yellow and may have orange undertones but is bright and a highly saturated color. Obvious central depressions and holes clearly separate this thin- and often crumbly-fleshed species from *Cantharellus* clusters.

Hymenium:

Again, similar to *C. fallax* group, the outer region of the individual trumpets is the fertile surface which is typically smooth to rugose, but not lamellae-like. The hymenium will be white to a pale-yellow but may not be evident in especially young fruitbodies in which the hymenial layer has not yet formed. Spore print is a orange/cream-tinted white.

Stipe:

The stipe is not a distinctive structure but a continuation of the individual pileal regions (becoming the hollow internal portion of the stem) and the hymenial (outer) regions. The stipes of the individual trumpets fuse together irregularly forming a tangled mass of trumpets and holes from a single large base.

C. odoratus in situ

C. odoratus

C. odoratus in situ

Urnula craterium

Inedible

Description:

Urnula craterium are the harbingers of Spring and an indication that morels will soon fruit. This species is common across North America (especially East of the Rockies) and certainly abundant here in Alabama. It belongs to the family *Sarcosomataceae* in the order *Pezizales* of the class *Pezizomycetes*. The name *Urnula* in Latin means "little urn" while the species name *craterium* is a specific Latin epithet for a bowl in which wine and water were mixed. Hence, the name *Urnula craterium* is almost literally translated into a little urn of the type in which water and wine are mixed. However, the common name is typically "devil's urn", likely due to its dark flesh.

Ecology:

U. craterium begin growth in early Spring as some of the first larger fungi to be found and continue to fruit until late Spring. They often grow in clusters or (in my experience) in a line along the sides of dead and decaying logs/branches. They seem to prefer oak but aren't picky about their hardwoods. If the branch/log is partially buried, it will sap extra water from the ground and provide an ideal fruiting habitat.

Fruitbody:

U. craterium begin as thin finger-like growths, of some dark brown/grey/black shade (reminiscent of, but much softer than *Xylaria*). The fruitbody elongates with a star-shaped pore at the apex which widens and deepens through development to form the urn. The central depression (urn interior) will not reach the bottom of the stem and will eventually widen into a circular (or more likely oblong when clustered) cup. This inner portion forms the hymenium. Like many ascomyces, disturbing the hymenium by blowing on it or tapping it may cause a chain reaction triggering the forced dispersal of spores into a small plume! The outside of the fruitbody will change from a darker grey to a velvety black while the inside of the cup lightens from black to brown.

U. craterium, young with urn just opening

U. craterium urn opening

Fully opened urn, note tattered margin

KB

Gomphus

Requires special
Prep or

Not as good as

SPAM

Description:

Gomphus is a genus in the Family *Gompha-ceae* and Order *Gomphales* (shared with many club fungi) which takes on vaguely vase or cantharelloid shapes. The *Cantharellus*-like shapes were once enough to classify them as relatives of *Cantharellus*, but molecular study demonstrate these similarities are superficial. There are two predominant species in North America, *G.*'s *clavatus* and *ludovicianus* – though neither are commonly reported in the South-east they both are present. *G. clavatus* is sometimes called the "pig ear" mushroom. This genus is considered edible but with diverging reports on quality.

Ecology:

Gomphus are mycorrhizal and known to associate with pine where they may be found nearby their relatives in the genus *Turbinellus*. They fruit in the Summer and Fall but tend to be found at higher elevation and cooler temperatures meaning they are unlikely to be found near the gulf.

Fruitbody:

The fruitbody is cantharelloid in shape, vase-like with little to no central depression, per se, but often extremely upturned margins. The color ranges across shades of grey to lilac and some tans often with the margin displaying more saturated hues. The fruitbody is solid and colored similarly to the outside of the fruitbody. Most striking are the ridges which make up the hymenium, most similar to *Craterellus foetidus*, but with the depth of these ridges ranging significantly from find to find. Fruitbodies may be found growing alone, gregariously, or clumped into a massive emergence similar to *Polyozellus multiplex*.

G. clavatus, tan/lilac

G.clavatus, deeper ridges

Fresh *G. clavatus* emerging from pine duff

G. ludovicianus, solid stipe

Craterellus look-alikes

Hydnum repandum group
The Hedgehogs or Sweet Tooth

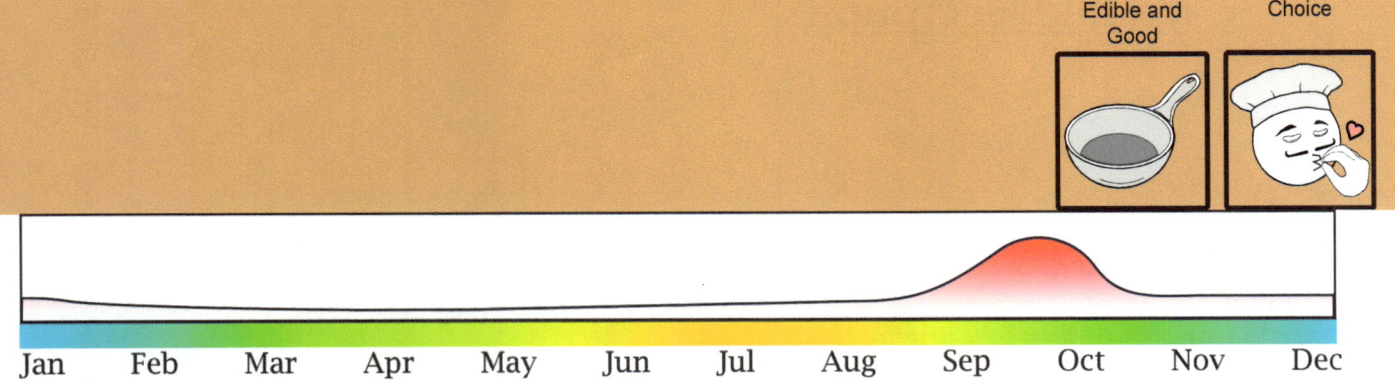

Jan Feb Mar Apr May Jun Jul Aug Sep Oct Nov Dec

Typical Color Palette

Shape

Convex to Flat

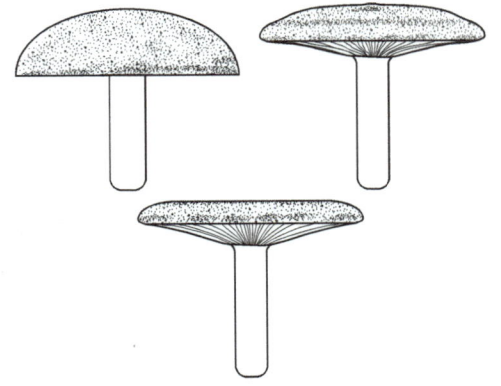

Hemenium: Teeth

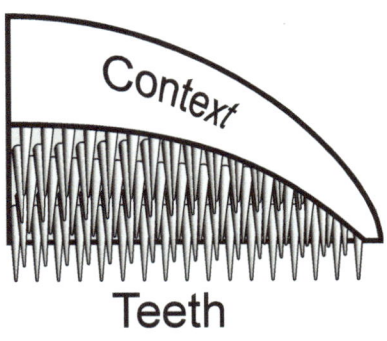

Context

Teeth

Typical size range

H. repandum group

20cm

Growth

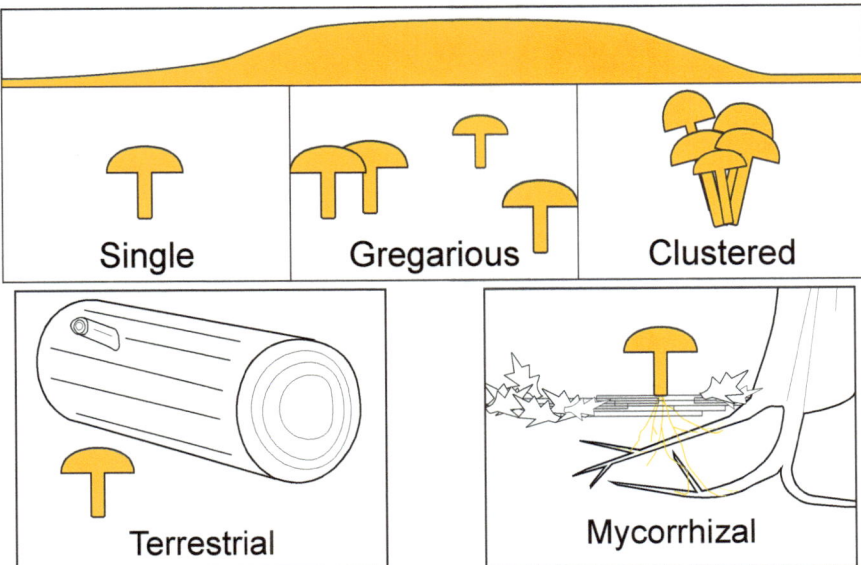

Single

Gregarious

Clustered

Terrestrial

Mycorrhizal

Hydnum form mycorrhizal relationships with hardwoods and conifers.

Hydnum repandum group

87

General Desciption

Description:

Commonly called hedgehogs or sweet tooth mushrooms, these toadstool-shaped mushrooms have an outstanding set of chompers hidden beneath the cap. *Hydnum repandum* is a European taxon that until recently we used as a species or subgenera-level placeholder name. Swenie et al., (2018) provided us with a species-level division of our Southeastern *Hydnum* which includes *H.*'s *aerostatisporum, albidum, alboaurantiacum, albomagnum, canadense, cuspidatum, mulsicolor, subconnatum, subtilior, umbilicatum,* and *vagabundum*. This book will be lumping all of these species together to describe the *Hydnum repandum* group as those edible and tasty *Hydnum* species.

This genus is located in the Family *Hydnaceae* in the Order *Cantharellales*. While not particularly closely related, *Hydnum* shares the general texture and consistency of *Cantharellus*. This will be an important feature used to distinguish this genus from those look-alikes which have radically different textures.

Ecology:

This wide group is mycorrhizal with hardwoods or conifers and specific tree associations can help you determine which species is which should you choose to investigate. These fungi fruit Summer through early Winter. Found growing alone, scattered, gregariously, or in clusters, sometimes with fused bases.

Pileus:

Cap shape is convex, flat, or infundibular (upturned) with a smooth or irregular margin (typically related to maturity). The pilus (cap) and context is fleshy, meaty, or chanterelle-like in texture but otherwise externally glabrous/bald with possible large scale-like or irregular growth in the center of the cap, sometimes a pore. Colors are typically muted and range from white, yellow, tan, ochre, peach, or orange-cinnamon.

Hymenium:

Consistent with their common names, *Hydnum* sport teeth as their hymenial surface. The hymenial surface ranges from free to decurrent. The individual shape of the teeth varies from short and round cones/nubs in younger specimens to pendular and oblong

Hydnum teeth, somewhat oblong

Hydnum teeth, more even and white in color

Hydnum cap, maybe waterlogged

Darker colored *Hydnum* pileus

or irregular in more mature specimens. The teeth are soft and easily flex or break when touched. In fact, they can be downright delicate, forming a layer of broken teeth at the bottom of your foraging basket at the end of the day. These teeth are typically more pallid than the pileus, being stark white, pink/peach cream, or various lighter shades of yellows, tans, and ochres.

Stipe:

Typically, centrally connected to the cap, but commonly off-center especially when the cap shape is irregular. The stipe is even or tapered with the wide end attaching to the cap (especially in decurrent hymenial instances) but may be bulbous at the base. Stipe coloration is generally lighter than the cap and maintains the same color range but may be more highly colored than the teeth. Similar to *Cantharellus*, the stipe is more highly fibrous than the cap context, but still meaty and firm.

Hydnum teeth, wide and multipronged

Hydnum bisected

Hydnum stipe snapped to show texture

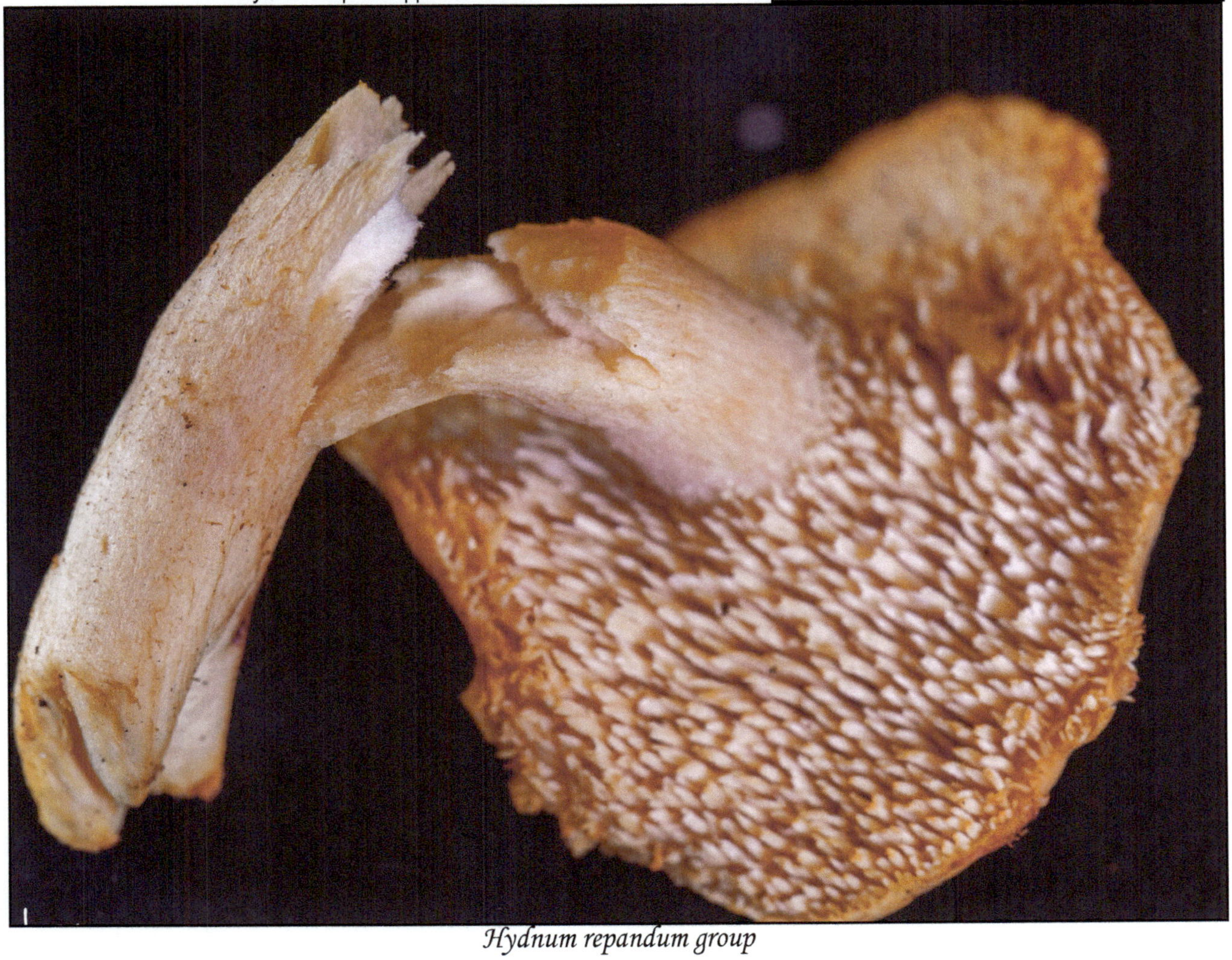

Hydnum repandum group

General Desciption

Inedible

Description:

There are surprisingly few genera of mushrooms which have both the toadstool shape (cap and stem) and teeth as the hymenial surface. Not including those with drastically different shapes (such as *Auriscalpium vulgare*) we are left with *Hydenellum*, *Hydnum*, *Phellodon*, and *Sarcodon*. While these genera have a wide range of features, this book will focus on the primary differences between *Hydnum* and the others. To keep these divisions clear, I have expanded upon the relevant taxonomical relationships in the associated figure. The fact that these four genera all sport teeth for hymenium is an example of convergent evolution, a term used to describe superficially or functionally similar structures with different origins (such as the wings of a bird vs a bee vs a bat). Here, this realization allows us to use the genetic relationships (represented as taxonomical relationships) to find features which discriminate or group these taxa.

Hydnum of the Family *Hydnaceae* and the Order *Cantharellales* which is shared by Families *Cantharellaceae* and *Clavulinaceae*, both of which primarily form softer-fleshed mushrooms which can be meaty in texture (think chanterelles). *Hydenellum*, *Phellodon*, and *Sarcodon* are all genera in the Family *Bankeraceae* of the Order *Thelephorales* which is shared with the Family *Thelephoraceae* (genera included being *Thelephora* [fiber fans] and *Polyozellus* [including the 'blue chanterelles']). The Order *Thelephorales* is dominated by fibrous, corky, and tough-fleshed specimens with indeterminant growth

Sarcodon with scaled pileus

Hydenellum concrescens, mature specimen

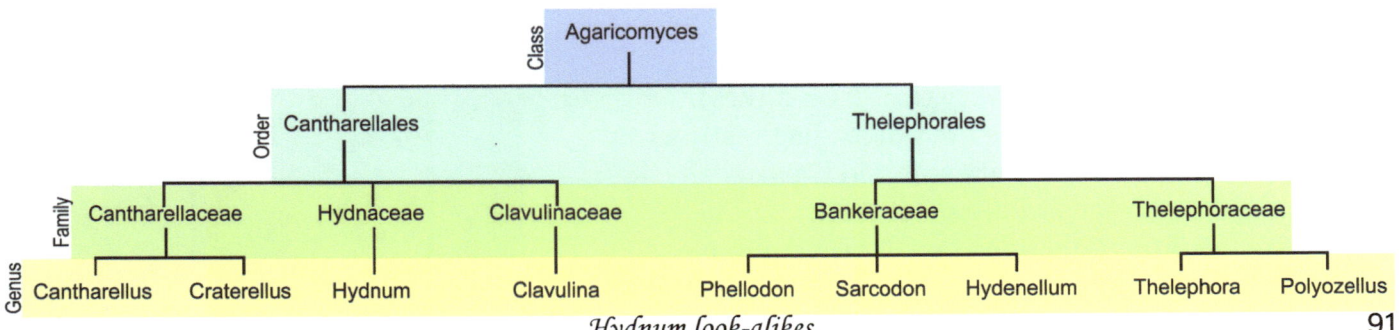

Hydnum look-alikes

of the fruitbody. While these larger taxonomical divisions should rarely be used as the foundation of identification characteristics (because they are incredibly variable), this is one of the few times it's an excellent choice. In this particular case, if a toadstool-shaped mushroom with teeth is found, the texture will be the first feature to note. Can you easily tear it (*Hydnum*), or is the texture corky or fibrous (*Hydenellum, Phellodon,* or *Sarcodon*)? Is there forest debris (sticks, leaves, etc.) trapped in the fruitbody flesh? If so, you do not have *Hydnum*.

Some of the species within the look-alike genera are in fact edible, but most are inedible and these delineations will not be discussed here.

Ecology:

All of these groups are mycorrhizal, individual species have their preferred host preferences, but as a whole all of these fungi will be found in wooded areas. The season with which these genera fruit is also wide and overlapping with highest fruiting likely to occur during the Summer and Fall and into early Winter.

Pileus:

The pilus (cap) of *Hydenellum, Phellodon,* or *Sarcodon* ranges in color but may take on more substantial saturation and dark colors than the *Hydnum repandum* group but many of which are white or lighter colored (remember we're taking about three whole genera!). The pilus of these genera can be smooth/glabrous/bald or ornamented with fibrous tufts or even scales (check out *Sarcodon imbricatus*) radiating from the center to margin. Zonate rings of different colors or textures are also possible in the look-alikes, but not in the *Hydnum repandum* group. Our look-alike genera can also take on some impressive cap sizes (30+ cm in diameter), though are easily found in less impressive size ranges.

Hymenium:

Along the hymenium both the *Hydnum repandum* group and look-alikes have teeth, but the shape and texture of these teeth differ dramatically. Young or immature teeth start as small downwards pointing cones or nubs. As the fruitbody develops, these teeth elongate and may take on particularly flat/oblong shapes (*Hydnum*) or pendulous but mostly equal shapes (only tapered at the very tip) (look-alikes). However, these shapes alone are not as diagnostic as the texture. *Hydnum* teeth are soft and break easily (perhaps less-so for especially short teeth). Look-alikes *Hydenellum, Phellodon,* and *Sarcodon* have more robust teeth which, while soft to the touch when

Hydnellum concrescens cap with concentric rings

H. concrescens, mature with concentric rings

H. concrescens with young teeth developing

Hydenellum sp. cap

92   *Hydnum look-alikes*

fresh, are much more tough and elastic (bending more than breaking).

Stipe:

The stipe is less likely to be a clear delineating structure between the *Hydnum repandum* group and look-alikes as the look-alikes have a wide range of structures and colors available between species. However, like the rest of the fruitbody, *Hydenellum, Phellodon,* and *Sarcodon* have indeterminant growth and often grow around or encapsulate forest debris which may only be apparent by investigating the base of the stipe. On the whole, *Hydnum* have unornamented stipes, if the stipe has some obvious feature, it is *not Hydnum.*

Sarcodon with decurrent teeth

Hydnellum concrescens, with engulfed pine litter

Hydenellum sp. with long pendulous teeth and growth rings in context. Texture is corky and tough

Fleshy Polypores

General Desciption

This section will cover the fleshy polypores, specifically those which may be harvested for sales and their closes look-alikes – many of which are also edible. The term 'fleshy' is only applicable for young or prime specimens as all of these fungi will become tough and inedible with advanced age. There are many polypores which are fleshy when young or at peak maturity but here we will discuss the genera *Grifola*, *Laetiporus*, *Sparassis*, *Polyporus/Cladomeris* as well as their look-a-likes *Bondezarwia* and *Meripilus*.

These fungi all develop with indeterminant growth, meaning that haptomorphosis (engulphing detritus) is common. All of the above are saprobes which prefer cooler weather for fruiting so be on the lookout in Spring and Autumn near dead or dying hardwoods.

Primary features to look for in differentiating these sometimes massive and amorphously shaped fungi include color, size of fronds, and pore layer. Though the size and shape of the pores is of use for identification, many of these fungi will develop grossly enlarged pores which split and become maze-like in maturity. Use your newfangled mushroom knowledge to determine if the specimen is young or old.

Due to the extensive breadth of the Order *Polyporales* this book cannot hope to cover every remote look-alike. Those non-edible look-alikes being excluded from this edition are those which are especially tough, woody/corky, or would otherwise not be considered for foodstuff following handling. Those primary genera include *Climacodon*, *Inonotus*, and *Pseudoinonotus*.

Prime *Sparassis americana* bouquet with rooting stalk

Harvest of *Laetiporus cincinnatus*

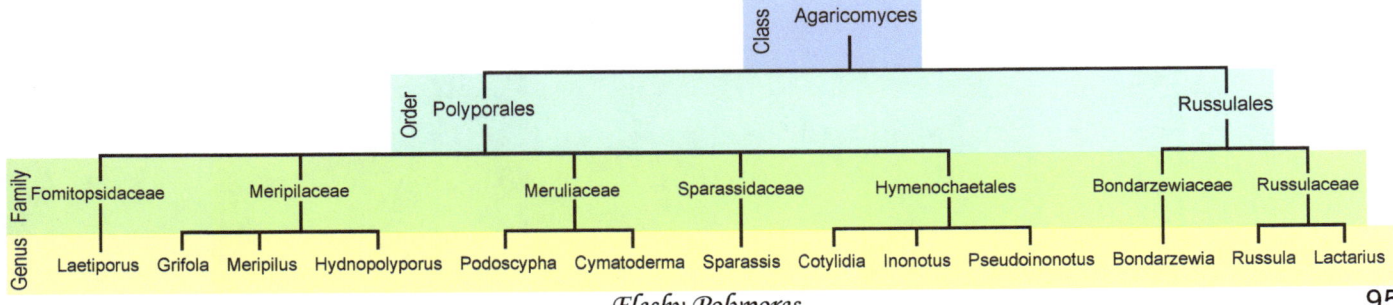

Grifola frondosa
Hen of the Woods, Maitake, Sheep's Head

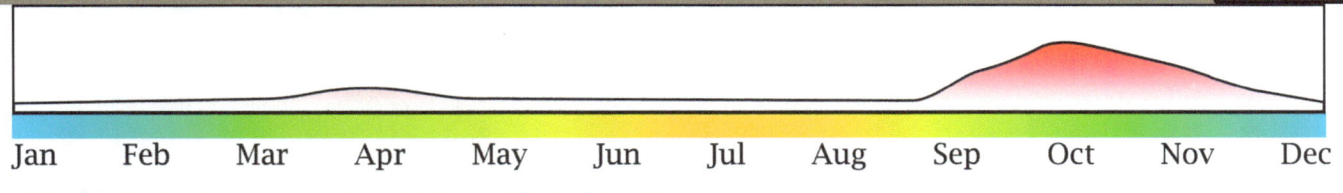

Typical Color Palette

Shape

Rosette

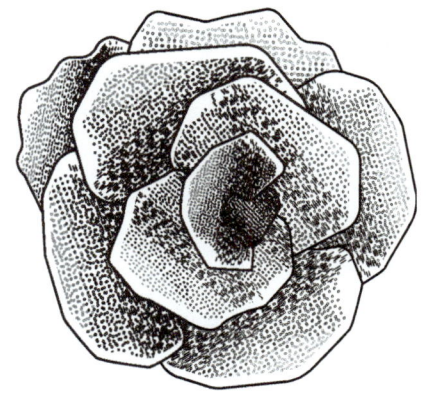

Hemenium: Pores

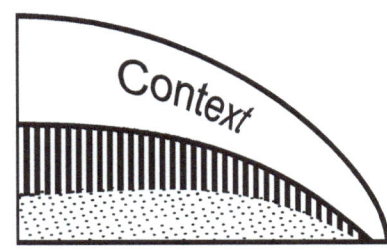

Pores/Tubes

Typical size range

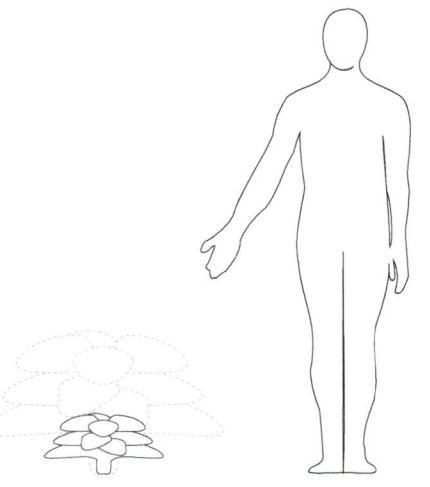

Growth

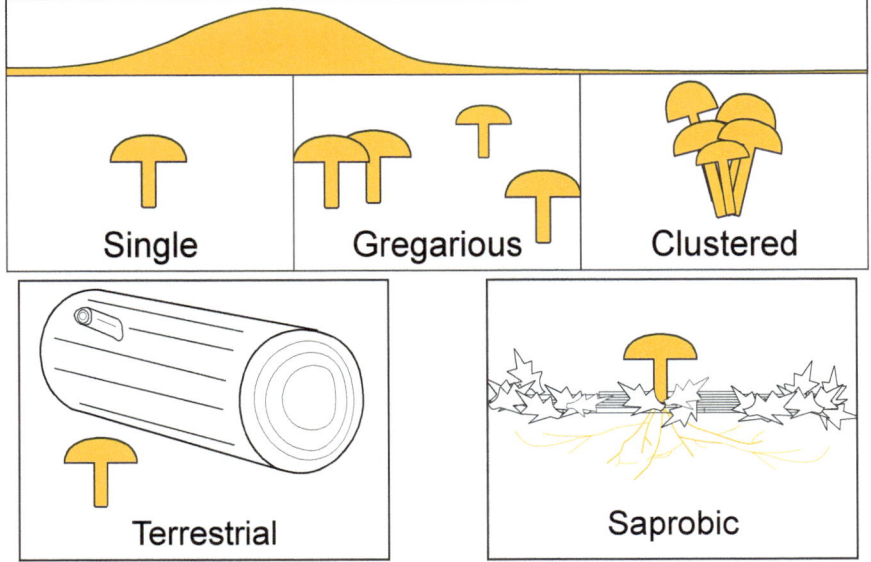

Grifola frondosa forms a butt rot on dead or dying oaks but may be found on maple and rarely other hardwoods.

Grifola frondosa

97

General Desciption

Description:

An exceptionally popular edible mushroom with a laundry list of common names which most commonly include hen of the woods, maitake, sheep's head, and ram's head. These fungi are easy to identify, easy to target, but also easy to overlook on a forage. Like several of the polypores listed in this section, the flesh is thick, meaty, and robust.

Ecology:

Grifola can be found in Spring or in far greater numbers in the Fall. They will fruit at the base of trees as the organism forms a white butt-rot. Technically they fruit from the wood itself but are almost always found so low that we consider them terrestrial. The organism itself is parasitic/saprobic on oaks (mostly) and maples though are occasionally found on other hardwoods. These can be found growing individually, or in gregarious packs surrounding a single or several tree bases.

Your best bet to find them are to seek older oak growth and check it weekly in the fall, especially after the first cool rain. I have seen these grow in close association with *Armillaria* which are also parasitic saprobes. This is unlikely to be a fungal relationship, but rather an ideal time/environment to chow on compromised oak. You're unlikely to find this fungus growing in especially hot regions or near the gulf (within 100-200km). Search in higher elevation and higher latitude regions.

Fruitbody:

The overall shape of *G. frondosa* is unlike the typical toadstools and much more amorphous. There is a pseudostipe, a stump-like mass from which a multitude of branches grow. These individual branches may be rounded towards the connection points but flatten as they reach their edge to become frond- or paddle-like. Sizes range from small immature specimens a couple of inches tall or in diameter, to monsters several feet wide. The fronds should be thick and substantial and the base a solid chunk of mushroom. When you cut into this fruitbody, the flesh should be white and easy to cut with a sharp knife, even where thickest it should be no harder to slice than a Daikon radish or broccoli stem at the hardest.

The color of the fruitbody ranges from white

Young *G. frondosa* with tiny fronds

Larger fronds of a prime specimen

Darker *G. frondosa* being prepped

A view of the underside

through several shades of tan and grey to grey-black. The fruitbody should not stain or bruise brown or black upon normal handling. The colors are typically lightest at the growth regions which are the edges of the fronds/paddles and the connection points to the central base.

Hymenium:

G. frondosa has a porous hymenium which changes somewhat dramatically with age. These pores should be stark white but in advanced age may become tinted yellow. When young and immature, the pores will be small and especially shallow. As the fruitbody matures, the pores will widen and greatly extend in length. Longer pores are still suitable for consumption but may be slightly tougher than those younger specimens. The pores will develop along the individual frond's stalks.

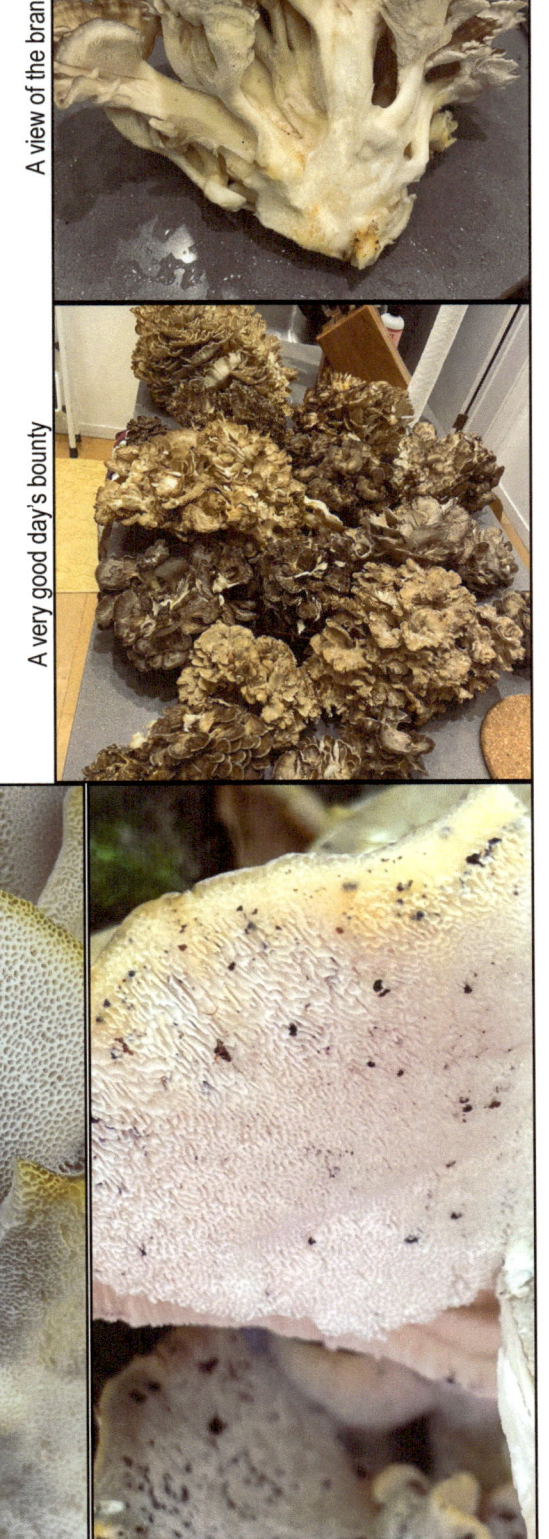

A view of the branching

A very good day's bounty

Three stages of *G. frondosa* hymenium maturity. The final one is not fit for sales

Grifola frondosa

99

Polyporus umbellatus
Umbrella Polypore

GB

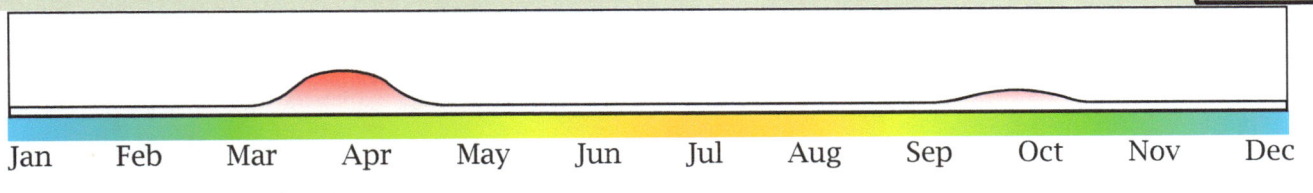

| Jan | Feb | Mar | Apr | May | Jun | Jul | Aug | Sep | Oct | Nov | Dec |

Typical Color Palette

Shape

Branching

Hemenium: Pores

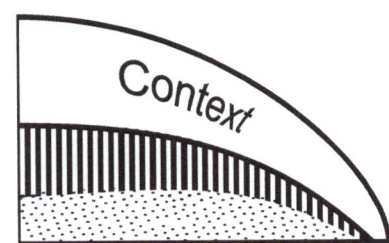

Pores/Tubes

Typical size range

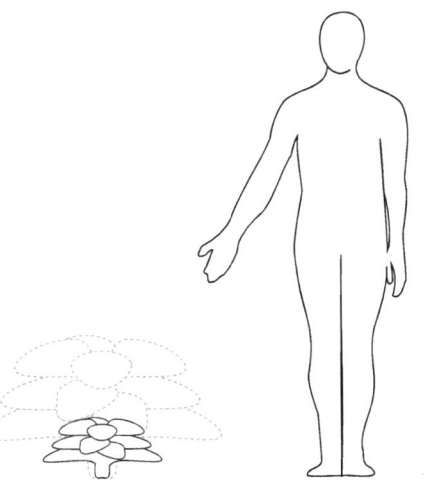

Growth

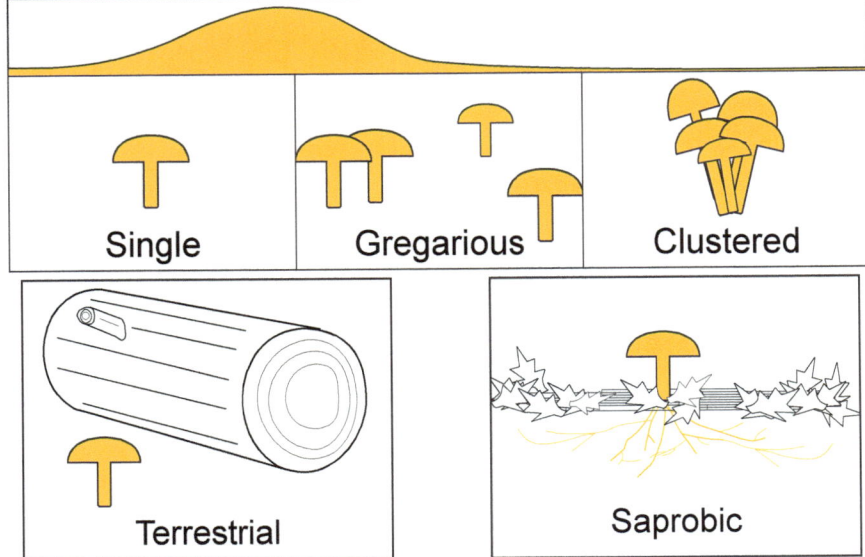

Single   Gregarious   Clustered

Terrestrial   Saprobic

Polyporus umbellatus forms a butt rot and fruits terrestrially at the base of ash, beech, and oak. While rare in Alabama, these may be more easily found in Northern or Mountaine Alabama.

Polyporus umbellatus

General description

Description:

Called the umbrella polypore, this fruitbody is an especially rare find. Many seasoned mycologists never find this fungi so count yourself lucky if you do, and don't forget to mark your GPS as they do tend to fruit in the same location for several years. The name *umbellatus* is a literal Latin to English translation of "umbrella". Previous taxonomical references may call this *Cladomeris umbellatus* or (for the very old references) *Grifola umbellatus*. After reading the following description, you may better understand why this fungus was once thought to be closely related to *Grifola frondosa*. Supposedly this mushroom is delicious, perhaps those describing it can taste the jealousy of those who have yet or may never find this elusive fungi.

Ecology:

A butt rot forming saprobic fungus which fruits terrestrially at the bases of ash, beech, and oak. These fruit during the early Spring, just after (or overlapping) the *Morchella* and other ascomycota pop (April-ish) but are also reported to fruit in mid Fall with the majority of the other edible polypores in this section. This species is reported to grow in most of the world but is rarely documented in the Gulf states. That being said, it does certainly grow in Alabama, but may be more likely to fruit in montane regions or further from the actual coastline. Like *G. frondosa*, these fruitbodies may be found singly or gregariously scattered around the base of the host tree(s).

Fruitbody:

The shape of the fruitbody is very unique, despite the fact that the component shapes are so common. The overall structure might be thought of as dozens of mushroom caps at the end of a broccoli-like branching stalk. Specifically, the fruitbody has a distinctive branching stipe very similar to that of *Grifola frondosa*. Like *G. frondosa*, the base of the stalk is the thickest and it becomes more narrow with each branch. The unique part about *P. umbellatus* is that these branches do not end in flattened shelves or plates, but rather an individual toadstool-shaped cap. Each cap is rounded and ranges from 1 cm to over 5 cm in diameter. These caps begin as convex/planar and become mostly flat with upturned edges or a slightly depressed center in age. The overall cap color

P. umbellatus in situ from above

Cap shapes and some branching structure

A good representation of the internal branching of the stipe is a dusty tan/brown with slight textures of fibrous striations or a somewhat scale-like appearance. This author thinks the caps look very similar in texture/color to grey-capped *Gerronema strombodes*, yellow undertones and all. Though many specimens seem much closer in color and visual texture to the cap of a young *Grifola frondosa*.

The overall fruitbody ranges in size from clumps no larger to a fist to those over near ½ a meter wide. Like many other fungi, the specific proportions (tall vs wide) are variable, but they seem to rarely grow to or over 30 cm tall.

Hymenium:

Most of the other polypores which have a 'cap and stem' or toadstool shape have a distinctive region at the meeting of the cap and stipe where the hymenial surface ends – but *P. umbellatus* has a porus hymenial surface which runs down the branching stalks to almost reach the base. These pores are small but easily visible to the naked eye and look very similar to those of a young *Grifola frondosa*. The hymenial surface is white to cream with tan/yellow undertones, especially in age. Importantly, the stalk on the underside of each cap widens to meet the cap, rather than being a more distinctive structure as in many toadstools.

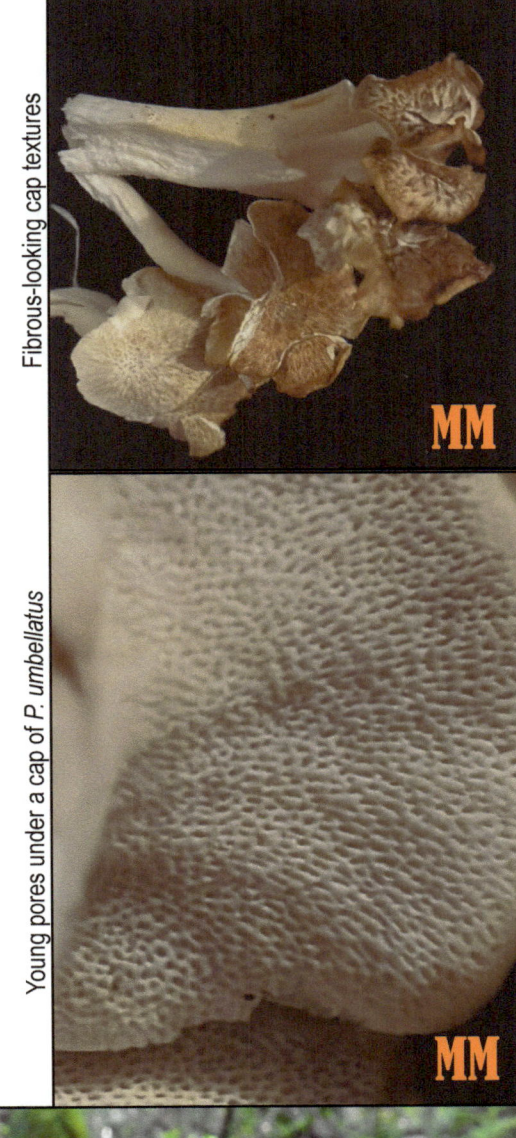

Fibrous-looking cap textures

MM

Young pores under a cap of *P. umbellatus*

MM

A wide profile of *P. umbellatus in situ*

GB

Polyporus umbellatus

Laetiporus
Chicken of the Woods

Adverse reactions uncommon

Choice

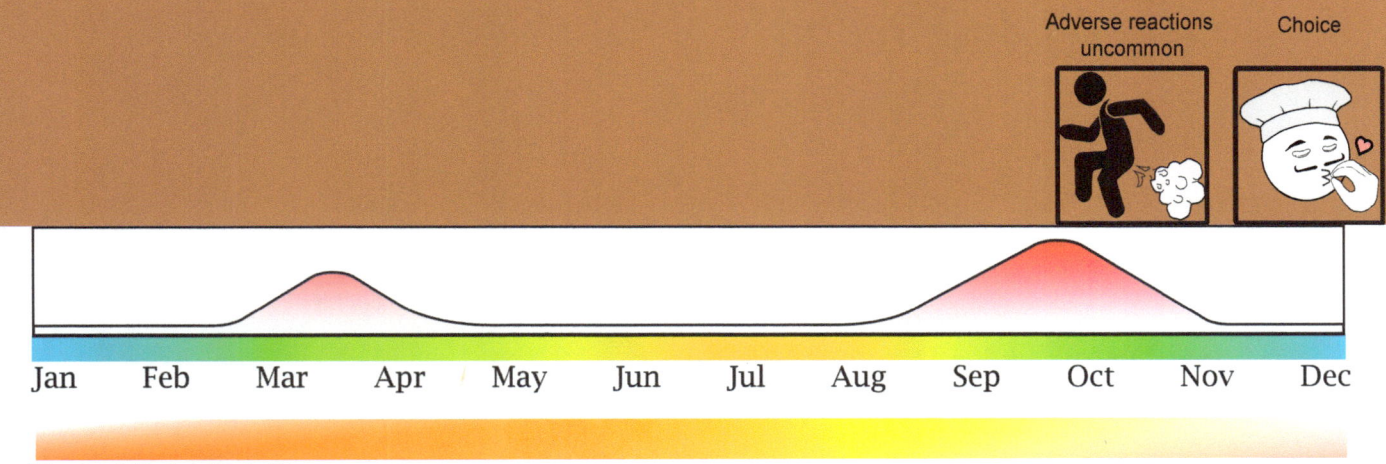

Jan
Feb
Mar
Apr
May
Jun
Jul
Aug
Sep
Oct
Nov
Dec

Typical Color Palette

Shape

Shelves or Rosette

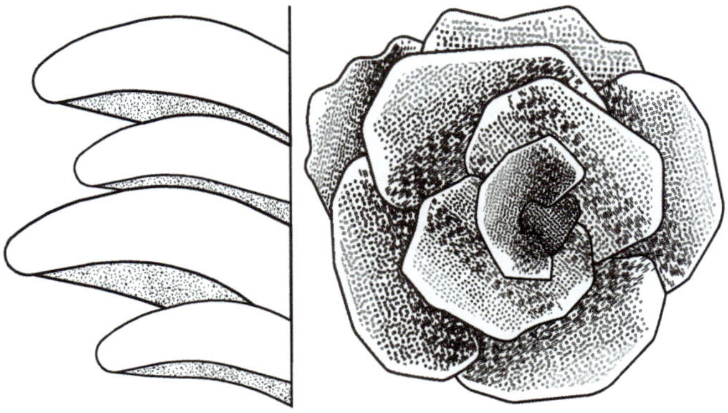

Hemenium: Pores

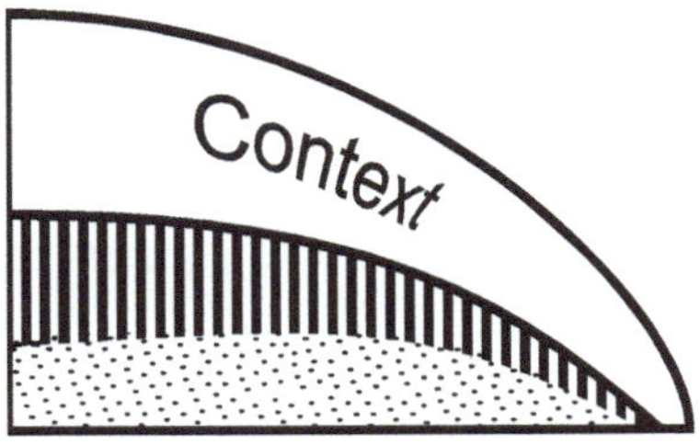

Context

Pores/Tubes

Typical size range

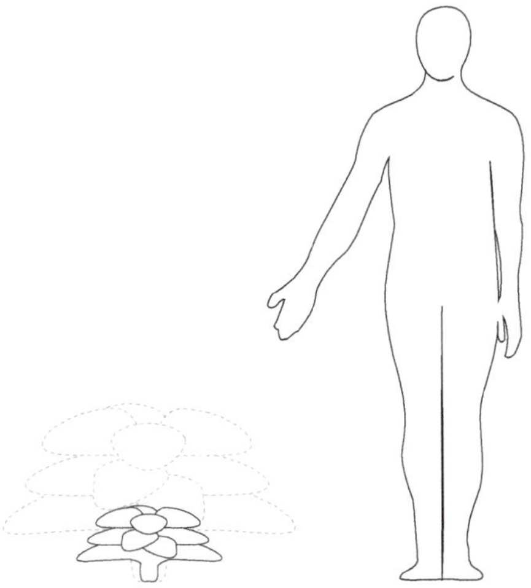

Growth

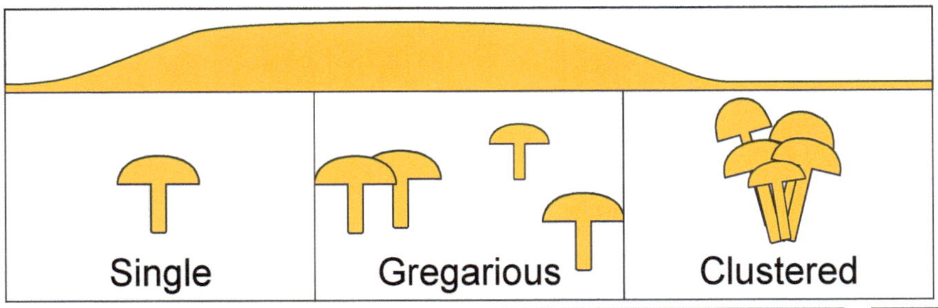

Single
Gregarious
Clustered

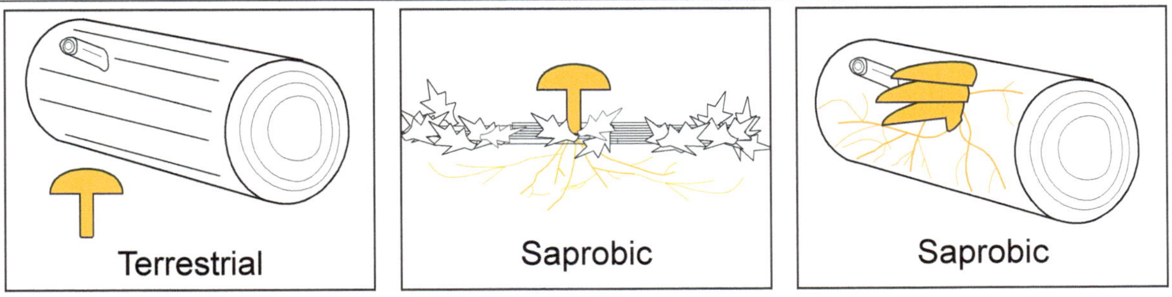

Terrestrial
Saprobic
Saprobic

Laetiporus forms either a butt rot or heart rot on dead or dying hardwoods, especially oak.

General description

Description:

    Laetiporus (lay-tee-poh-rus) are known as the "Chicken of the Woods" due to their texture which is akin to chicken breast meat. The flavor is chicken-like, certainly meaty, but a stock made from these mushrooms would not be a perfect match for chicken stock. There are three species of *Laetiporus* in the Gulf states which are suitable for harvest and sales plus one (*L. percisinus*, the peach chicken) which is not approved for sales and will not be discussed here in depth. The species are *Laetiporus cincinnatus* (sin-sih-nat-us), *sulphureus* (sulf-yur-ee-us), and *gilbertsonii var pallidus* (gill-bert-sone-ee-i var pall-id-us). All of these are edible and tasty, however *Laetiporus* (especially cincinnatus) have been known to cause gastric upset in sensitive individuals. This GI distress may be from the fruitbody being undercooked, the individual having an innate sensitivity, or a sensitivity which has developed over time.

    As a highly sought-after mushroom which is easy to identify, Laetiporus has been the center of some controversy regarding the host tree. Specifically, many have reported that *Laetiporus* growing on/from the wood of eucalyptus or yew are in some way more likely to cause GI distress, or even be mildly toxic. These fears can be eschewed as they have never been confirmed (see Beug et al., 2006). However, all should be cooked thoroughly and eaten in moderation the first time.

Ecology:

    All of these species of *Laetiporus* are parasitic saprobes, *L. cincinnatus* causing a brown butt rot, *sulphureus* and *gilbertsonii* causing a brown heart rot. This means that *L. cincinnatus* will be found terrestrially, near the base of host trees: oak, or from their roots. On the other hand, *L. sulphureus* and *gilbertsonii* will be found growing higher up on standing wood or on fallen logs. All if these species prefer to fruit in the Autumn but may be found in Spring, or from late Summer to early Winter.

    While *L. cincinnatus* and *sulphureus* are commonplace in the South and East of the United States, *L. gilbertsonii var pallidus* is a species unique to the Gulf coast. *L. gilbertsonii senso stricto* is known as a West coast clade strikingly similar to *L. sulphureus*

'Antlers' of emerging *L. cincinnatus*

Especially wide frond of *L. cincinnatus*

Prime *L. cincinnatus*.

A bountiful harvest of *L. sulphureus*

but genetic analysis revealed that a species native to the Gulf coast and Caribbean is best considered a variety (var) of *L. gilbertsonii*. Hence, we have *L. gilbertsonii var pallidus* with which the varietal name describes the pale color (pallid(us) *Latin* for pale), a discriminating characteristic.

The ecology of these *Laetiporus* is the best way to discriminate between species which is an especially good idea for sales or consumption purposes.

Fruitbody:

Laetiporus is another genus which can produce colossal fruitbodies >1 ft across. This description may be a bit hard to interpret for those non-terrestrial fruitbodies which develop as overlapping shelves and not a discrete entity. When *Laetiporus* grows sideways, as from a log/wood or a steep hill, the fruitbody will form overlapping shelves which can spread out through the width of the colonization of the growth media. This means a completely colonized fallen tree which is 20 ft long may develop fruiting along this entire length, and with individual fruits stacking on top of one another, growing into one another, or even forming distinctive rosettes along the top of the media. *Laetiporus* growing along these flat regions (especially common to the butt-rot forming *L. cincinnatus*) will develop an antler-like young growth which expands rapidly (inside of a day or week) to form large and wide overlapping shelves. These shelves are connected via rounded, more robust pseudostalks to a central mass. The vertical haptomorphic growth of *Laetiporus* can form some very odd shapes, but most will resemble a rosette pattern.

The flesh of *Laetiporus* changes somewhat dramatically as it matures and ages. The raw flesh of young *Laetiporus* is very tender and similar to raw chicken breasts. *L. cincinnatus* does tend to be drier and have a slightly foamy texture compared to the others, perhaps this is related to the larger amounts of water which seems to be pumped into young *sulphureus* and *gilbertsonii var pallidus*. Regardless, all of the *Laetiporus* will exude moisture from the harvest site wound when harvested young.

Laetiporus harvested at a more mature state will present dramatically larger fruitbodies but some portions of which will have toughened, particularly the central regions. When these larger specimens are found, the tender portions of the fruitbody are the most ideal for collection and may be restricted to the whole, or edges of the fronds. The tougher portions will be more difficult (through still easy) to cut with

Laetiporus

L. sulphureus cap edge with yellow growth region

Pumpkin-orange surface of fresh *L. sulphureus*

Mature, but harvestable *L. sulphureus*

a knife in a perpendicular direction to the grain and may be more likely to snap or break. In my limited experience, these tougher portions can be eaten, but require more effort to prepare in a more limited series of dishes and may be more inclined to induce GI upset or distress.

Over mature or old *Laetiporus* will commonly become bleached, dry, crumbly, and take on a fetid odor. Please don't bother with these.

The color of all the *Laetiporus* (sans *L. persicinus*) is a bright orange with variations in hue and saturation to include yellow oranges to deeply saturated pumpkin oranges as well as more peach or pallid versions common to *L. gilbertsonii var pallidus*. *L. persicinus* runs from cream to various shades of brown with a hymenial surface which bruises a darker brown on even gentle contact. The fruitbody is typically oval/round and lacks the overlapping shelves or antlers typical of other *Laetiporus* species.

Hymenium:

The underside of *Laetiporus* is almost completely smooth in early and mid-development and will usually not become obviously or deeply poroid until maturity. These pores will run down the fronds and on the underside of any pseudostalks. Most importantly, is the color of the hymenial surface which is used as the major distinction (besides ecology) between *L. cincinnatus* and the others. *L. cincinnatus* has a white (or sometimes cream) colored hymenium. On the other side is the sulfur yellow hymenium of *L. sulphureus* (from whence it derives the name) and more pallid yellow of *L. gilbertsonii var pallidus*.

L. sulphureus, leaking after harvest

L. sulphureus young porous hymenium

L. sulphureus young porous hymenium. Pores are small and shallow.

Laetiporus

Laetiporus sulphureus, young and freshly emerging (left) and dried/old/stinky (right)

Laetiporus cincinnatus, young and freshly emerging (left) and dried/old/stinky (right)

Sparassis
The Cauliflower Mushroom

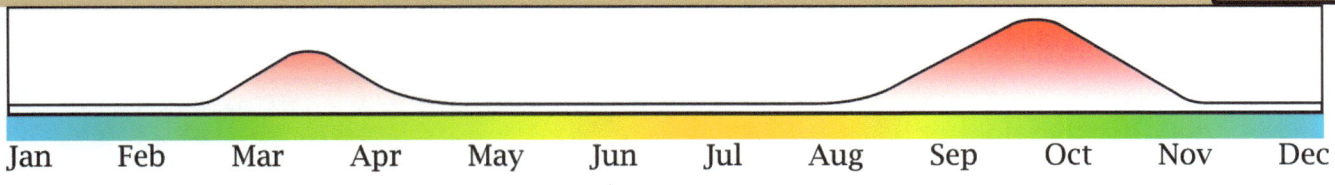

| Jan | Feb | Mar | Apr | May | Jun | Jul | Aug | Sep | Oct | Nov | Dec |

Typical Color Palette

Shape

Coral

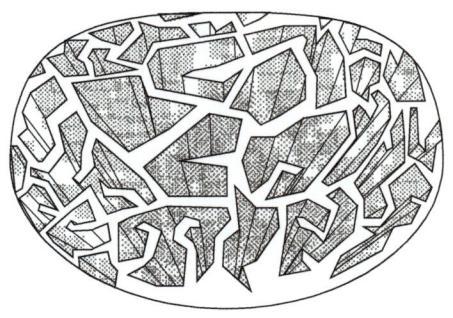

Hemenium: Smooth

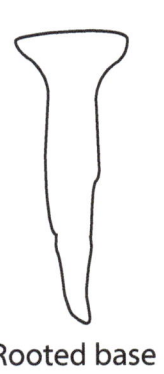

Rooted base

Typical size range

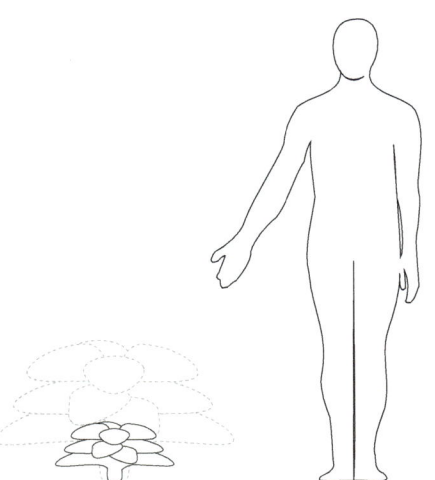

Growth

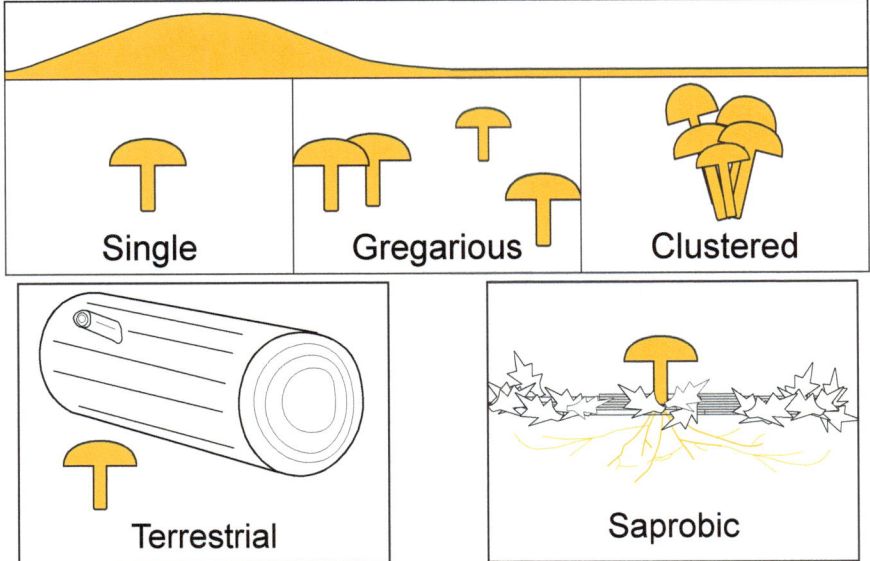

Sparassis prefer coniferous hosts but may easily be found with oak and a few other hardwoods. The fungi lives in the deeper roots so fruitbodies will often have a long tapering 'root' which is actually the stem.

Sparassis

General description

Description:

Colloquially known as the cauliflower mushroom. This fruitbody may be better described by mycologist Alexander Smith as looking like a bouquet of egg noodles, but that doesn't have the same ring to it. Unlike the other polypores in this section, Sparassis takes on a more coral-like structure and does not produce large pores on the underside. This description is less applicable to *Sparassis spathulata* which is still very coral-like, but as for a pasta-metaphor I would suggest lasagna strips. These species represent two different taxonomical divisions within the genus with similar morphology. As luck would have it, very few mushrooms resemble *Sparassis* of either type, and none that do are toxic.

Ecology:

Weakly parasitic and saprobic forming a brown rot at the base of coniferous trees and sometimes oak. *Sparassis* will fruit for several years around the same dying/dead tree, typically in the late Summer through Fall. The fungus itself seems to prefer a deeper substrate and as such the fruitbody almost always has a root-like structure connecting it to the deeper mycelium.

Fruitbody:

Sparassis americana is morphologically indistinct from the non-Eastern US variants such as *S. crispa* or *S. radicata*. The fruitbody is typically fist-size to well over a foot across and may be over 20 cm tall. As described above, the fruitbody appears as a mass of curly or wavy and flattened lobes which are packed or stacked together at the base of a tree. The color ranges from creamy whites to fleshy tans and eventually yellowed beige in age. The individual lobes (noodles) may take on a multi-toned appearance up close. The lobes on the outside are attached to a sturdier irregularly branching internal structure strikingly similar to the white matter of a brain. When young, fresh, and prime *Sparassis* has a unique fragrance which may be especially desirable for delicate dishes. The entire structure is edible including the core which should be easily cut with a knife.

Sparassis spathulata has thicker, wider, and less ribbon-like lobes. The general color scheme is the same, but each lobe may have some striations from

A prime specimen of S. americana

Close up of the egg-noodle like texture

Young S. spathulata

The interior of S. americana

the base to the top as well as a white (or much lighter) growth region at the tip of the lobe (usually that portion furthest from the base). When young, the fruitbody appears generally round as a coral-like structure with several angular holes between the growing lobes which form a lattice-like pattern. As the lobes develop, they become more distinct and may in age become more frond-like. If the prime/mature specimen has very thin lobes it is a classic *S. spathulata*, however if the lobes are thick (>1 cm) you may have a variation known as *Sparassis spathulata f. herbstii* (see Petersen et al. 2015). I would also describe these as having a structure more akin to the immature *S. spathulata* with lobes never becoming as distinct and with a more prominent white growth region at the tips/edges. Like *S. americana*, the entire structure is edible including the core which should be easily cut with a knife.

To recap, *Sparassis americana* looks like a bouquet of egg noodles while *S. spathulata* looks more like a bouquet of conjoined lasagna noodles.

Hymenium:

The hymenium is smooth and non-porous as well as being indistinct by eye as it encompasses the superficial layer of the entire lobe.

A bouquet of egg noodles in honor of A. Smith

A more superficially rooted stipe of *S. spathulata*

A prime specimen of *S. spathulata*

Fistulina hepatica

Beefsteak

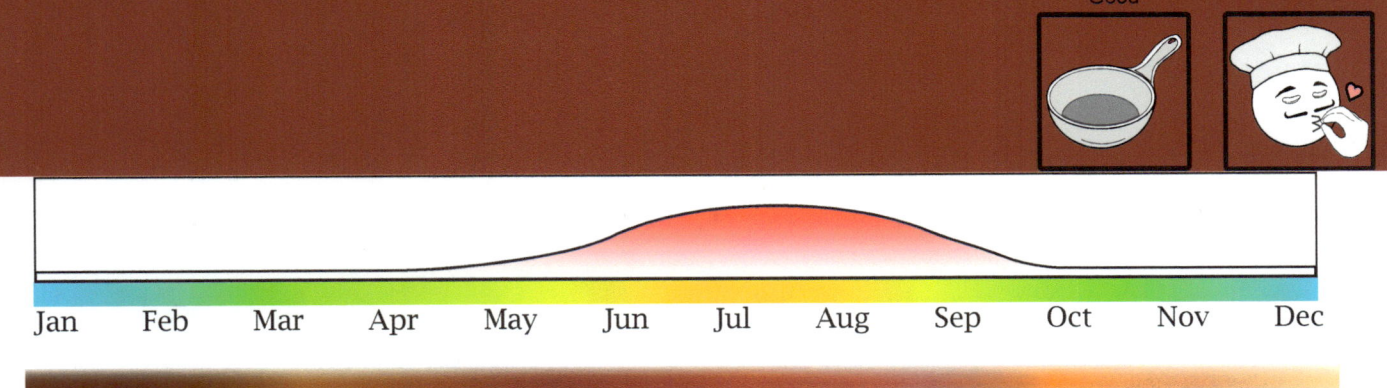

Jan Feb Mar Apr May Jun Jul Aug Sep Oct Nov Dec

Typical Color Palette

Shape

Shelf, from above a spade

Hemenium: Tubes

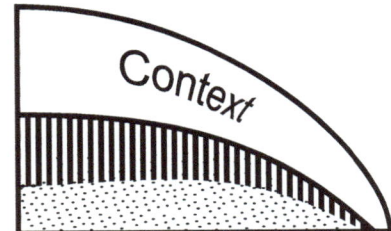

Pores/Tubes

Growth

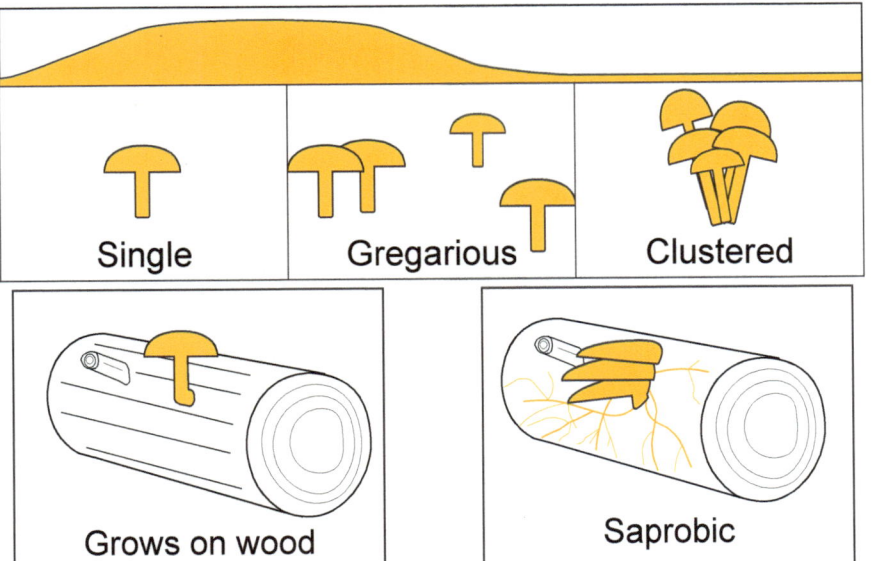

Single

Gregarious

Clustered

Grows on wood

Saprobic

Typical size range

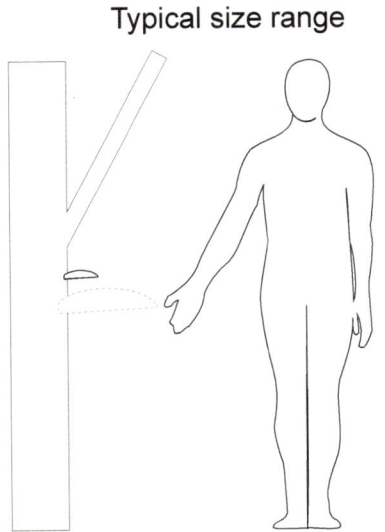

Fistulina hepatica grows on the wood of oak or chestnut.

Description:

One of the fruitbodies referred to as 'beefsteak' or the 'beefsteak mushroom' due to its almost perfect camouflage as a slab of raw beef growing from the side of a tree. Importantly, the common name beefsteak has also applied to the genus *Gyromitra* (especially in the American Midwest, see *Morchella* look-alikes), of which some are toxic (*G. esculenta*). In this author's opinion, the term beefsteak is much more aptly applied to *Fistulina hepatica*.

The name '*Fistulina*' (fist-you-lee-nah *or* fist-you-lie-nah) is Latin for 'little tube' in reference to the rather unique pore body of this genus. *Hepatica* (heh-pat-ih-kah) derived from '*hepat*' is Latin for 'liver' in reference to the color and texture of the fruitbody. Together the name *Fistulina hepatica* refers to a liver-like species in the genus with little tubes – both of which end up being important features for the identification of this fungi.

F. hepatica is one of the very few fungal fruitbodies in this text to be considered edible raw (the others are the jelly mushrooms) and this author has enjoyed munching them straight from the tree. The taste is unique, a tart, cranberry-like umami flavor with a texture akin to a very solid gelatin (or perhaps raw liver, but this author has yet to bite into raw liver). If this description sounds unappetizing, I urge you to try for yourself.

Ecology:

F. hepatica is saprobic creating a brown rot on the wood of oaks and chestnut (Cartwight 1937) and can often be found towards the base of trees or stumps. Fruiting occurs through the Summer and early Fall.

Fruitbody:

F. hepatica is a soft-fleshed polypore that has a distinctive shape due to it having a stem. The fruitbody appears as a longer, often yellowish-pink appendage which quickly expands into the scallop shaped cap with stalk or an amorphous lump. Upon expansion the color loses the yellow and becomes a pink or whitish pink, sometimes with early red development. As the fruitbody matures the pink colors deepen to various shades of red and cooked-beef browns and the stalk may widen enough to blend in

F. hepatica in situ

A more mature, browning, *F. hepatica*

Close-up texture of young *F. hepatica*

Young pink hymenium

with the shape of the scallop-shaped cap. During early development the fruitbody will likely have evenly spaced dark glandular dots which fade and become smaller in maturity. During this phase of maturity the fruitbody may begin to exude blood-red liquid from either the cap or pore-layer. When this liquid dries on the fruitbody it often leaves shallow craters (very similar to the scrobiculi of *Lactarius*).

The hymenial surface of *F. hepatica* is poroid, but unlike most polypores, the pores are individual tubes which are not fused to one another (run your fingernail along the hymenial surface or use a hand lens and you can see this). If you are uncertain about the identity of your find and do not wish to cut into the fruitbody, these free tubes (shallow to moderate in depth) are one of the best indications of this genus (remember *Fistulina* means 'little tubes'). In development these tubes may be very shallow and pink in color but should quickly become cream to white (sometimes with a yellow undertone).

The context (flesh) of the fruitbody takes on two different, often overlapping textures/colors (all of which feels and tastes the same). The first of which is a watermelon-flesh like visual texture which is often more mottled white and pink but may have some striations to it. This is the less pretty of the two and while commonly encountered, is less likely to be the star of online or published photographs of this fungus. The second of which is the more classic well-marbled raw beef visual texture in which the meat-like color and texture is striated/marbled with white/cream/yellow bands. This second textural appearance is more likely to be present above the hymenial surface while the first may be found more towards the top (pileal or ahymenial surface). Regardless of which texture/colors predominate, the fruitbody is easily torn, juicy, and very palatable.

F. hepatica has very few look-alikes, especially once the fruitbody has been thoroughly investigated though there have been some instances of people mistaking *Haplopilus* (the only poly-pore genus which is considered toxic) for them and becoming sick. Haplopilus has wide (stretched near the base of the fruitbody) pores which are fused and does not have the unfused tubes which are specific to *F. hepatica*.

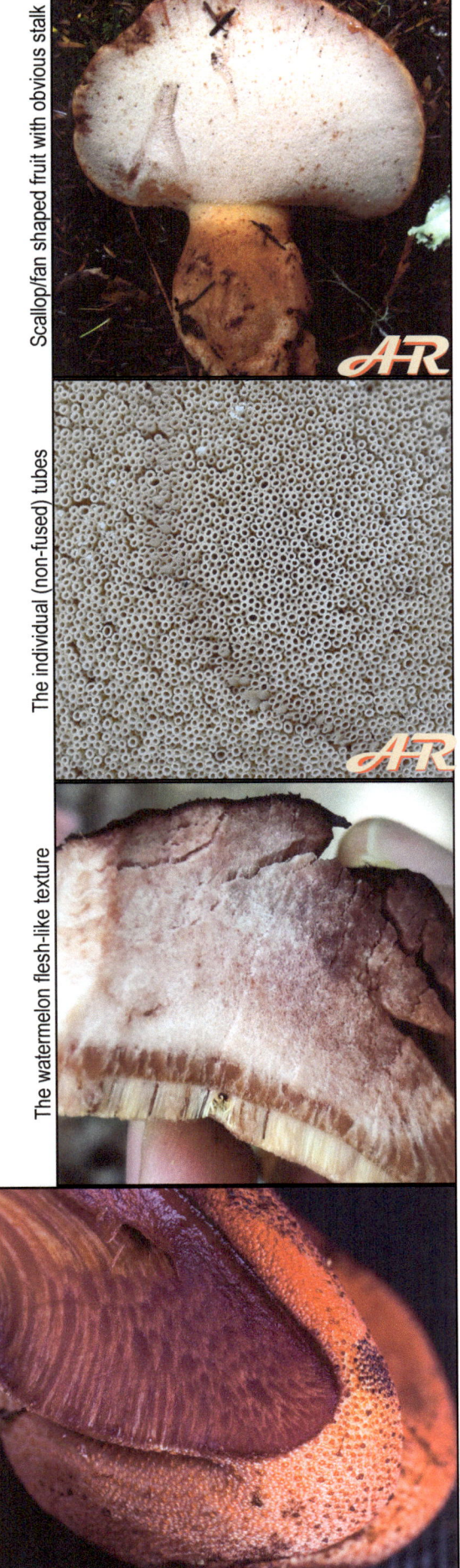

Scallop/fan shaped fruit with obvious stalk

The individual (non-fused) tubes

The watermelon flesh-like texture

The meatier visual texture with light 'marbling'

Fistulina hepatica

117

Other Polypores

Meripilus sumstinei

Description:

Known as the Black staining polypore due to the fact that this polypore – stains black! This polypore is commonly confused with both *Grifola frondosa* and *Laetiporus* due to their overlapping fruiting season, general structure, and size. This fungus is edible when young and the flesh is tender, but due to its tough fibrous nature it requires special preparation and has a greatly reduced repertoire of dishes it may contribute to. Often, the fruitbody is divided, frozen, and used for stocks imparting an intense "mushroomy" flavor.

Ecology:

This parasitic fungus causes a white rot and is found fruiting at the base of dead or dying hardwoods (predominantly oak; sometimes from buried roots or stumps). They are prolific fruiters creating fruitbodies which return for several years in the same location. Fruitbodies appear in the Summer and early Fall with a more substantial overlap in the *Laetiporus* season than the *Grifola* season.

Fruitbody:

Fruitbodies seem to be directly related to the size of the organism's host, growing in small rosettes in mulch-laden flower beds on buried roots or several feet across along dying old growth oaks. Like many of the other polypores, a central pseudostipe (more akin to an amorphous mass) pushes many overlapping (rosette-like) fronds out. These fronds/paddles are typically much wider and thinner than its look-alikes (*G. frondosa, B. berkeleyi, L. cincinnatus*). The color ranges from whites, various greys, some browns, to black.

M. sumstinei has three unique features. The first is that the fruitbody will stain black following even modest handling. The staining does take time to set in (sometimes around an hour) and is most evident on the hymenium due to the contrast. The black staining will also occur without handling in the event that region of the fruitbody have dried or otherwise

Large mature specimen of *M. sumstinei*

Especially thick fronded specimen

Young, fragrant, and lighter-colored *M. sumestinei*

Fistulina hepatica

been damaged. Check the edges of the fronds and in heavy growth regions where the fronds connect to the stalk.

The second feature is the aroma. *M. sumstinei* has a pungent cloying (almost artificially sweet) odor which permeates the woods around it. I have 'sniffed out' *M. sumstinei* on many occasions going so far as to use the smell as a marker for which trail I took! This smell will fade with the mushroom's age.

The final feature unique to *M. sumstinei* is the extreme fibrous nature of the fruitbody making it difficult to cut (perpendicular to the grain) with even a very sharp knife. The fruitbody will be much more tender towards the edges. This feature is the best to use as a discriminating characteristic if you are having difficulty determining the difference between these large polypores. Tear a frond by hand and you will quickly see these fibers.

Hymenium:

In young age or immaturity, most of the polypores have very small, undeveloped pores. *M. sumstinei* will maintain a very small, shallow

pore layer even into maturity. The pore layer is white but will stain black (sometimes slowly) upon even gentle handling. Like the rest of these polypores, the hymenium runs down the branching structures of the fronds.

Older *M. sumestinei* with widened, shallow pores

Black staining of margins and damaged regions

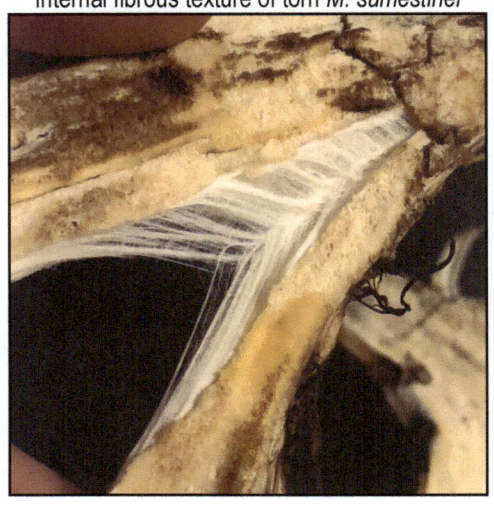

Internal fibrous texture of torn *M. sumestinei*

Bondarzewia berkeleyi

Requires special Prep or

Not as good as

SPAM

Description:

Called Berkeley's polypore (named for mycologist Miles J. Berkeley) this impressive fungus can create massive fruitbodies. *B. berkeleyi* are considered edible, particularly the tender edges of the younger fronds. The rest of the fruitbody becomes far too tough for most foodstuff applications. This fungus is often confused with *G. frondosa* and *L. cincinnatus* but us easy enough to tell apart.

Ecology:

B. berkeleyi is another parasitic fungi which causes a butt rot and is found fruiting at the base of dead or dying oaks and other hardwoods. Fruiting occurs at about the same location (from the same tree) for several years from late Summer through Autumn. The growth is rapid (perhaps just slower than *M. sumstinei*) so a small fruit can become very large very quickly.

Fruitbody:

B. berkeleyi is one of the fungi which produce the largest fruitbodies on a regular basis, measuring over a foot across and tall and weighing dozens of pounds. Most similar to *G. frondosa* and *M. sumstinei* in gross morphology, *B. berkeleyi* has a large amorphous pseudostipe from which fronds develop. The fronds are typically much thicker at both the edge and connection to the central mass than the other polypores listed here. These fronds can appear as smaller distinct entities, or as massive sweeping fans swirling over 360 degrees around the central mass like a screw. These larger sweeping fronds make *B. berkeleyi* especially distinctive when present.

B. berkeleyi presents concentric rings of color on the surface of each frond within the range of tans, beiges, and creams. When old, the fruitbody will become darker (browns) and either dry out or melt into an especially odorous pile.

Hymenium:

Depending on the individual fruitbody, the hymenial surface will range from white to beige to tan, discoloring and becoming darker in maturity (lighter than the surface). Importantly, the pores begin much wider and more prominent during development than any of the other polypores discussed here. The pores are less round and quickly become a thick, distinctive layer which is more maze-like (the pores become distorted taking on longer, sometimes twisting or branching shapes when viewed directly). The pores do not bruise or stain.

120

Large *B. berkeleyi* with small overlapping fronds

Young frond growing with wide angular pores

Wide sweeping fronds of *B. berkeleyi*

Shallow angular pores of immature specimen

Elongated maze-like pores in mature specimen

Hydnopolyporus fimbriatus

Requires special
Prep or
Not as good as
SPAM

Description:

One of the *Sparassis* look-alikes, *Hydnopolyporus fimbriatus* and *palmatus* are very similar in general shape and size to *S. spathulata* (especially if you exclude *S. spathulata f. herbstii*). There have been reports of these being eaten as mistaken for *Sparassis* with no ill effects, and documented in Boa (2004) to be edible or used as foodstuff internationally. This author has never tried them and cannot provide a description of how much preparation may or may not be involved in cooking them. Regardless, they should not be included for sales. The genus *Hydnopolyporus* only contains these two species and is being taxonomically shuffled from *Meripilaceae* into the Family *Irpicaceae* with the crust forming Genus *Irpex* which is known for its "irpicioid" hymenium (flat oblong teeth). This is leading to a nomenclature shift and possible merge to *Irpex rosettiformis*.

Ecology:

Both *H. fimbriatus* and *palmatus* fruit on hardwood in tropical and subtropical regions during the warm or hot months. The growth directly on wood (even if buried) is a prime distinguishing characteristic from the terrestrial – 'rooted' parasitic/saprobic ecology of *Sparassis*.

Fruitbody:

The fruitbody takes the form of several fused lobes which create a latticework very similar to *S. spathulata* but in my opinion more open with individual fronds being more prominent. Importantly, these lobes are typically thinner (especially thinner than *S. spathulata f. herbstii*) and sometimes diaphanous (allowing light to shine through). The edges of *H. fimbriatus* are usually smooth but can become shredded and droopy in maturity. The edges of *H. palmatus* form many small projections like a palm frond, though these tips are more likely to be rounded than sharp. Both species have striations from the growth base to the tips of the individual lobes, making them even more easily confused with *S. spathulata*.

Hymenium:

The hymenium of *Hydnopolyporus* is another feature which will distinguish it from *Sparassis* as they have notable pores which overstretch and break into oblong or irregular tooth like structures.

A convincing look-alike, *H. fimbriatus* on wood

H. palmatus with overlapping fronds

Rounded projections on *H. palmatus* lobes

H. palmatus with irpicioid teeth

Other Fleshy Polypores

121

Family Meruliaceae including Podoscypha and Cymatoderma spp.

Inedible

Description:

Both *Podoscypha* and *Cymatoderma spp.* are in the family *Meruliaceae* and have fruitbodies which, in the right circumstances, may be confused with *S. spathulata*. However, even quick observation will quickly highlight their differences. At least one species, *Podoscypha nitidula*, is documented as edible as are two species of *Cymatoderma* (*C. dendriticum* and *elegans*; Boa 2004), but this book will consider them inedible as a group until more information is available.

Ecology:

These are two genera only likely to be found in tropical and subtropical regions which means the gulf coast and similar regions are distinctive possibilities. They fruit in the hot months. *Podoscypha* fruits terrestrially and *Cymatoderma spp.* grows on decaying wood.

Fruitbody:

The size of *Podoscypha* is variable from species to species, but typically presents as very small (<5 cm tall and <10 cm wide) for *Podoscypha petalodes*, the most likely to be found in our region. The lobes are flat, forming wavy or even curly fans which overlap in an irregular fashion. Sometimes they look like small bowls on a stalk, almost akin to a depressed *Coltricia cinnamomea*. These cups grow into one another to form the odd lattice-like structure. This author thinks they look much more like *Thelephora vialis* with more individual, non-tattered lobes and a less distinctivly rosette shape. The colors of this genus range widely but seem to remain in the realm of earthy or fleshy hues with horizontal striations common.

In this author's opinion, *Cymatoderma* forms some of the most wonderful chalice-like fruitbodies. These fruitbodies range in size from 3 cm to well over 15 cm. The colors are typically light and in the case of *C. caperatum*, the edges become lilac, reminiscent of *Trichaptum biforme*. As the fruitbody matures, the growth at the edges may become irregular, scalloped, or otherwise not contiguous with the cup-shape.

Multiple petals/lobes of *Podoscypha petaloides* forming a good look-alike for *S. spathulata*

Wide lobes of *Podoscypha aculeata* forming a convincing look-alike for *S. spathulata*

Other Fleshy Polypores

Hymenium:

Both genera have smooth hymenia which may form a distinctive layer when compared to the stalk/stipe. This layer is thin and fleshy/soft.

Inedible

Cotylidia spp.

Chalice-like *Cymatoderma caperatum*

Description:

Unlikely to be confused with *Sparassis* until the fruitbodies become a mass of fans which, from a distance can have a similar appearance to *S. spathulata*. Interestingly, this genus is currently located in the Family *Hygrophoraceae* suggesting it is more closely related to the wax caps than any of the polypores but recent genetic advances may place it in the Order *Hymenochaetales* with many other polypores.

Ecology:

As a genus, *Cotylidia* are found widely and seem to fruit from Summer through late Fall. The larger fleshy species may be tropics and subtropics bound. Overall this is a fairly undocumented group of fungi which seem to have mycorrhizal relationships but may be opportunistic saprobes.

Fruitbody:

Overall, this genus produces small wide-brimmed cup-like structures somewhere between *Thelephora*, *Podoscypha*, and *Cymatoderma*. The flesh ranges from tough (like *Thelephora*) to fleshy/delicate, but is usually thin. The fluted cup-like shapes can become highly irregular, flattened, or lobed especially if the individual fruitbodies grow into one another. Several species have a ¼ or ½ cup shape (see pictured) more akin to rounded palm fronds. The colors of the genus range from whites and creams to some more intense hues such as yellow.

Hymenium:

The hymenium appears as a smooth or wrinkled surface with coloration similar to that of the anhymenial surface (the rest of the non-hymenial surface).

Cotylidia sp. with palm frond-like structure

Piptoporellus

Description:

A genus which has been oddly absent from not only the local field guides, but also most documented finds. This genus started making an appearance, or perhaps was only noticed because of social media, in 2019 where is was dubbed the "Mystery Chick" due to its strong similarities to the local *Laetiporus*. Following the efforts of many interested parties in the Southeast, the fruitbodies were well described and eventually sequenced in Florida to uncover the mysterious genus – *Piptoporellus*. While the fruitbody has been consumed as mistaken for *Laetiporus*, or by the bold for its own sake, the texture is akin to a densely foamy rubber with little to no flavor and as such we cannot regard it as food stuff.

Ecology:

Fruiting throughout the Summer and early Fall, *Piptoporellus* is a saprobe with a very specific host – live oak (*Quercus virginiana*). Not much else has been verifiably documented about this fungus as even the species is either undocumented or not yet named.

Fruitbody:

Piptoporellus range in color from orange sherbet and creamy warm hues to whites and tans which lose their saturation in age to become somewhat tan/grey. The surface is often zonate, ranging from glabrous to finely velvety but almost always with amorphous grooves and valleys. From a distance, the texture of the cap is the best way to distinguish this genus from *Laetiporus*. Fresh young specimens have a fruity to soapy scent and a soapy to insipid/bland flavor. The pores are white to cream and begin shallow to become elongated in age and closer to the media connection point. The overall shape is shelf-like or similar to a shell or half circle, usually with a point of connection to the wood which is lower than that of the pileus providing a greater depth at this connection point. The context is a strikingly orange-cream color which contrasts with the white pores. This flesh is not like the meaty flesh of *Laetiporus*, but akin to an air or fluid-filled foam, easy enough to cut but surprisingly durable to tear against. For those who have handled *Laetiporus*, the texture and composition of *Piptoporellus* should easily set them apart.

Piptoporellus in situ

Piptoporellus pore surface

Piptoporellus pileal surface

Piptoporellus context and pores in cross section

Other Fleshy Polypores

Inonotus hispidus & quercustris

Description:

Inonotus is a genus of 30 or so species of saprobes which typically decay dead hardwoods with a white rot. Species within the genus typically form medium to large fruitbodies of various shapes (though usually shelf-like). Two of these species in particular can take on superficial similarities to *Laetiporus*, *Inonotus hispidus* and *I. quercustris*.

Ecology:

Growing on the dead wood of hardwoods, both of these species prefer to grow on oak (*Quercus*) and may be found growing throughout the year at various levels of the tree.

Fruitbody:

These species take on a wide range of morphologies which substantially overlap with one another and will be described together. The gross shape is typically that of a shelf, half circle, or overlapping shelves often drooped slightly from the point at which it grows from the tree. Early fruitbodies may be round to hoof-shaped and expand outwards with maturity to form the complete shelf-shape. The growth region along the margin is lighter in color compared to the rest of the fruitbody, typically whites and creams with warm undertones. The pileal surface takes on a wide range of colors from fairly bright orange (those which are most likely to be confused with *Laetiporus*), to tans and browns usually with reddish undertones. While the fruitbody is not zonate, there is often a region of saturated color just medial from the lighter outer growth region.

Importantly, both species are overtly hairy, velvety, or hirsute, though this texture may be lost with age and environmental damage. The pores are tan to dark brown and the context (flesh) is also dark brown or will darken with age.

Inonotus quercestris, above

Inonotus quercestris, below

I. q. cross section

Inonotus hispidus with gutation

Inonotus hispidus cross section

Cap and Stalk

General Desciption

This section will cover those edible fungi and their look-alikes based on the loose macro-morphological description of a 'toadstool'. For this book, the definition of a toadstool is those mushrooms with a classic cap and stem shape. Previous books or descriptions may use the term 'toadstool' to specify toxic mushrooms but here we only use it as a description of the general shape. Some mushrooms that fit this description have already been covered (*Cantharellus*, *Hydnum*, etc.) so most of those genera covered here will have distinctive gills (lamellae) and be in the taxonomic Orders *Agaricales* or *Russulales*.

Major features to be aware of when considering these groups of mushrooms are similar to most other sections of this book but may emphasize lamellar characteristics as well as color and texture of the pileus (cap). These mushrooms were included for sales purposes because they are easily recognized or identified with high confidence by the novice forager. That being said, there are vast amounts of potential look-alikes for those with little to no experience that this book cannot hope to cover. However, we do hope to emphasize those most important features so that you can gain experience with confidence – but also recommend the novice forager proceed slowly here.

Macrolepiota procera (not discussed)

Stropharia cluster (not discussed)

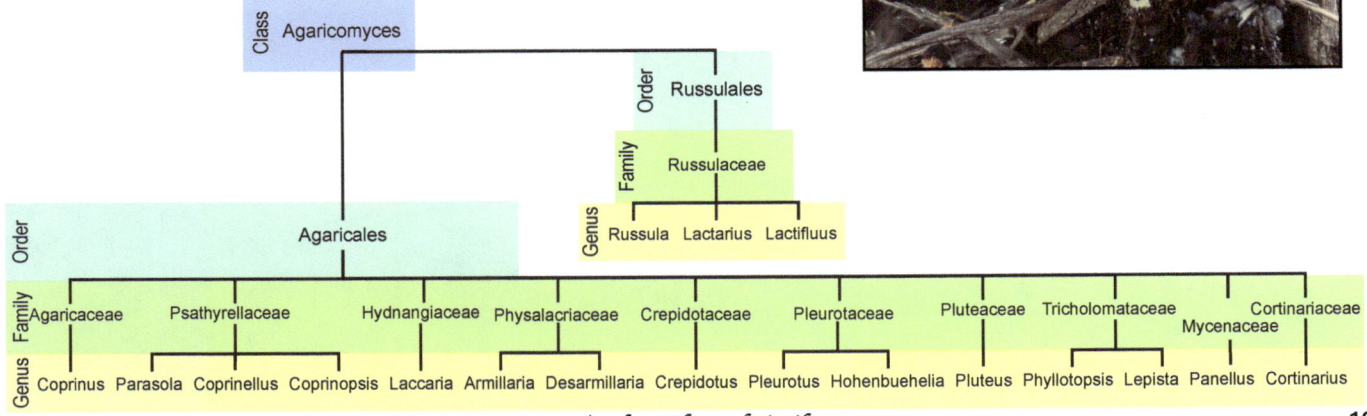

Toadstoods and similar

Pleurotus
Oysters

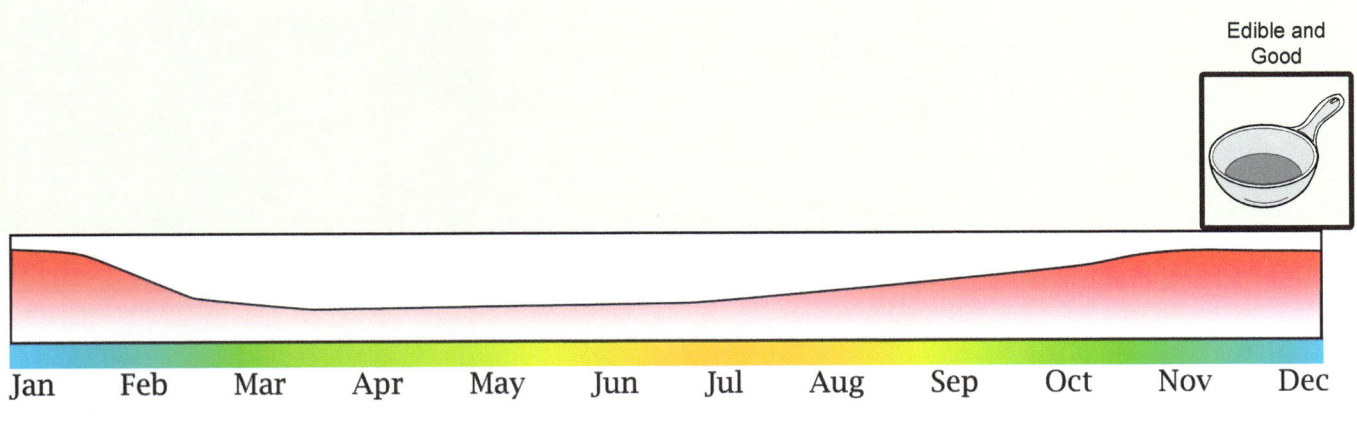

Jan Feb Mar Apr May Jun Jul Aug Sep Oct Nov Dec

Typical Color Palette

Typical size range

Pleurotus species

20cm

Shape

Convex to Flat, off-center stipe

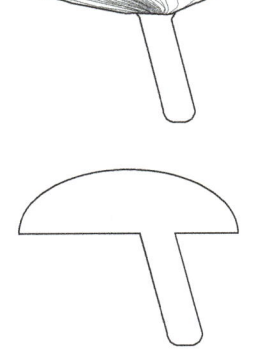

Hemenium: Lamellae

Decurrent
Deep

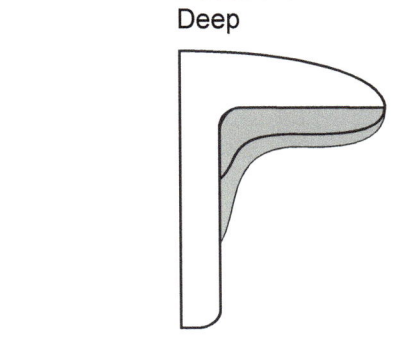

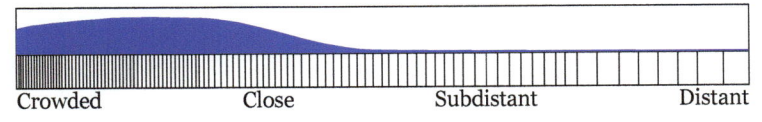

Crowded   Close   Subdistant   Distant

Growth

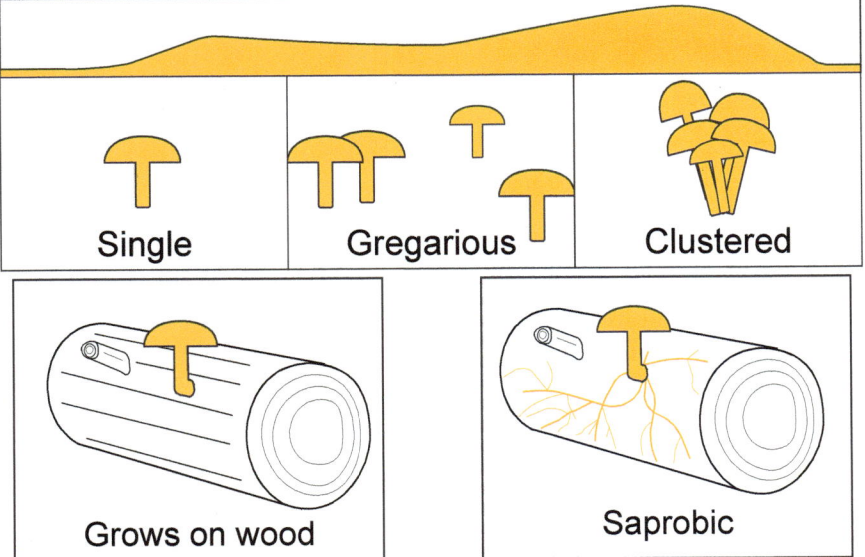

Single   Gregarious   Clustered

Grows on wood   Saprobic

Pleurotus is an unpicky decomposer of wood and commonly found on downed logs or dead trees throughout the year, but especially in cooler or colder months.

Pleurotus

129

General Desciption

Description:

Often called Oyster mushrooms, *Pleurotus* are a commonly encountered cool to cold season mushroom which are easy to identify. This genus is commonly cultivated due to being a voracious decomposer with little preference for its host. Of all of the mushrooms discussed in this book, this is the most commonly found genus in supermarkets or farmers markets and is a good introduction to fungal fruitbodies outside of the button mushrooms or portabellas (all *Agaricus bisporus*) which rule the supermarket. Alabama and the surrounding states have three primary species, *Pleurotus ostreatus* (the 'true' oyster), *P. pulmonaris*, and *P. laevis/dryinus*. There are likely many other species hiding within that range, but often without discriminating features we will lump them together.

Pleurotus dryinus/levis (maybe found spelled *laevis*) (we likely only have *P. levis* in substantial number) are explicitly excluded for wild harvest for sales. The rationale for this exclusion is not clear, but it may be due to the superficial resemblance to *Tapinella atrotomentosa* (not pictured) which is mildly toxic.

Ecology:

Pleurotus are saprobes found most commonly on hardwoods. They do not seem to be particularly picky about their host wood and because of this are easily cloned and cultivated. Similar to *Hericium* (lion's mane), they will typically fruit following a cold spell or a cool rain. However, *Pleurotus* can be found growing year-round and the season may help inform the species (but I think there is considerable overlap). Specifically, *P. ostreatus* and *dryinus/levis* prefer cool to cold weather while *P. pulmonarius* is more likely to fruit when hot outside. Importantly, bugs have also discovered that many oyster mushrooms grow year-round and as such most warm weather fruitbodies are larval hotels. The best *Pleurotus* for harvest are found when the mosquitos aren't out biting.

Pileus:

The overall fruitbody is almost always a cluster of caps with a common origin emerging from a break in the growth media (like a crack in the bark). Each cap with its own stipe which originates in the central

Popular as a cultivatable genus

P. pulmonarius in the Summer

P. pulmonarius in the Summer

P. pulmonarius in the Summer

mass or directly from the media. These caps do not fuse into one another since their growth is determinant leading to several shelving caps with distinctively off-center stipes. These caps emerge small, usually darker than the initial fruiting mass and unfurl quickly to take on off-center convex caps or flattened caps with a slightly inrolled margin. Eventually the edge of the margin will push up making an almost cup-shaped fruit. This process is especially stunning on cultivated blocks with dense fruiting.

The cap color ranges from various shades of grey and tan to stark white. There are species with more saturated colors, especially *P. citrinopileatus* (yellow) and *P. ostreatus var. columbinus* (blue/steel-grey) but these do not grow natively or if found are usually feral (escaped from domestic growth). The pileus is minutely fibrous up close or with a hand lens, but otherwise glabrous for all except *Pleurotus dryinus/levis* which can become densely fuzzy.

Hymenium:

Pleurotus as a genus have deep, dramatically decurrent lamellae (gills) which often run almost the entirety of the fruitbody, from margin to growth media. These gills are crowded to close and typically a similar color, or lighter than the pileus. In most cases the gills are stark white. Pleurotus will all drop a thick white spore print.

Stipe:

Often taking up more than half of the mass of the total fruitbody, the stalk on *Pleurotus* can become wide and thick – especially in larger fruiting or often in cultivated clusters. They can appear thinner and more rounded as in *P. pulmonarius*, but there is overlap in ratios of pileus to stalk width. More often than not, if you see an especially large (wide capped) fruiting of *Pleurotus*, especially if they are more pigmented and growing in cool to cold weather, you're looking at *P. ostreatus*. Pure white (or very pale) with thinner stipe and smaller overall size growing in warmer weather may be a better fit for *P. pulmonarius*. If you find one with a fuzzy (sometimes outrageously so) stipe, check *P. dryinus/levis*.

Older waterlogged *Pleurotus*, note the fraying margin

Far too old *P. levis*, not fit for harvest

P. pulmonarius in the Summer

Pleurotus look-alikes

Pluteus cervinus

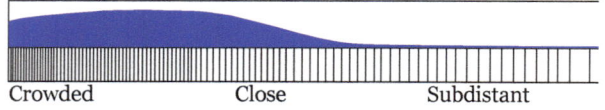

Crowded   Close   Subdistant

Requires special
Prep or
Not as good as
SPAM

Description:

Called the Deer mushroom or the Deer Shield. *Pluteus* is loosely translated from *Latin* to mean shield while *cervinus* (*cervus*) is *Latin* for deer. In fact the genus *Pluteus* is colloquially referred to as "shield" mushrooms, which is impressive for a genus of over 300 species, most all of which would make rather delicate shields. All of which are wood munching saprobes.

Pluteus cervinus (and to a lesser degree *P. petasatus*) are commonly confused with *Pleurotus* due to a rather scant collection of overlapping features including their color, growth media, and season of fruiting.

Ecology:

Pluteus as a genus are almost always found growing on dead wood, either standing or fallen and sometimes untreated mulch. *P. cervinus* prefers hardwood but can be found on coniferous wood. This species fruits most abundantly in the cooler months and may be one of the first basidiocarps (fruits from the Division *Basidiomycota*) to be found in Spring.

Pileus:

The cap ranges from 3 cm to over 15 cm in diameter and is almost always round with a flattened convex shape that may have a very gentle umbonate center (some young specimens may be outright campenellate). The color takes on a small range of tans to browns and the fibrils radiating from the center are very fine giving the pileus a glabrous (bald) texture. Sometimes the pileus can even be a bit shiny, or perhaps polished.

Hymenium:

White at first but quickly becoming pink to tan/pink as spores develop. The deep, crowded gills are free of the margin – a substantial difference from Pluteus' exaggeratedly decurrent lamellae. All *Pluteus* will drop a pink (or pink-ish) spore print.

Stipe:

The stipe of *P. cervinus* connects centrally to

Mature, pink-gilled *Pluteus*

Young, free gills of *P. cervinus*

Pileus of *P. cervinus*

132   *Pleurotus look-alikes*

the cap and is unornamented, smooth (glabrous) and often seems just barely strong enough to bear the weight of the cap without folding or snapping.

Crepidotus / Hohenbuehelia

Inedible

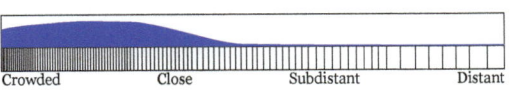

Crowded — Close — Subdistant — Distant

Description:

This is a 'catch all' section used to describe those features very common to the two named genera *Crepidotus* and *Hohenbuehelia*. These two genera include several species which are confused with *Pleurotus* on a regular basis. Specifically, they are confused with "baby oysters" as they are smaller, more fragile (usually), and can grow in large number or in similar patterns to *Pleurotus*.

Ecology:

These genera grow on dead wood and can be found throughout the growing seasons (Spring - late Fall).

Pileus:

The fruitbody is akin to a scallop shell adhered to wood – no stalk to speak of (or a very short one if so), just a convex to flat pileus emerging from the wood. These genera contain species with a wide variety of colors and patterns, though most are muted such as whites, greys, and browns. Patterns and textures are also varied, but overall, the features are generally soft. If you pull at one, you will find the texture to be vastly different from *Pleurotus* (which are meatier) as the fruitbody is often more delicate and the context is especially thin. Almost all of the species in these genera are very small and rarely reach more than 4-5 cm in width.

Hymenium:

Crepidotus and *Hohenbuehelia* have lamellae (gills) which run from the margin to the connection point. Importantly, *Crepidotus* will drop a brown spore print (often discoloring the lamellae to be similarly colored) while *Hohenbuehelia* have a white spore print.

Stipe:

Unlike *Pleurotus*, both *Crepidotus* and *Hohen-*

Crepidotus from below

Crepidotus from below

KB

Crepidotus from side

Crepidotus from below

Pleurotus look-alikes

buehelia lack a distinctive stipe. They may have some small region which is not cap from which the cap emerges, but at best we can only call these pseudostipes.

Inedible

Hohenbuehelia petaloides

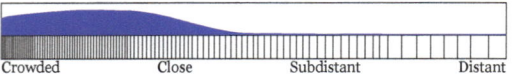
Crowded　Close　Subdistant　Distant

Description:

In this author's opinion – this is the most convincing look-alike for *Pleurotus* and is a bit different than those *Hohenbuehelia* described above.

Ecology:

Growing most commonly in mulch or in woody detritus from the forest floor, the saprobe *H. petaloides* can be found in the late Summer through early Winter. These may be found growing alone but are commonly encountered growing gregariously.

Pileus:

The fruitbody takes a shape often described as petaloid which describes the cup-like shape of a single petal from say, a rose or other flower with rounded, concave petals. This rounded or fluted shape not only provides substance to the species name, but also makes for a convincing look-alike to a mature *Pleurotus* fruitbody. Extreme examples can become overlapping or even tangled masses of these fluted fruits. Note that these fruitbodies are never round and will often have a slit or groove on one side almost as if they had grown around a branch or similar object. The color of the pileus ranges from light tans to darker greys.

Hymenium:

This author finds the lamellae (gills) present on *H. petaloides* to be shallower (but perhaps not 'shallow') than *Pleurotus* gills. The lamellae are crowded and extremely decurrent.

Stipe:

The stipe is not an obvious feature as it seems the lamellae slowly fade into nothing and lack any abrupt stop. The remaining stalk may be more darkly colored than the rest of the fruitbody.

H. petaloides in situ

H. petaloides, showing lateral fissure

H. petaloides, pileal texture

H. petaloides, tapering gills

Sarcomyxa serotina &
Panellus stipticus

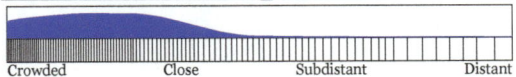

Inedible

| Crowded | Close | Subdistant | Distant |

Description:

Panellus is a medium sized genus in the Family *Mycenaceae* which used to encompass any "pleurotoid" shaped mushroom with white spores which respond to a particular chemical test when viewed under a microscope (amyloid). In fact, this designation landed several of the species in the *Pleurotus* genus (once upon a time), which have been removed since. So, it should come as no surprise that as far as *Pleurotus* look-alikes go, there are several in this group – many of which may have gone by different names. *Sarcomyxa serotina* (previously known as *Panellus serotinus*) is even given the common name the "late oyster" due to their tendency to fruit in the late fall, following most *Pleurotus* flushes. Since Alabama and the other gulf-coast states are warmer climates, this seasonal difference is unlikely to be noticed.

Panellus stipticus, also called the bitter oyster or luminescent panellus is less likely to be confused with *Pleurotus* due to its much smaller size – though the shape is still similar enough that some may think they are baby oysters. Interestingly, this is one of the species of fungus which actually glow in the dark. I have been unable to detect the glow from either the mycelium or fruitbody with the naked eye, but some especially bright specimens do exist.

Sarcomyxa serotina is considered edible but may be bitter in taste. *Panellus stipticus* is considered inedible.

Ecology:

Both of these fungi grow on dead wood, primarily deciduous hardwoods but sometimes coniferous wood. They form a white rot appearing as gregarious to tightly clustered growing on the side (or just underneath) their wood hosts. Fruiting occurs, as the colloquial name "late oyster" implies, later than *Pleurotus* in many parts of the country for *S. serotina*. However, their fruiting in the gulf states will overlap the fruiting of our cold-loving *Pleurotus ostreatus*. In particularly warm regions of the state (Southern and low altitude) this species may not be present or otherwise may not fruit at all. *Panellus stipticus* fruits earlier in the Fall and may continue to fruit into the late Fall and even Winter if the temperatures are mild.

Pileus:

S. serotina ranges from 3 cm to over 10 cm in

Sarcomyxa serotina in situ

Mature P. stipticus cluster

Anastomosing gills and pseudostipe of P. stipticus

Cracked, mosaic pilus of P. stipticus

Pleurotus look-alikes

135

length and takes on a wide palette of colors on the pileal surface, most often a shade of green, green-tinted tans/yellows or even dark brown but overall has a darker or more saturated color than *Pleurotus*. The shape is "pleurotoid" but can be more specifically described as scallop-shell shaped and convex to flat. The margin is usually inrolled to some degree and glabrous (bald) but may be slightly sticky when young or whetted. The context is somewhat thick (like *Pleurotus*) and white.

Panellus stipticus is much smaller but maintains the same general shape as *P. serotinus*, with a far less-fleshy context. These fruitbodies can be far smaller than your pinky nail to ~4 cm across. The pileal surface is textured with a shattered mosaic-like pattern. The color ranges from white to ochre to tan, though may appear fluorescent green when completely dark.

Hymenium:

Both species have lamellae (gills) which are moderate in depth and crowded to close. *S. serotina* had adnexed gills while those of *P. stipticus* are free to adnexed. Both commonly sport short gills, but *P. stipticus* also has anastomose cross veins. The lamellae of *S. serotina* range from white(ish) to yellow and tan while those of *P. stipticus* are much more consistently colored with their caps and come in various tans.

Stipe:

Both species have a pseudostipe which most often appears as a small ball-like protuberance from the growth media from which the cap unfurls. This pseudostipe is often lighter in color than the rest of the fruitbody, often appearing white. This structure can become 'leggy' or elongated to more closely resemble a true stipe – usually when the fruitbody is young and being pushed into a more favorable position for airflow (especially in *P. stipticus*).

Phyllotopsis (sub)nidulans

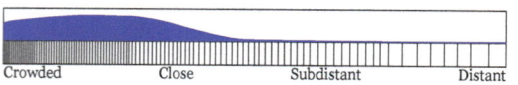

Crowded   Close   Subdistant   Distant

Inedible

Description:

Colloquially called the "mock oyster" or "orange oyster", *Phyllotopsis nidulans* belongs to the Family Tricholomataceae which is a more hodgepodge family containing many genera which are differ drastically from one another. *P. nidulans* is similar in shape and size to *Pleurotus* species but has a few characteristics which easily set it apart. Theis species is not known to be toxic, but oftentimes comes with fishy or

P. stipticus, with anastromose gills

Extremely long pseudostipe

Sarcomyxa serotina, underside

RP

Sarcomyxa serotina

AR

136   *Pleurotus look-alikes*

rotten egg-like odors which deter most people from trying them. This book will consider them inedible.

Ecology:

Saprobic on almost any deadwood which still has bark present and forming a white rot. Growing gregariously, clustered with overlapping caps, or in fused clusters. Fruitbodies appear in cooler months of Spring and Fall and may be present during warmer Winters.

Pileus:

As implied by their common name, *P. nidulans* are primarily some shades of orange, usually a cream-colored orange on the pileus. The pileal surface is lightly to intensely (usually more of the latter) fuzzy/hairy with these fibers providing much of the white-cream color to the otherwise more saturated orange cap. The fibers are more densely present towards the base of the pleurotoid shaped caps (closer to the growth media), such that the margin often appears to have a more saturated orange color. Especially brightly colored specimens are more likely to be an Eastern North American species called *P. subnidulans*. The margin is often inrolled giving the fruitbody a convex shape, though often with a flattened top.

Hymenium:

Medium depth lamellae (gills) form the hymenial surface which are crowded to close in *P. nidulans* and more distantly spaced (close to subdistant) in *P. subnidulans*. Both have very common short gills. The lamellae are also orange, usually a more saturated orange than the cap (which is also more likely to become washed out or sub-bleached) These gills run from the margin all the way to the pseudostipe or directly to the growth media connection point in a range from decurrent to adnexed (though these terms hardly apply).

Stipe:

The stem or stipe is either nonexistent or very short best described as a pseudostipe – more of a connection point than anything else.

P. nidulans individual caps

Note the lack of stipe

More saturated orange gills with short gills

P. nidulans overlapping with hairy/fuzzy pileus

Pleurotus look-alikes

Armillaria and
Honey Mushrooms

Desarmillaria

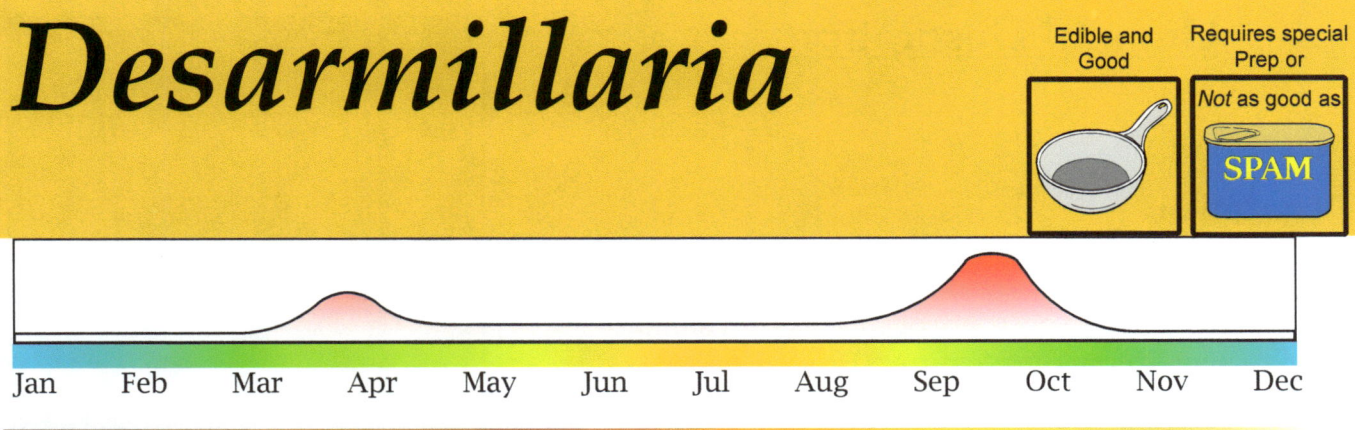

Edible and Good

Requires special Prep or *Not* as good as SPAM

Jan Feb Mar Apr May Jun Jul Aug Sep Oct Nov Dec

Typical Color Palette

Shape

Convex to Flat, central stipe

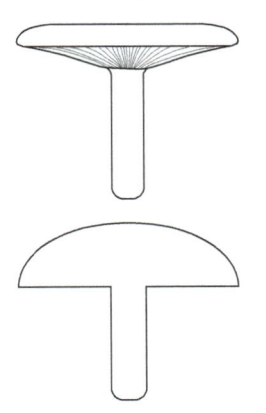

Hemenium: Lamellae

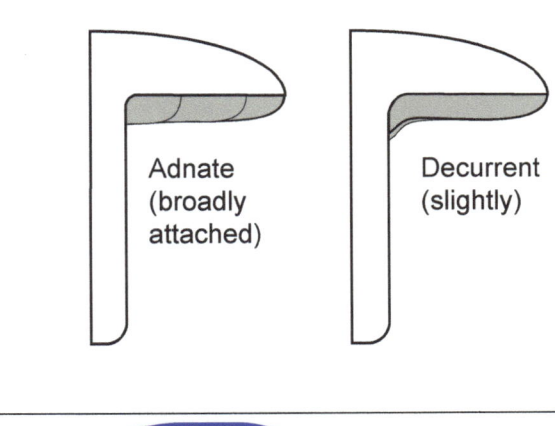

Adnate (broadly attached)

Decurrent (slightly)

Crowded   Close   Subdistant   Distant

Growth

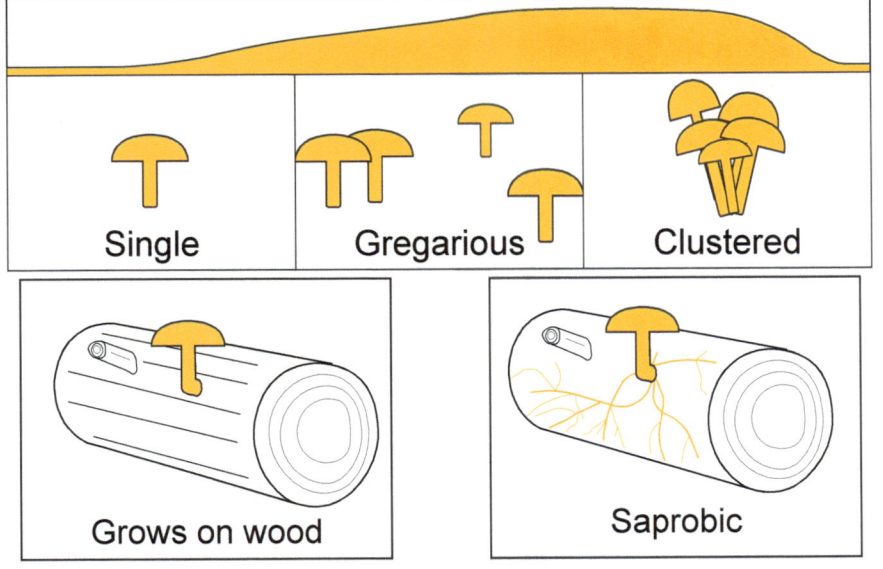

Single

Gregarious

Clustered

Grows on wood

Saprobic

Typical size range

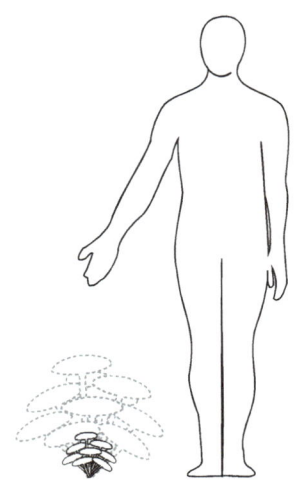

Armillaria is a fiece decomposer with a propensity to parasitize hardwoods such as oak growing primarily at the ground level. Look for black rhizomorphs under bark which decorticate the wood.

Armillaria and Desarmillaria

General Desciption

Description:

Colloquially known as the "Honey mushroom," the genus *Armillaria* (including the newly minted *Desarmillaria*) contain a variety of species with similar edibility and overlapping features. Here, we will describe three species native to the Southeastern United States including *Armillaria gallica, mellea,* and *Desarmillaria caespitosa/tabescens*. "*Armillaria*" [arm-ih-lar-ee-ah] is Latin for 'bracelets', a reference to the stunning annulus (ring, or partial veil) of *Armillaria gallica*. "*gallic(a/o)*" is Latin for 'French' an homage to where they were first officially described. The common name "honey mushroom" is a reference to the Latin "*Mel*" or "*Melle*" which means 'honey' and is an appropriate description of the range of colors these mushrooms take.

Recently, an effort to split the genus *Armillaria* has been made which has landed the 'ringless honey mushroom' (previously *Armillaria tabescens*) in an entirely separate genus called *Desarmillaria*. The Latin epithet "des" refers to 'a lack of' in reference to the Armillaria or bracelet/ring/annulus – so a translation is the 'ringed mushroom without the ring'. Furthermore, the North American species was renamed "caespitosa" since it is genetically distinct from the European *D. tabescens*.

Armillaria species also form a unique relationship with an *Entoloma* species (*Entoloma abortivum*) which result in an aborted mushroom form referred to as "shrimp of the woods". This mushroom is not discussed in this edition of this book but is worth investigating for those seeking to expand their mycophagic repertoire.

Ecology:

Armillaria and *Desarmillaria* are both weakly to extremely parasitic to immunocompromised trees, shrubs, or other woody plants where they cause a white rot. They are also happy to munch on decaying wood and spread from one food source to the next via long black rhizomorphs (mycelial cords) which are surprisingly easy to find. Both genera fruit in the cooler months of Spring or Fall, but *Armillaria* are more likely to produce larger fruitbodies in the Fall. This author has observed that *Desarmillaria caespitosa* is more likely to fruit in domestic settings such

Emerging *Armillaria*

Distinctive cap ornamentation of *Armillaria*

The soft, persistent annulus of *A. gallica*

The vegetable-like snap of *Armillaria* stipes

as in yards and other manicured regions. Regardless, most clusters of either genera are so likely to be found at the base of trees that in some regions their common names refer specifically to this feature (see опеньки, meaning "near the stump" in Ukrainian). (*Des*)*Armillaria* are most commonly found clustered, but may be found singly or gregariously growing, especially when the media (such as on top of felled wood) is atypical.

The overall size of the fruitbody is likely due to the size of the underlying organism and ranges from a small handful-sized cluster to massive fruitings of near a meter wide. *Desarmillaria* tends to run on the smaller side of this range while *Armillaria mellea* runs on the larger side.

Pileus:

The pileal (cap) surface is not a good way to tell these species apart as the features are well conserved and the intensity of these features vary from specimen to specimen. First and foremost is the color, which ranges from pale/dull yellow to almost mustard and from tans/ochres to near buckwheat honey. The range of color on a single cap is also subject to a range with darker centers and lighter margins which are either a smooth transition or a more abrupt, two-toned one. Unfortunately, this wide color palette also overlaps with many other cool-weather mushrooms so don't rely on this feature for identification.

Next are the small scales on the pileal surface which are clusters of fibers which may appear lighter or darker than the rest of the cap or may be washed off entirely. However, when present, this dotted/scaled appearance is a good indicator of (*Des*)*Armillaria* (when the mushrooms in question are in a cluster).

The cap shape ranges from campanellate/bell-shaped to convex and eventually flat, often with some level of umbonation (the central, more pointed tip). When campenellate or convex, the sides sometimes become boxy with semi-flattened edges, especially following environmental conditions such as rain which make the margins heavy with water leading to some droop.

The context (inner flesh) is white to cream in color and can become thick in the larger specimens (especially *Armillaria mellea*). This context is soft and makes the caps good for eating, though they may be slightly bitter on occasion.

Hymenium:

Lamellae (gills) of (*Des*)*Armillaria* are close in spacing and of medium to deep in depth. They connect to the stipe in a range from adnexed to slightly

Tight clusters of young *Armillaira* growing at the base of wood.

A range of honey-like colors in *Armillaria*

The distinctive yellow hues of *A. gallica*

A. gallica stipe

decurrent. The lamellae range from white to some shade near that of the cap and will darken when they dry. (*Des*)*Armillaria* drop a thick white spore print.

Stipe:

The stipe/stem provides many more important identification features including the anulus (or lack thereof), texture, basal clustering, and rigidity. As discussed above, *Desarmillaria* lacks the annulus altogether while both *A. mellea* and *gallica* have a ring. The thickness/robustness of this ring is an ideal feature for determining if you have found *A. mellea* which have the thick, prominent, and persistent ring compared with *A. gallica* which have a wispy, cobwebbier ring. The stipes of (*Des*)*Armillaria* are individual, non-branching, but all erupt from a central fused region.

Less prominent is the presence of a slightly bulbous base as seen in *A. gallica* and are absent in *A. mellea*. Furthermore, *A. gallica* often has yellow pigmentation at the base of the stipe. *Desarmillaria* lacks both bulbosity and additional pigmentation. In fact, *D. caespitosa* tend to have much thinner stipes as compared to their cap size than *Armillaria* species. Regardless of size (length or girth), the stipes are fibrous and tend to produce an audible crack when snapped in half lengthwise. While fibrous, the stipes are still edible, but are often discarded in favor of the softer, more palatable caps.

Lepista nuda
The Wood Blewit

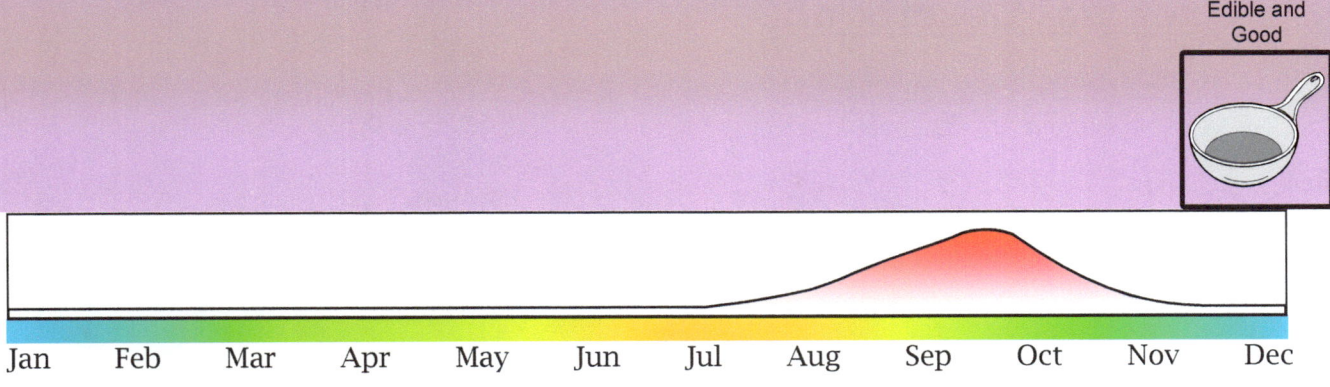

Jan   Feb   Mar   Apr   May   Jun   Jul   Aug   Sep   Oct   Nov   Dec

Typical Color Palette

Shape

Convex to Flat, central stipe

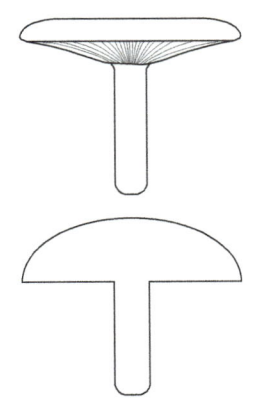

Hemenium: Lamellae

Adnate to Adnexed, sometimes sinuate, intermediate depth

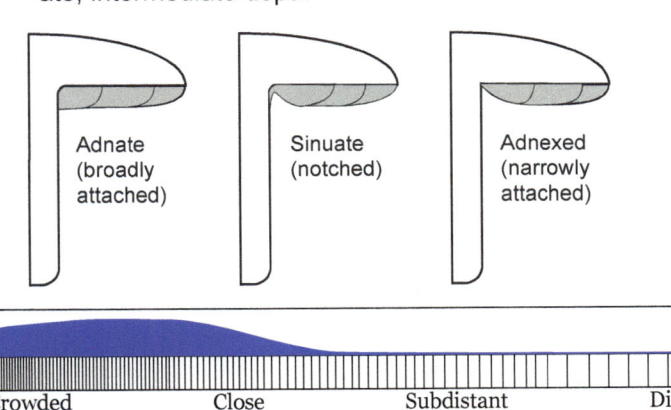

Adnate (broadly attached)   Sinuate (notched)   Adnexed (narrowly attached)

Crowded   Close   Subdistant   Distant

Growth

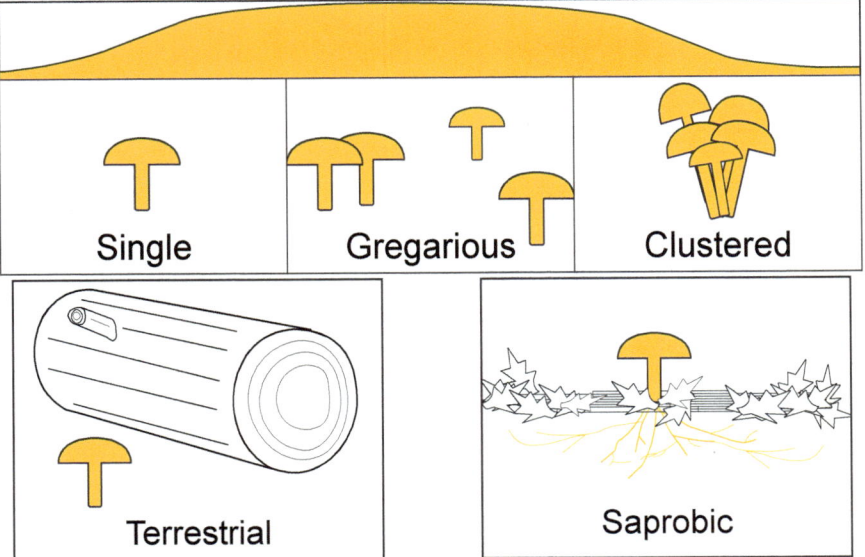

Single   Gregarious   Clustered

Terrestrial   Saprobic

Lepista are saprobes which are commonly found in leaf litter at the edge of the woods.

Typical size range

Lepista nuda

20cm

Lepista nuda

General Desciption

Description:

Often called the Wood Blewit or simply Blewit, this fungus is also accepted as *Clitocybe nuda* since *Lepista* is considered a subgenus of *Clitocybe* (Alvarado et al. 2015). The species name 'nuda' comes from its initial description in Herbier de la France in 1790 as the bald (or nude) counterpart to another purple hued mushroom which is believed to be *Cortinarius violaceous* (see look-alikes). The genus *Lepista* holds three species of interest for this book which are often mistaken for one another and have similar edibility. While they are all discussed here, only *L. nuda* is currently approved for sales in Alabama. These fungi are common and can be easily cultivated in garden beds or similar outdoor environments.

One of the most pronounced features of this group is the purple/violet coloration of the fruitbody. Unfortunately, this less-common color scheme is shared by some other mushrooms and can lead to frequent misidentifications. As always, this book urges the reader to consider color a non-primary identification feature for this, and most (but not all!) other mushrooms.

Ecology:

L. nuda is saprobic in the leafy detritus of the forest floor (deciduous mostly but also some coniferous woods) and especially common at the edge of a wooded area with large buildups of decomposing material. *Lepista* is a genus which is not picky about the temperature, but fruits most prolifically in Autumn. The other *Lepista*, *L.s tarda/sordida* may fruit in warmer weather. *L. tarda* is sometimes called the Field Blewit due to its propensity to fruit in grasslands.

Pileus:

The cap of *Lepista nuda* is very similar in size (5 cm to 18 cm) and shape to a store-bought portabella mushroom, beginning convex and opening to become semi-flattened with an in rolled margin or sometimes a slightly wavy margin. *L. tarda* and *sordida* tend to be smaller in stature and with thinner caps (especially *tarda*; less context material than the robust *L. nuda*) which are more likely to become upturned (infundibular) or wavy as they age. The pileal surface is glabrous (bald) and ranges in color from

Washed out purple/pink cap of *Lepista nuda*

Bifurcating stipes

Two-toned, hygrophorus pileus of *L. nuda*

Crowded pink/purple gills

highly saturated (but not dark) violet to a dingy tan. The color fades with age losing the violet tones in favor of the earthy tans and ochres. *L. nuda* and *sordida* are more likely to display the more intense violets.

The color of the pileus is often two-toned (hygrophanous) which seems to be a result of both moisture content and age. In fact the somewhat unique patterns of this hygrophanous coloration can be very helpful for identification, looking like the cap is faded due to too much moisture.

Hymenium:

Lamellae (gills) which are adnexed to adnate (sometimes sinuate), crowded to close, medium in depth, and contain frequent short gills. The color ranges from an intense violet to muted pink to purple tinted ochre to cream to downright tan. Like the cap, the color saturation of the gills fades with age and environmental exposures. *L. tarda* is more likely to have muted lamellae color which are slightly more widely spaced.

Stipe:

L. nuda has a short, thick, stipe which is often bulbous at the base. The colors are like the cap, though less intensely saturated, and less likely to fade noticeably with age. This means that the muted violet or pink colors are maintained outside of extreme environmental degradation. *L. tarda* or *sordida* both have thinner stipes which may be slightly longer in relation to their cap diameters. The base will often contain pillowy white fibers which fade into the substantial mycelial mat. The texture of the stipe (on all three species discussed here) are similar to a brushed cotton-like fiber, thin and soft by eye. Note the more colored flesh just below this fibrous layer in the images. This is a good discriminating feature for these species but is easily overlooked.

This finely fibrous stipe points to *Lepista*

Young caps and gills can be a deep purple hue

Young caps and gills can also be a light pink hue

Lepista nuda

147

Lepista nuda look-alikes

purple *Cortinarius*

Inedible | Requires special Prep or *Not* as good as SPAM

Description:

Cortinarius was once the largest genus of fungi with over 400 individual species. It has recently been divided into several genera with overlapping features. This book will consider them a large, single genus until such a time as the components and their relationships undergo further clarification. As such a genetically and morphologically diverse group, there are some species which are considered tasty edibles (*Cortinarius caperatus*, not discussed further), while others are distasteful, or even still some which are deadly toxic (*Cortinarius orellanus*, containing the kidney destroying toxin orellanine). To simplify the description of this large genera this book will focus on those three primary species of *Cortinarius* which bear a superficial resemblance to *Lepista nuda*, and discuss those other, less taxonomically clear species and specimens to rule out.

As a whole, the genus (almost all of the species) expresses a partial veil which is uniquely fibrous. Rather than splitting during growth like a typical annulus, this fibrous membrane break as individual threads, creating a web-like connection of the remaining strands along the margin and stem called a cortina. From this, the genus received the common name web-caps and genus name *Cortinarius*.

Ecology:

Cortinarius fruit all year (sans in snowy Winter conditions) but those species which are most likely to resemble Lepista appear most often in the Autumn (with a significant overlap in the fruiting of *Lepista*). *C. violaceous, iodes, iodeoides,* and other purple/violet colored species are mycorrhizal and fruit singly, gregariously, or in small clusters. *C. iodes/iodeoides* most often associate with oaks while *C. violaceous* is more promiscuous with other hardwoods and conifers. If the basal stipes are connected for those growing in clusters, it is usually a very slightly fused connection and not a shared basal mass.

Unknown species of *Cortinarius* which resembles *L. nuda*

C. violaceous in situ

Cortinarius iodes

Pileus:

The pileus (cap) of the species discussed here have a range of purple, violet, tan, and yellow colorations which vary significantly from specimen to specimen. *C. violaceous* may be more consistent in coloration than the others as it takes on dark violet colors which sometimes become near black or with brown undertones. *C. iodes/iodeoides* are indistinguishable by the cap alone as they are lighter purples with spots, streaks, or smears (which can cover the entire cap) of yellow-ish tans which can give them striking patterns. Furthermore, *C. iodes/iodeoides* are typically viscid (sticky) when young or whetted and this glutinous layer dries to become a metallic sheen as well as glue leaves and detritus to the drying pileus. *C. violaceous* has a more textured pileus which is never viscid. This texture is fuzzy or like many small soft scales of clumped fibers and is a good indicator (when other features of *Cortinarius* are present) that the specimen is *C. violaceous*. Other species may also be shades of violet, purple, or other overlapping colors.

All the above mentioned *Cortinarius* will have convex caps which can become flattened in age. The only way to easily discriminate between *C. iodes/iodeoides* is to lick the cap (they are not toxic) – if bitter you have *C. iodeoides*, if insipid (bland) you have *C. iodes*. Most species of *Cortinarius* may have cortinal remnants dangling from the margin.

Hymenium:

All *Cortinarius* have lamellae (gills) and drop a rust-brown colored spore print. The range of gill coloration, spacing and depth is vast, but all will develop some rusty colors in age. *C. iodes/iodeoides* have medium depth gills with close spacing. *C. violaceous* has medium depth gills which are more widely spaced (maybe subdistant) but still close. All will have frequent short gills. Lamellar attachment ranges from adnexed, adnate, sinuate, or notched.

Stipe:

For the genus at large, *Cortinarius* have a wide range of stipe/stem shapes and include many bulbous bases and even abruptly bulbous bases and range to thinner even shapes. For example, *C. violaceous* has a thicker stipe with a bulbous base which can become less evident with some specimens (especially the taller ones). *C. iodes/iodeoides* can also be easily found with squat bulbous based stipes, but are more commonly found with taller, thinner stalks which seem even in shape.

The genus also contains a wide array of stipe ornamentation and even the texture of the fibers in the stipe. While almost all of them contain some remnants of the partial veil (the cortina), the persistence of these web-like fibers ranges significantly. *C. iodes/iodeoides* have thicker fibers which can take on a metallic sheen (same as the cap) which may mask or emphasize the fibers. *C. violaceous* has a fuzzy or slightly wooly texture on the stipe, though typically less than that of the cap.

Other *Cortinarius* may take on remarkably similar shapes, colors, and size to Lepista nuda, but the presence of a cortina and depositing rust-brown (or perhaps cinnamon) spores are dead giveaways for the genus *Cortinarius*.

Unidentified *Cortinarius sp.* note cortina in bottom specimen

Laccaria

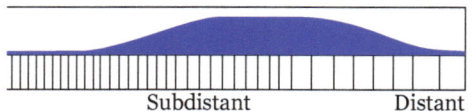

Subdistant   Distant

Inedible   Requires special Prep or

Not as good as SPAM

notched lamellae of a *Laccaria*

Lilac mycelium and fibrous stalk

Laccaria ochropurpurea

Dismantled *L. ochropurpurea*

Description:

Another genus with several purple members which share the fruiting season with *Lepista*. This genus tends to be taller and lankier with thinner caps so is much less likely to be confused with *L. nuda*. Those purple species in our region are *Laccaria amethystina*, *ochropurpurea*, and *vinaceobrunnea*, but other purple species exist elsewhere such as *L. amethysteo-occidentalis* and *gomezii*. Some species of this genus go by the common name, 'deceivers' due to their propensity to change color as they age (usually becoming more muted of brown/tan/dingy). These purple *Laccaria* are considered edible, but not of high quality.

Ecology:

Laccaria amethystina and *ochropurpurea* are mycorrhizal with many trees in the Order *Fagales* including beech, oak, birch, and walnut as well as some coniferous trees East of the Rockies. *L. vinaceobrunnea* is far more discerning in its mycorrhizal relationship with the Southern live oak (*Quercus virginiana*) and is relegated to the gulf coast. All will grow singly or gregariously in the cooler months and may appear in greater numbers when the soil has been modified with nitrogen-containing substances (such as ammonia).

Pileus:

Caps range in size from 1 cm to over 6 cm and are typically small in relation to the length of the stipe and with a thin context (this is true for most *Laccaria*). The cap is convex, flattening and becoming upturned (infundibular) in age. There is often a central pit/pore/umbonation in the cap, but the depth of the pore is shallow (does not lead to a hollow stipe as in *Craterellus*). The pileal surface is mostly glabrous (bald) but short fibers/hairs may be present, especially towards the center of the cap where they can become scurfy. The cap color ranges from a deep, saturated violet when young and whetted/moist to a very light (whitish) grey with tan undertones when older/drier and with a vinaceous to tan intermediary. *Laccaria amethystina* is likely to display the more saturated violets while *L. vinaceobrunnea* may appear more washed-out or pink/vinaceous or with tan undertones. In contrast, *L. ochropurpurea* has a white/cream/

Lepista nuda look-alikes

light grey cap with lilac undertones.

Hymenium:

Lamellae (gills) which are somewhat shallow (though this may be in part to the short cap), contain many short gills, are subdistant to distant and connect to the stipe slightly adnate, adnexed, to slightly decurrent. The lamellae are thick and waxy for the size of the cap, but brittle. *Laccaria* drop a white spore print. *Laccaria amethystina, ochropurpurea,* and *vinaceobrunnea* have gills which range in color from deep violet/purple (especially in *L. amethystine*) to vinaceous, pink, or washed-out violets (especially in *L. vinaceobrunnea*). Both versions may fade to cream/tan/ochre.

Stipe:

Laccaria as a whole lean towards long, thinner (gangly) stalks, though they may often be found with bulbous bases or a crimp/groove running vertically for some length of the stipe. Most of this genus have copious fine fuzzy mycelium at the base of their stipe and the color of this mycelium is an important indicator for species-to-species identification (though it often fades substantially with age). For *L. amethystina* the stipe is colored similarly to (though perhaps less saturated than) the pilus while *L. vinaceobrunnea* typically sports much lighter colors (again similar to the pilus) but may be very light, contrasting the violet/pink of the hymenium. *L. ochropurpurea* expresses the very light colored stipe, similar to the cap with lilac undertones. Furthermore, *L. ochropurpurea* usually has a much thicker, robust stalk - more likely to have substantially bulbous bases than those other purple *Laccaria.*

Laccaria have a very particular texture to their stalks, not just the fibrous scales and slight ornamentation seen on some species, but the size of the fibers themselves is exceptionally thick. The robust fiber is perceivable from a distance and can help spot-ID this genus. Note the texture in the images.

Stipe textures

| *Lepista nuda* | *Cortinarius* | *Laccaria* |

Coprinus comatus
Shaggy Mane

AR

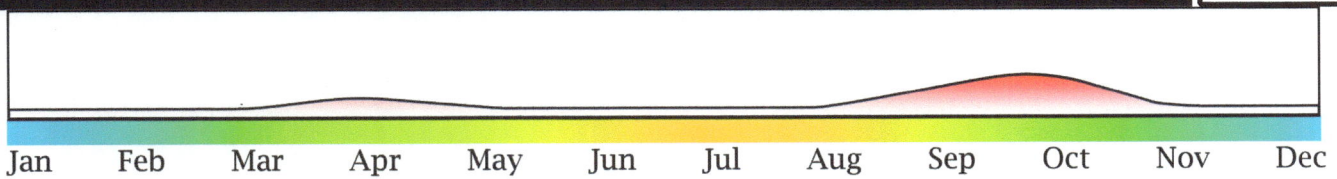

| Jan | Feb | Mar | Apr | May | Jun | Jul | Aug | Sep | Oct | Nov | Dec |

Typical Color Palette

Shape

Egg to Bell shaped to Convex

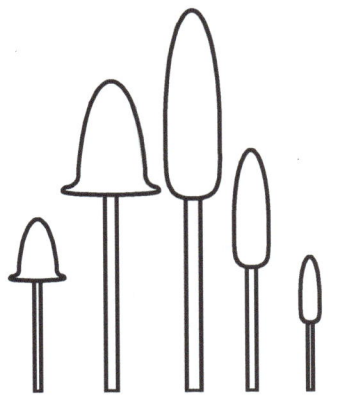

Hemenium: Lamellae

Free and Deep

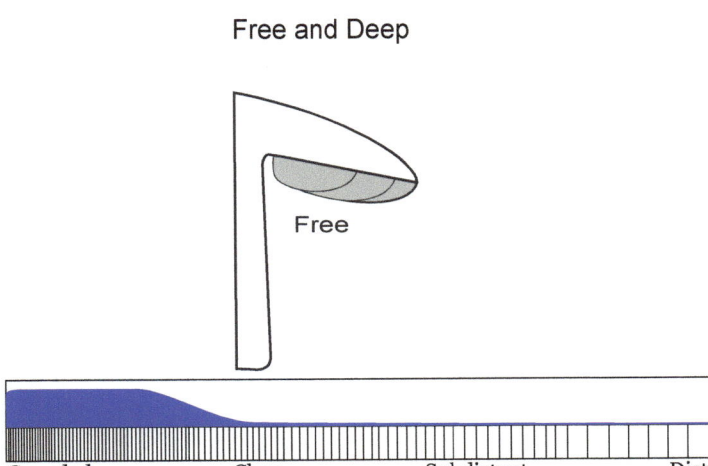

Free

| Crowded | Close | Subdistant | Distant |

Growth

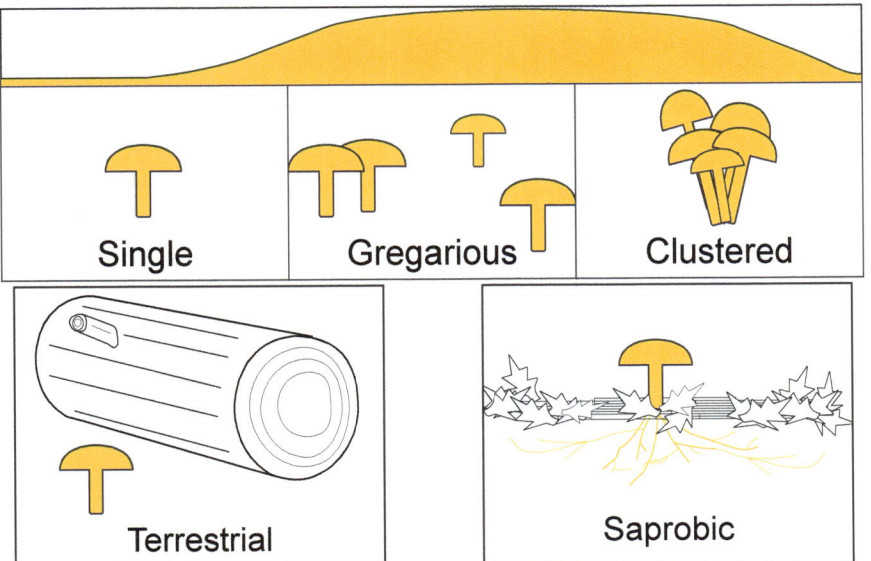

Single

Gregarious

Clustered

Terrestrial

Saprobic

Typical size range

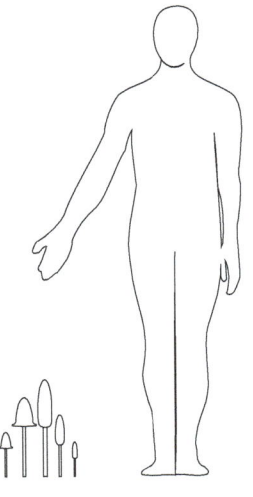

Coprinus comatus is a saprobe which enjoys composted media, fruiting commonly in leafy/pine detris, in lawns, or anywhere high nitrogen content is available.

Coprinus comatus

153

General description

Description:

Called the "Shaggy mane" or referred to as part of the many deliquescing mushrooms as an "ink cap" or specifically as the "shaggy ink cap". Coprinus is a smaller genus in the Family *Agaricaceae* setting it apart from the many look-alikes and other "coprinoid" mushrooms in Family *Psathyrellaceae* (including Genera *Coprinellus*, *Coprinopsis* and *Parasola*). While the Latin epithet "*copr*" refers to dung while "*Coprinus*" means belonging to dung (Hallock, 2015), a reference to those mushrooms which thrive in nitrogen rich areas including dung, compost, or fertilized soils. Fortunately, *Coprinus comatus* isn't found on dung, unlike many of those other mushrooms sporting the '*copr*' root.

Coprinus comatus has a very unique feature which sets it and a handful of others apart from most every other mushroom, rather than dropping spores, the cap melts. This process is called 'deliquescing' and involves enzymatic destruction of the cap turning it black and liquid such that the spores are suspended in the 'ink' and washed or carried away. It was previously thought that once this process has begun that any deliquescing portion of the cap have been rendered inedible, but the truth is that the ink is edible – albeit with an interesting flavor – and can be used as a substitute for squid ink or for specialty culinary dying or preparation.

Ecology:

Coprinus comatus is most commonly found fruiting in nitrogen rich soils which often include composted material, highly decomposed plant material, or lawns. They often grow in small clusters or gregariously, sometimes in fairy rings and most often in later Summer through Fall. While not necessarily a cool or cold weather species, *C. comatus* are rarely reported in consistently hot regions and may be more common in montane or Northern latitudes.

Pileus:

The overall shape of *Coprinus comatus* is also unique such that the rounded cap is so tall that the fruitbody can appear cylindrical. Overall, the shape ranges from egg-like to tall and cylindrical with a rounded top. The surface is often covered with clumps of soft fibers which appear as scales of some sort.

Especially tall/long and finely scaled caps in various stages of deliquescence

Egg shaped and soft-scaled C. comatus caps

Coprinus comatus

Fruitbodies range from 5 cm to over 20 cm presenting impressive columnar structures in these larger sizes. The color ranges from a stark white to dingy creams, often with discolored scales in tans and browns, and of course the jet-black of the ink in mature specimens.

Hymenium:

 C. comatus has lamellae (gills) which are free of the cap, extremely crowded (tightly packed), and are surprisingly deep compared to the depth of the contex (cap flesh). The gills begin white, fade into a pinkish-tan, and eventually turn inky black. The gills and thin context begin to deliquesce beginning at the margin. As the enzymatic reaction slowly climbs towards the center/top of the cap, a small network of the thread-like framework emerges which coils at the shortening margin. This can lead to some truly impressive, yet ephemeral, opportunities to image these beautiful fruitbodies.

Stipe:

 Besides the especially columnar stature of *Coprinus comatus*, the stipe contains a feature which better separates it from the other coprinoids – a ring. Externally, the stipe is white, mostly bare of ornamentation but may present soft scales at the base where various layers of the margin once attached. The annulus or scales are delicate, fading very quickly, and often found clinging to the margin of the cap rather than where it should be – on the stalk! Perhaps this makes it a poor identification feature. When sliced down the middle, the stipe sill also be hollow sans a thread of fibers running the length of the stipe.

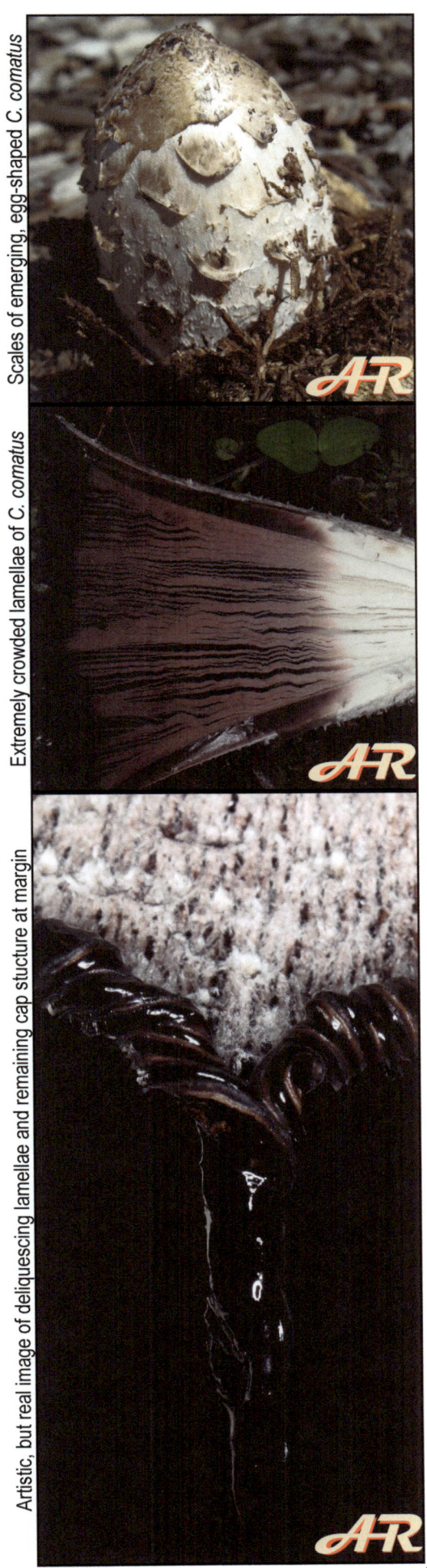

Scales of emerging, egg-shaped *C. comatus*

Extremely crowded lamellae of *C. comatus*

Artistic, but real image of deliquescing lamellae and remaining cap stucture at margin

Coprinus comatus

General Description

Requires special
Prep or

Not as good as
SPAM

This section will discuss all look-alikes as a single group. Since *C. comatus* is such a unique mushroom - we will only consider similarly shaped and colored mushrooms as well as those which deliquesce. Unfortunately, these groups have substantially overlapped macromorphological features which makes describing them far too complex for this book. Consider these descriptions tentative and know they are greatly abridged. Fortunately, almost all 'coprinoids' – those with deliquescing lamellae are edible, though not always very good.

   'Coprinoids' include the genera *Coprinus*, *Coprinellus*, *Coprinopsis*, and *Parasola* which almost all have free gills, black spores, and thin context. Similar, non coprinoids include the genera *Psathyrella*, *Panaeolus*, and some other little-brown mushrooms (LBMs) such as *Conocybe* or *Bolbitius*.

Coprinus sterquilinus

Inedible

   Coprinus sterquilinus looks similar in shape, stature (though usually smaller), and color to *C. comatus*, but with a thinner context and growth almost exclusively from dung or straw/hay. This species is similarly edible to *C. comatus*, but this book discourages eating fungi which grow directly from dung, let alone selling them.

Genus *Coprinopsis*

Adverse reactions
uncommon

   Coprinopsis is a genus which includes several of the larger coprinoids with white, brown, grey or darker caps with large amounts of either thread-like or granular velar remnants. There are also many which are extremely small, and many of these size

Coprinopsis variegata, deliquesced

Coprinopsis variegata

Coprinopsis atramentaria

look-alikes

Coprinopsis variegata growing from a log

Coprinopsis variegata growing from mulch

Coprinellus disseminates at base of tree

Coprinellus micaceus, note minute granules

groups which grow prolifically on hay and animal feed. This genus contains the species *Coprinopsis atramentaria* which (along with some allies) contain the compound 'coprine' which has similar effects to the drug Antabuse – which causes raised blood pressure, nausea, vomiting, and 'hangover' effects when consumed with alcohol. I have personally consumed, and quite enjoyed, *C. atramentaria* but made sure to not consume alcohol for the next day or so.

Genus *Coprinellus*

Inedible

Coprinellus is another genus in the Family *Psathyrellaceae* which is more likely to take on yellow, brown, and reddish hues on the cap but still contains the same whites, browns, and greys as the genus *Coprinopsis*. This genus is also likely to contain velar remnants on the cap giving them grainy or thread-like ornamentation. The two most seen species in the Southeast United States are *Coprinellus miceaceus* and *Copninellus disseminates* due to their abundant growth and showy clusters.

C. miceaceus push through the soil or well-decomposed wood in tight clusters of yellow-tan caps which begin taller than they are wide. The caps are striated and usually have grainy white velar material peppered on them.

C. disseminates erupts from either the ground around or directly from the sides of logs or stumps and commonly standing deadwood as many small (½ – 2 cm) overlapping caps. Each of the caps is convex with slightly flared edges, colored as whitish grey lines emerging from a central rusty tan tip. Each cap sits atop a thin white stalk all emerging from the media together or adjacent to one another.

Coprinus comatus look-alikes

Genus *Parasola*

    Parasola is a genus in the family Psathyrellaceae which have lamellae that often deliquesce. However, this genus is less likely to be confused with *C. comatus* as their stature is much smaller and the entire pilus is extremely thin (sometimes see-through). This genus also has a thin and hollow stipe and free gills, though most species lack the ornamentation of the stipe to seem "shaggy" and may – if anything – appear scaled. They do not have velar remnants on the cap but will almost always have a brown central region at the apex/center of the cap.

Parasola emerging en mass in mulchjed garden bed

Coprinellus domesticus with especially fine velar material

Coprinellus domesticus emerging and mature with small velar granules

Coprinus comatus look-alikes

Family Russulaceae
Lactarius, Lactifluus, and Russula

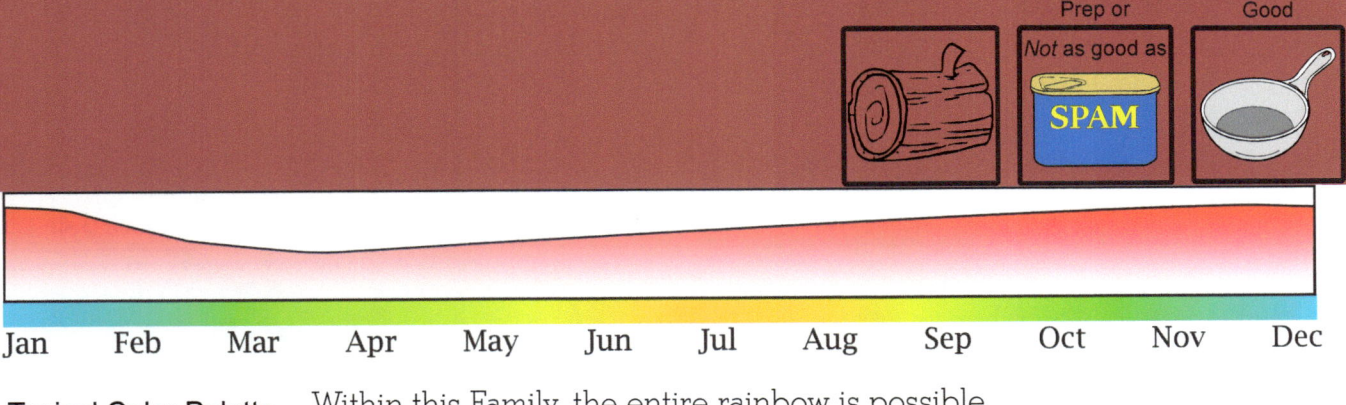

| Jan | Feb | Mar | Apr | May | Jun | Jul | Aug | Sep | Oct | Nov | Dec |

Typical Color Palette   Within this Family, the entire rainbow is possible

Shape

Convex to Flat, central stipe

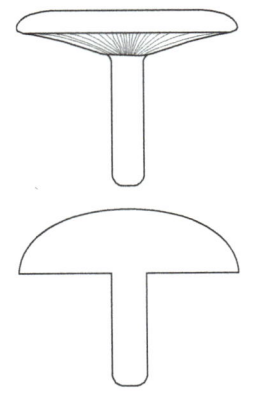

Hemenium: Lamellae

Ranging from shallow to deep and
Adnexed to slightly decurrent

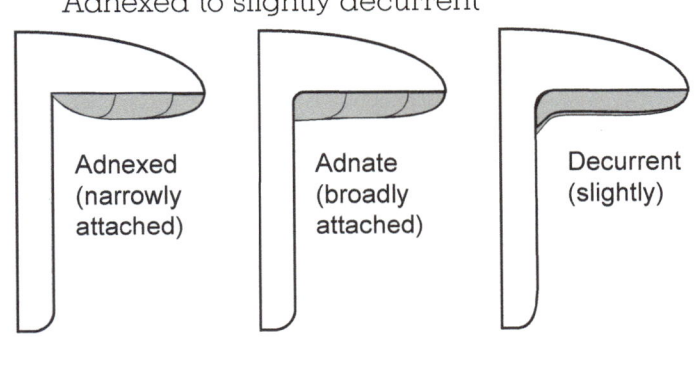

Adnexed
(narrowly
attached)

Adnate
(broadly
attached)

Decurrent
(slightly)

Growth

Russulaceae growth patterns are different between genera and
species with Russula popping up as singles or gregariously and
many Lactarius growing in tight clusters.

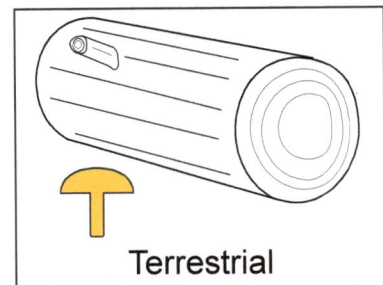

Terrestrial

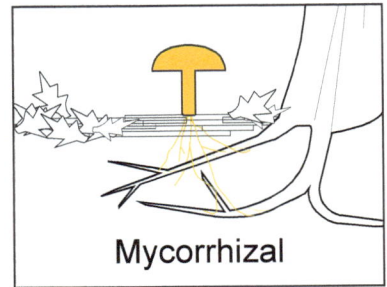

Mycorrhizal

Russulaceae are typically mycorrhizal forming a vast array of relationships with different plants. Unless it's snowy or very dry, there's almost
always something from this family fruiting in your local woods.

General Desciption

General Description

Fruitbodies from this Family can be readily identified as such by their very similar range of cap shapes, the texture of the flesh, and obligate mycorrhizal associations. Overall, this family is extremely diverse in individual species, but contains relatively few genera. This book will concern itself with the genera *Russula*, *Lactarius*, and *Lactifluus*. Unfortunately for the novice taxonomist, the species can be difficult to confidently discriminate and identify. Fortunately for the novice mycophagist, relatively few species are toxic and those which are inedible are often so because they smell or taste fetid, acrid, bitter, or spicy (like a mouthful of black pepper).

Those species approved for commercial sales in Alabama are fairly easy to identify with few look-alikes, but due to the overlapping features of some of these species this book urges the picker to also use other resources until they have an exceptionally confident handle on the genus *Lactarius*. As a part of this training, I urge you to consider smelling and tasting most fruitbodies from this Family. Specifically, the taste-and-spit test of all but those foul-smelling *Russulaceae* will yield important identifying characteristics. Those species covered in this book will all taste insipid (mild, lacking flavor) when raw but many others will have very distinctive smells and tastes – many of which are unpleasant.

Description:

This Family of fungi is unique in that at the cellular level, the tissue contains clusters of rounded cells (swollen hyphae) called sphaerocysts (Brundrett et al. 1996). Don't worry, you won't have to break out the microscope and check every toadstool for these sphaerocysts because their presence in the tissue causes the tissue texture to be crumbly. This feature is restricted to Family *Russulaceae* and is especially prominent in the Genus *Russula* –appropriately known as the "brittle gills". Overall, the texture of fresh fruitbodies in this Family are easy to snap across either the cap or the stipe and are unlikely to be fibrous as so many of the other mushrooms described here are.

Ecology:

This family forms a wide variety of mycorrhi-

A red-capped *Russula*, from below

Unidentified *Russula* sp.

Lactarius subplinthogalus with scalloped margin

Russulaceae

zal associations, predominantly with hardwoods and coniferous trees. Fruitbodies from this Family appear throughout the non-frozen season, with each species having their own preferred season.

Pileus:

The typified range of cap shapes for this Family is a flattened convex which continues to slowly expand until the cap margins rise giving the cap an infundibular shape. The Family *Russulaceae* actually has an exceptional variety of potential shapes (including Secotioid and Gasteroid) but the relevant species will all be Agaricoid (toadstool-shaped).

Hymenium:

Lamellae (gills) ranging in colors from stark white to beautiful indigo or sienna orange, often staining or bruising different colors – a veritable rainbow is possible in this taxonomic Family.

Spore deposits are light, falling into the "pale-spored" grouping of toadstools. Specifically, they range from pure white through cream, dingy yellows, to ochre-tan. Often a substantial spore-print is necessary to see some of the nuance of color in these spores.

Stipe:

This family produces stipes without a ring/skirt/annulus which are glabrous (bald, not fuzzy or hairy). Most are stout in shape and typically equal. The genus *Lactarius* alone may contain a unique ornamental feature called "scrobiculi" which means "little potholes" which are a result of a dried layer of slime. Almost all should be easy to snap in half without being overtly fibrous.

Genus *Lactarius*

Description:

Commonly known as the "Milk mushrooms" due to their propensity to exude a milky latex substance when cut or damaged. The color, smell, taste, and staining ability of this latex can be of great importance to anyone interested in becoming familiar with this genus. Though many porous fungal fruitbodies may exude watery liquid from their hymenium (most commonly when too wet) in a process called guttation - the exudation of latex upon damage is unique to the genera *Lactarius* (Latin: *lac(t)* = "milk") and *Lactifluus*. The presence of milk/latex is also a great way to distinguish these genera from *Russula*, which often shares shape and stature.

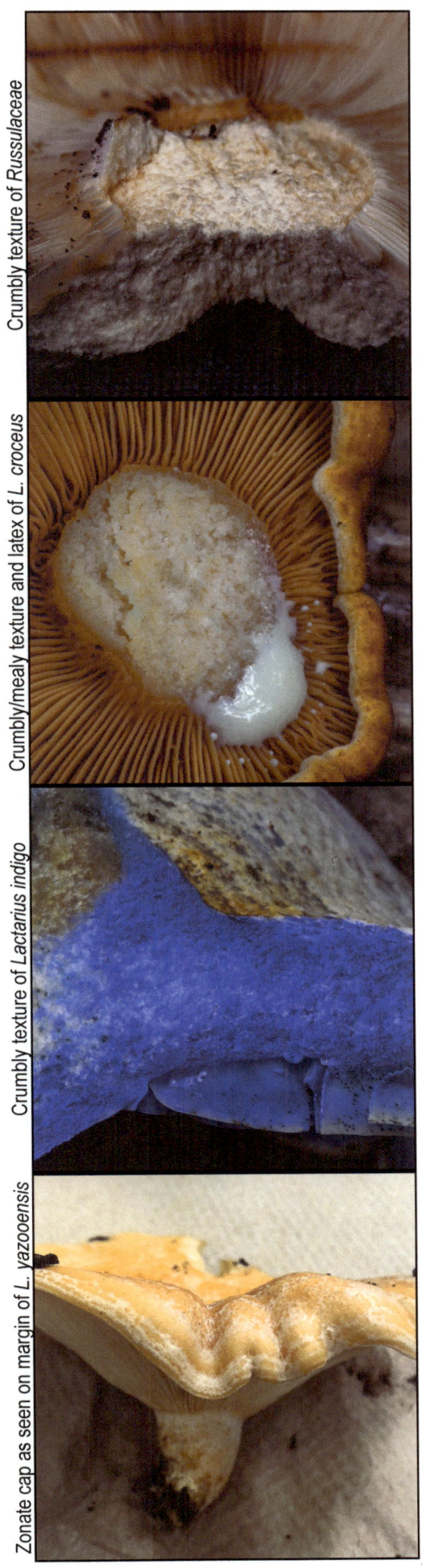

Crumbly texture of *Russulaceae*

Crumbly/mealy texture and latex of *L. croceus*

Crumbly texture of *Lactarius indigo*

Zonate cap as seen on margin of *L. yazooensis*

Lactarius

163

Ecology:

All members of this genus are considered mycorrhizal (Heilmann-Clausen et al. 1998) and as such will be found fruiting in forested areas and abundantly when host trees move sugars around their roots (Late Spring-Late Fall).

Pileus:

Lactarius have a crisp to mealy context (cap tissue) with a variety of textures, colors, and sizes (1 cm – 20 cm). The shape has a fairly consistent range centered around flattened convex with in-rolled margins, often with a slight central depression and becoming infundibular (cup-like) in maturity. Because of the consistency of the range of shapes (as with Family *Russulaceae*), members of these groups can often be identified to family by eye.

Unlike other members of the Family *Russulaceae*, only the genus *Lactarius* (and a rare branch called *Multifurca*) have radial striations (rings) on the cap. Not all *Lactarius* have this feature, but if you spot it, you'll know you have a *Lactarius*.

Hymenium:

All *Lactarius* have lamellae (gills) with attachments at or near adnate with some deccurent or adnexed tendencies. Lamellar depth is usually intermediate to deep and ranges from crowded to distant. The exudation of milk/latex is typically most prominent from a cut to the gills and the features of which should be noted. One feature which often eludes those unfamiliar with this genus, is the ability of the latex to stain either the gills or other surfaces (regular white paper is a great media to try), though this reaction may take several minutes or require some drying. Importantly, many *Lactarius* will have only scant latex production or, as in older specimens, will not produce any to the naked eye.

Stipe:

Unlike the fibrous stalks that most fruitbodies use, *Lactarius* have stipes with a meaty to mealy texture which is often dependent on the species, maturity, and environmental factors. When infested by bugs, the stipe is usually the first hotel opened. Stipes are primarily even in stature and may be longer or shorter than the diameter of the cap. Another unique feature of this genus is the potential for the development of scrobiculi (singular: scrobiculum) which means "pothole" and is a result of a dried slime layer which occurs during the development of some *Lactarius*.

Scrobiculi of *Lactarius*

Dried yellow-tinged latex of *L. subpurpureus*

Distant adnate gills of *L. subplinthogalus*

Slightly zoned cap of *L. subpurpureus*

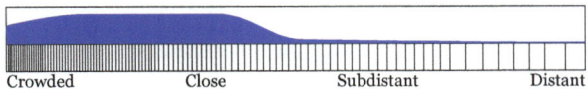

Lactarius indigo **complex**

Crowded	Close	Subdistant	Distant

Edible and Good

Description:

Colloquially and appropriately called the indigo milk cap, this *Lactarius* is one of the more stunning fungi in our region due to its intensely saturated blue-indigo color. While purples may be commonplace, blue is an especially uncommon color in the fungal world and as such, mushrooms like these are very fun to find and easy to identify. *Lactarius indigo* is actually a complex of a couple variations including the smaller *L. indigo var. diminutivis* (Singer et al. 1980), and the classic *L. indigo var. indigo* and perhaps some others with more pallid or green-tinted colors. The blue palette is shared with two look-alikes discussed next; *L.*'s *paradoxus* and *chelidonium*, but *L. indigo* is a solid, striking blue.

L. indigo, as well as *L.*'s *paradoxus* and *chelidonium* are all a part of the section *Deliciosi* within the genus *Lactarius* and are all edible – if a bit grainy (think of a pear).

Ecology:

As *L. indigo* is mycorrhizal with hardwoods such as oak and gumball trees (Liquidambar) as well as coniferous trees, it can be found in most wooded areas and fruits most prolifically in the Spring and Fall. This mushroom is especially common along the gulf coasty and as such can often be found in significant numbers in Alabama growing singly or gregariously, though sometimes close enough to one another to appear clumped.

Pileus:

Aside from the radical indigo-blue coloration of this entire fruitbody, the cap is adorned with a layer of fine white fuzz which appears as radial stripes emanating from the center out towards the margin. Often the fine white fuzz is cut with regions of intense blue shining through between the blue rings. The margin is often in-rolled until mature while the center is often slightly depressed. The flattened convex shape can become grossly infundibular in advanced age, when the color fades and becomes pallid. The diameter ranges from 2 cm to over 10 cm.

Hymenium:

As in all of the *Lactarius*, lamellae form the hymenial surface and have an adnate attachment and fork often. While the entire fruitbody is capable of

Range of blues in *L. indigo*

In-rolled margin and blue lamellae of *L. indigo* Note the radial rings on the margin

White fuzz and scrobiculi of *L. indigo*

Cobalt-blue latex of cut *L. indigo*

producing the bright blue latex, the gills seem able to produce the greatest quantity when cut or damaged.

Stipe:

Those *Lactarius* within section *Deliciosi* are especially likely to have the oval/ellipsoid potholes along their stalks called scrobiculi. In *L. indigo*, these scrobiculi are often more intensely blue then the slightly lighter stipe color. The shape is even and generally much shorter than the diameter of the cap.

Lactarius chelidonium

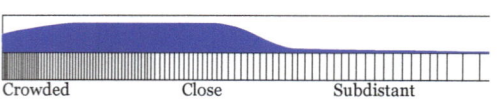
Crowded   Close   Subdistant

Requires special Prep or *Not as good as* SPAM   Edible and Good

Description:

One of the equally edible look-alikes for *L. indigo* which is <u>not</u> approved for sales in Alabama. While confused with *L. indigo*, this species is far more likely to be confused with *L. paradoxus* due to their highly overlapping features.

Ecology:

Growing in association (mycorrhizal) with pines during the cooler Fall months. *L. chelidonium* often grows gregariously or in small clusters, rarely with attached stipes.

Pileus:

Bald to minutely fuzzy, the cap of *L. chelidonium* takes on orange-tinted tan colors with green undertones which become more apparent in age or with damage. This fruitbody will lack the concentric rings, except for some bits along the margin. Like others in section *Deliciosi*, the cap is a flattened convex with in-rolled margins prior to becoming completely mature. The context will bruise a teal-green if snapped apart.

Hymenium:

Lamellae which have an adnate attachment but may lean slightly decurrent. The gills are an orange-tan or yellow-tan color and bruise a teal (blue-green) color. While the fruitbody and gills will bruise this teal color, the latex is scant and will emerge as a dingy yellow before staining the fruitbody green.

Stipe:

Even, shorter than the diameter of the cap and a more pallid color than the cap. Unlike *L. indigo*, scobiculi (pothoels) will not be present. The stipe is hollow and filled with a cottony material.

Green staining of *L. chelidonium*
Purple/tan pileus without striations/rings
Orange exterior and white cottony-interior
Green staining of the context of *L. chelidonium*

Lactarius paradoxus

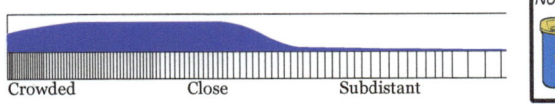

Crowded   Close   Subdistant

Requires special Prep or *Not* as good as SPAM   Edible and Good

Description:

Easily confused with *L. chelidonium* due to the multicolored fruitbody and highly conserved shape/texture/and growing season. *L. paradoxus* stands somewhere between *L. indigo* and *L. subpurpureus* (not discussed but see main image for Family *Russulaceae*). This fruitbody is just as edible as *L. indigo* and *L. chelidonium* but is not approved for sales in Alabama.

Ecology:

Growing in late Summer through Fall in association with their mycorrhizal partners (oak and pine), *L. paradoxus* will grow singly, gregariously, or near enough to one another to be considered clustered. These fungi are especially common in the Gulf states.

Pileus:

From above, these fungi may look like *L. indigo* due to their white-ish color with blue undertones. Upon further inspection the concentric rings/striations are much more subtle and green-purple undertones may be detectable. In fact, the range of colors may have you call it more purple with green splotches. Like the others in section *Deliciosi* discussed here, the cap ranges from 2 cm to over 10 cm and is a flattened convex shape with in-rolled margins until mature.

Hymenium:

The adnate lamellae (gills) of *L. paradoxus* look far closer to that of *L. subpurpureans* being a light purple-tan color which are crowded to close and a medium depth. Forking is likely near the stipe. Gills are stain green giving the hymenium and leading to confusion with *L. chelidonium* which has more orange-colored gills. Latex of *L. paradoxus* is scant and a reddish-brown which readily stains the flesh green.

Stipe:

Interestingly, both *L. indigo* and *L. subpurpureus* sport scrobiculi, but *L. paradoxus* will not have them. Like others in this section, *L. paradoxus* has a short stipe relative to the cap diameter which is colored similarly to the cap. The stalk is hollow.

Weather-bleached cap of *L. paradoxus*

Purple/tan color of *L. paradoxus* hymenium

Young blue cap with purple gills, *L. paradoxus*

Green staining of *L. paradoxus*

Lactarius

Lactifluus corrugis and volemus

L. corrugis

L. volemus

Description:

Called the corrugated milk-cap and voluminous milk-cap, respectively, both are included in the "Golden and Burgundy Milkies" group. These *Lactarius* are very similar to one another but with slightly different color and textural presentations. Unlike many other *Lactarius*, these are fairly easy to identify despite their wide-ranging size and proportions. Both of these species, when not dry, produce copious amounts of latex when cut. Both species also have a mild to strong fishy smell when fresh that can become unbearable if left in the back of the refrigerator for too long.

Ecology:

Both grow commonly in mixed woods in the Eastern United States and as with all *Lactarius*, are mycorrhizal. Typically found growing alone or scattered in Summer through Fall.

Pileus:

Cap diameters for both species range from 2 cm to over 12 cm and are broadly planar to infundibular in maturity. Young specimens have a planar-convex shape with in-rolled margins which quickly unfurl as well as a slightly depressed center. These young specimens may be minutely velvety to pruinose (a frosted, powdery appearance) which is especially common and dense for *L. corrugis*. The color pallet for each species is shown, highlighting the highly saturated burgundies and cinnamon range of hues. While the colors of each species overlap substantially, *L. corrugis* usually has a more pronounced pruinose pileus and, importantly, a wrinkled to corrugated pattern.

Hymenium:

Both species have close to crowded forking lamellae (gills) which attach to the stalk in an adnate configuration. *L. corrugis* has a tan to brown-tinted lamellae color while *L. volemus* has whiter, creamier, or more yellow-tinted gills. Copious latex from both species is exuded white and stains all part of the fruitbody brown. Taste of the latex is mild.

Stipe:

Stipe length varies greatly from substantially shorter to longer than the cap diameter. The stalk is more-or-less equal but may have a tapering base, a feature which is slightly more pronounced in *L. volemus*. One significant feature not equally shared

Creamy gills with brown stains, *L. volemus*

Pileus of *L. volemus*

Brown staining and filled stalk, *L. volemus*

Pileus of extra wide *L. volemus*

between these species is the finely velvety stipe of *L. corrugis* which is also likely to be a cinnamon color with creamy-yellow undertones. *L. volemus* on the other hand has a more glabrous (bald) stipe which lacks the cinnamon color and is rather a yellow-tinted cream, sometimes with more vibrant yellows and orange undertones. Both stipes are usually firm, thick, and not hollow until aged.

Lactifluus hygrophoroides

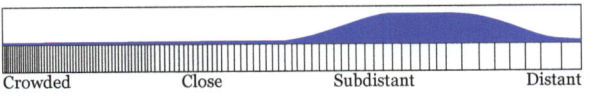

Crowded — Close — Subdistant — Distant

Edible and Good

Description:

This genus shares the prefix epithet lact (Latin: lac(t) = "milk") with Lactarius but also the Latin suffix fluus = "flow," to roughly translate into "flowing milk." Interestingly, the genera *Russula* and *Lactarius* are more closely related than *Lactifluus* is to *Lactarius*, despite their shared morphological features and exudation of milky latex upon damage (especially to the gills). The only species of this genera which is suitable for sales in Alabama is *Lactifluus hygrophoroides* [Lack-tih-floos high-grow-for-oh-ee-des] (previously classified as *Lactarius hygrophoroides*).

L. hygrophoroides is also readily identifiable with few look-alikes and a part of the "Golden and Burgundy Milkies" group.

Ecology:

Forming mycorrhizal associations with hardwoods, especially oaks throughout the Eastern United States, *L. hygrophoroides* fruits in the Summer-Fall.

Pileus:

One of the milk-mushrooms with a distinctive cap color and texture, a peachy tan or dull orange that ranges from glabrous (bald) to feeling very slightly fuzzy. The cap shape is broadly convex/flat but will likely lift the margin to become somewhat infundibular (cup-like) in age. The margin may become gently wrinkled with age. The cap ranges from 3 cm to 8 cm in diameter.

Hymenium:

Subdistant to distant lamellae (gills) with an adnate to slightly decurrent connection to the stalk. Gills are medium to deep given the size of the cap, and range in color from white to cream or pale yellow-tan. When cut, the gills exude copious white latex which does not change colors or stain the tissues. Taste of the latex is mild.

Lactarius

L. hygrophoroides with peachy-yellow stipe

Subdistand gill spacing and copius latex

Full stiple of L. hygrophoroides

The distinctive peachy-yellow cap

Stipe:

Another short-stalked species with a stipe (usually) shorter than the diameter of the cap. The stipe is equal to slightly tapered at the base and colored similarly (though sometimes more pallid) to the cap. The texture ranges from minutely velvety to glabrous (bald) and is solid to stuffed with cottony material inside.

Genus Russula

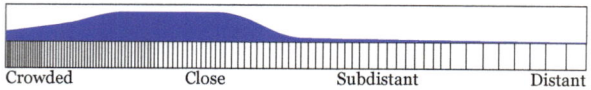

Crowded   Close   Subdistant   Distant

Description:

The genus *Russula* is interesting for a few of reasons. They tend to be the crumbliest fungi you're likely to find, they are exceptionally abundant and only stop fruiting in the dead of winter, they form mycorrhizal relationships with just about any tree you can imagine, they come in a rainbow of colors, and they are one of the very few groups of mushrooms to follow some straightforward rules regarding edibility. Recall the tissues of most Family *Russulaceae* contains clusters of rounded cells (swollen hyphae) called sphaerocysts (Brundrett et al. 1996; Anon n.d.) which make them crumbly. Most species of the genus *Russula* contain exceptional amounts of these sphaerocysts and are thus crumblier than an old cookie. In good fun, I urge you to throw these at any foraging partners to watch them explode on contact!

The most commonly found species of *Russula* are those with red caps and a white stalk which are a group of dozens to hundreds of species with overlapping features that require microscopy – and sometimes genetic analysis – to discriminate from one another. An interesting 'rule' which only applies to those <u>Red Capped Russulas of North America</u> is that if they do not taste acrid/bitter/peppery but are mild/insipid (without taste), they are edible. This rule does NOT apply to blackening, white-capped, or other Russula.

Ecology:

Growing mycorrhizal with hard woods, fruit trees, conifers, etc. Most species seem to have distinctive seasons, but as a whole the genus seems to always have some members fruit-

Red-capped *Russula*

ing outside of snow-covered Winter.

Pileus:

Ranging considerably in size from <1 cm to well over 20 cm with a veritable rainbow of possible colors (except blue). The textures also range substantially, but for the most part have a thin pileal membrane which can often be peeled off the context.

Hymenium:

All *Russula* have lamellae (gills) which range from slightly decurrent-adnate to slightly adnexed-adnate. Most species have white to cream colored gills with some notable exceptions which are not discussed here (including those which stain black). The gills are brittle and damage/crumble easily in most species. Spore prints are almost always some white/cream colors, sometimes tinted yellow/tan.

Stipe:

While often a bug hotel, the stalk is also brittle and can be snapped like old chalk. There are some species (*Russula compacta* or *brevipes*) for which the stipe is more robust, but not at all fibrillar.

Red-capped *Russula*

Russula

Russula crustosa & (parvo)virescens

Edible and Good

Description:

Colloquially known as the green or green-quilted *Russula*, these three species will be presented together here due to overlapping features and the same edibility as well as all being approved for sales in the State of Alabama. These three species are very likely to represent a much broader species complex which likely require genetic evaluation to interpret. Importantly, there are several other green-capped Russulas which form reasonable look-alikes that are not approved for sales covered next which includes R.'s *aeruginea, cyanoxantha, gracilis,* and *variata*.

Ecology:

All three are mycorrhizal with hardwoods (especially oaks) and some conifers, fruiting Summer through Fall.

Pileus:

All range from 3 cm to over 10 cm in diameter with a distinctive green cap which contains some crackling, quilted, or shattered texture to the color. The patches of more intense coloration are smallest for *R. virescens* (appearing more like broken safety glass) and substantially larger in *R. crustosa* and *parvovirescens*. *R. parvovirescens* takes on a blue-tint or a more teal coloration than the others and can often be separated based on this feature alone. *R. crustosa*, on the other hand, is typically more pallid, especially between the more highly pigmented mottled patches, and may have some yellow, cream, or tan hues.

All of these *Russula* will develop with a rounded convex cap which unfurls to become broadly planar-convex with in-rolled margins and a central depression. Often a membranous pellicle (the actual pileus) can be peeled from these mushrooms with a fingernail (as with many *Russula*). The cap is easily snapped in and is generally crumbly.

Hymenium:

These three *Russula* all have adnate lamellae (gills) which easily crumble and are most typically white to cream in color. They are medium in depth and will drop a white to cream spore-print.

Stipe:

The stipe is typically shorter than the diameter of the cap (for mature specimens), solid, white, glabrous (bald) and readily snapped in half.

R. crustosa young and mature

R. parvovirescens based on the blue-tint

R. parvovirescens based on the blue-tint

R. parvovirescens based on the blue-tint

Russula

Russula aeruginea, cyanoxantha, gracilis, olivacea, and variata.

Inedible

Requires special Prep or *Not* as good as SPAM

Description:

The species described here are those not approved for sales in Alabama, and are thus considered "look-alikes" despite being edible (though some are acrid in taste). *R.*'s *aeruginea, cyanoxantha, gracilis, olivacea,* and *variata* are all green-capped *Russula* which may be found in Alabama and the surrounding states. *R. cyanthoxantha* and *variata* are so similar that they will be considered together.

Ecology:

Each of these species is mycorrhizal and will be found in wooded areas Summer through Fall. *R. olivacea* seems to be present predominantly along the West coast but may be present across North America.

Pileus:

All of these species contain some amount of green in their cap color but will lack the distinctive quilted or cracked appearance of the pileus. *R. aeruginea* is the most straightforward with a plain green (think sage) cap which often presents with lines along the margin where the thicker tissue of the lamellae is detectable from above. *R. cyanthoxantha* and *variata* contain some amount of purple mottling or splotches. *R. gracilis* will have red-pink coloration along the margin with most of the green being confined to the center of the cap. *R. olivacea* also contains reds in the cap color and is often much more of an olive-colored green but sometimes is almost completely dark red.

Hymenium:

All have white to cream or slightly yellow-tinted lamellae with an adnate attachment to the stipe. Most species will have some forking of the gills, but with too much overlap to depend on as an identification feature between them. Importantly, *R. olivacea* will drop a yellow-orange tinted spore print which is just distinctive enough to help with identification.

Stipe:

All of these species will have a primarily white stalk which is equal to slightly bulbus or tapering at the very base (as is common in *Russula*). *R. gracilis* and *olivacea* will almost always have some pink shades on the stipe.

Russula

R. cyanthoxantha with purple mottling

R. aerugina based on the plain green

R. aerugina based on the plain green

R. aerugina based on the plain green

Hypomyces lactifluorum

Choice

Parasitic on fungi

Description:

The "lobster mushroom" is one of the classic go-to mushrooms for novices to forage – especially those foraging near/in pine-dominated land. This is because *Hypomyces lactifluorum* has a very unique appearance and is a parasite on species of *Russulaceae* – specifically *Russula brevipes* and *Lactifluus piperatus* which are not discussed here. *Hypomyces* is a genus of parasitic fungi in the Phyllum/Division *Ascomycota* which alone do not create fruitbodies but rather infect their fungal hosts and transform them into a completely new entity. Two of the species are known to produce edible fruitbodies (or rather create them), *H.'s lactifluorum* and *luteovirens*. Only *H. lactifluorum* is considered the lobster mushroom and is appropriate for sales in Alabama.

Ecology:

Since this fungus is a parasite on only a few other fungal fruitbodies, it will only be found where those fungal fruitbodies would themselves be found. Both *Russula brevipes* and *Lactifluus piperatus* grow in mycorrhizal partnership with conifers and are most likely to be found when pine trees are the predominant tree. *Russula brevipes* and *Lactifluus piperatus* typically fruit in the late Summer to Fall which is when *Hypomyces lactifluorum* begins to appear.

Fruitbody:

While superficially "mushroom shaped", the transformation process often begins during the fruitbody's development and changes it to become more amorphous (shapeless), though the underlying structure is usually still apparent. *H. lactifluorum* may appear as dense white splotches which quickly become a bright pumpkin-orange and spread over the host's fruitbody. The orange coloration may be yellow or red tinted. During this process the lamellae fuse and smaller shapes are absorbed into the greater structure. Beyond becoming a near fluorescent orange, the infected portions of the mushroom are completely chemically changed and will present as a much harder and denser fruitbody (think of a fresh potato).

When completely transformed, *H. lactifluorum* will have a texture of many small, hard bumps or ridges. When found, any soft portions (we have all grabbed a potato on its way out) should be cut off as they are usually old or perhaps infected with a secondary parasitic mold. The interior should be white or cream in color and hard/dense the whole way through. Though the 'skin' is usually a little bit harder, and may even present with cracks.

Hypomyces luteovirens presents very similarly but has a greenish-yellow top and yellow hymenial surface.

H. lactifluorus emerging as a 'shrump'

H. lactifluorum freshly dug up

Some lamellar shapes still present as ridges

A beautiful red-tinted specimen

Hericium
Lion's mane, Bear's tooth

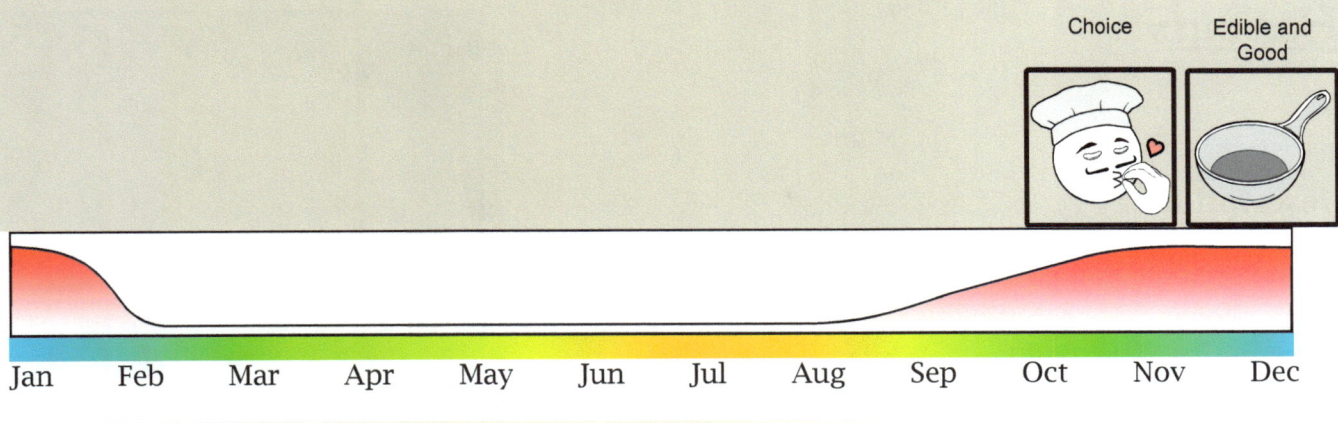

Jan   Feb   Mar   Apr   May   Jun   Jul   Aug   Sep   Oct   Nov   Dec

Typical Color Palette

Shape

Teeth hanging from singular or branched mass

Hemenium: Teeth

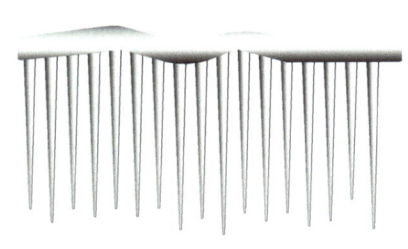

Typical size range

Growth

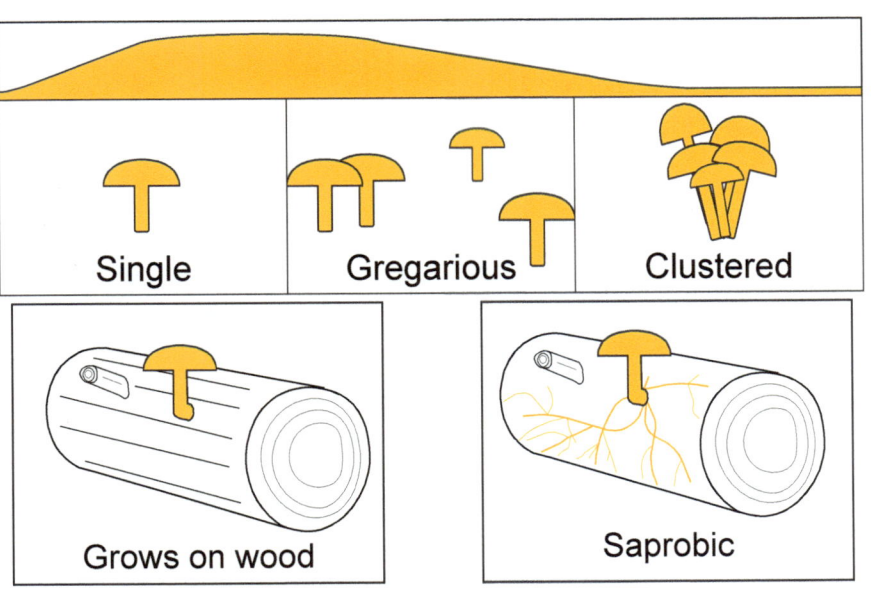

Single   Gregarious   Clustered

Grows on wood   Saprobic

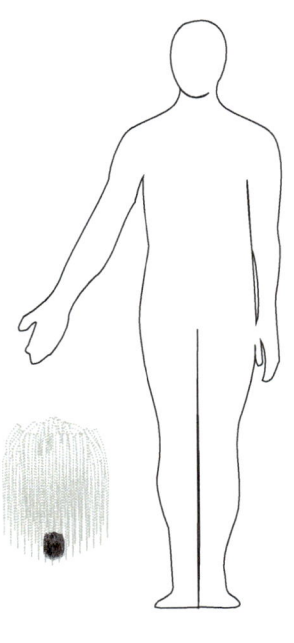

Hericium is a fierce decomposer of wood, especially oaks. Find them during the cool to cold months on dead or dying trees.

Hericium

Description:

A fungus of many names, lion's mane, bear's tooth, and hedgehog mushrooms. These are all apt descriptions of the dangling thin teeth which comprise the majority of the fruitbody. While the genus name *Hericium* is a literal translation from Latin to mean 'hedgehog', they are not related to the genus *Hydnum*, which also sports this common name. In Eastern North America there are three species of *Hericium*, each with a distinctive shape and few look-alikes, none of which are toxic. This combination makes this a perfect genus for beginners to start with, though they are beloved edibles of well-seasoned experts alike. The three species are *Hericium* (her-ih-see-um) *erinaceus* (air-in-ah-see-us), *americanum* (am-er-ih-kahn-um), and *coralloides* (kor-ah-loy-des).

Ecology:

Growing on hardwoods, especially oak, beech, and maple as either a saprophytic growth of dead wood or a parasite of dying trees. Fruitbodies can be found year-round, even with snow on the ground (though rare) but most prolifically during the late Fall and early Spring. The best time to look for Hericium is following Autumnal rains or near perpetual sources of water in cool to cold months. Due to the nature of consuming plant materials as they are damaged or weakened, *Hericium* are very often found high in trees and may require a ladder or the use of a fishing line with a weight attached to it to be thrown over the fruit.

Fruitbody:

All three species are white to cream in color and eventually yellow or turn a brownish color with age, often beginning with the tips of the teeth. The flesh will be soft and is easily torn by hand or sliced with a knife. The flesh often has a faint smell and taste of fresh seafood (not fish, fishy, or seaweed-like) but may be mild to insipid.

Hericium erinaceus is the most easily separated of the three as it does not branch but rather is a rounded structure with teeth emanating from all sides other than the connection point, which elongate in age and range from 0.5 cm to over 4 cm in some especially large specimens. Often, a sub-prime specimen will be found with appears to only have teeth dangling

Young *H. erinaceus* with short teeth

The flexible, soft, pendulous teeth of *H. erinaceus*

H. erinaceus with the top beaten up by rain

Internal structure of *H. erinaceus*

from the bottom, usually with a pitted top (see image) which is likely due to environmental damage such as oversaturation of rainfall. The teeth are long, even in diameter (not oblong) and pendulous ending in a bluntly pointed tip. These teeth are soft and flexible, and most will comfortably survive a ride in your mushroom basket without being ripped off (unlike those delicate teeth of *Hydnum*!). The major portion of the fruitbody it a solid or mostly solid (some holes may be present) white fungal flesh which is edible and tasty upon cooking. This species ranges dramatically in size from the size of a baseball to that of a beachball!

Hericium americanum and *coralloides* are similar in shape to one another but can often be discriminated from one another. These species have many branches from which the delicate (but flexible) teeth dangle. The teeth of these species are much shorter and sometimes appear as more of a wooly or bearded entity. *H. americanum* has longer branches and longer teeth while *H. coralloides* (from the word coral) typically form a more tight-knit branching structure with shorter teeth. All three of these species are considered tasty edibles and many (especially *H. erinaceus*) are being cultivated commercially.

H. coralloides with many short branches and short teeth

H. coralloides with many short branches and short teeth

H. americanum with long teeth

Long branching of *H. americanum*

Hericium look-alikes

Irpiciporus/Spongipellis pachyodon

Inedible

Description:

A very unique crust fungus which grows in small clumps or massive clusters which is often mistaken for *Hericium* due to its obvious teeth.

Ecology:

Often found growing on the sides of dead wood with the most prolific growth occurring during the cooler seasons.

Fruitbody:

Unlike *Hericium* this fruitbody is truly *effused-reflexed* (as the projecting fruit which has a distinctive top and bottom [partially pileate – being "L" shaped with hymenium on the side of the media and bottom of the projecting portion of the fruitbody]) with a distinctive 'cap' and long teeth which cascade downwards, often connected to one another or the growth media. These teeth are not rounded, but rather oblong and irregular, often fusing with one another to form odd shapes. The top-most portion of the fruitbody is a sterile tissue (non hymenial) but is the same color and texture as the teeth. Unlike a soggy *Hericium*, the cap does not have pits in it but is smooth and glabrous. Furthermore, the bulk of the fruitbody is fused to the media and projecting caps do not extend far. Finally, the texture of *I. pachyodon* is completely different than Hericium, being leathery or corky and tough to cut, let alone to rip in all but the youngest of specimens.

Donkia pulcherrimus

Inedible

Description:

Perhaps a better look-alike for *Hericium* than the rest, but seemingly less often encountered. Previously housed in the genus *Climacodon* and was considered related to *C. septentrionalis* which is covered in many field guides (but not here) as the Northern Tooth fungus. *Donkia pulcherrimus*, unlike its more

I. pachyodon growing up a log

I. pachyodon with cap and oblong teeth

Climacodon pulcherrimus

commonly discussed 'cousin', is a softer bodied fruit-body which is uncommonly reported (maybe due to hiding underneath wood).

Ecology:

Causing a white rot on hardwoods (especially those well saturated dead logs) in warmer climates, but cooler months (late Spring and early Fall).

Fruitbody:

D. pulcherrimus can develop to over 13 cm in width and is usually an oval to scallop-shaped fruit hanging along the side or underside of its substrate. Unlike the crusts and some of the polypores with similar shapes, the fruitbody can be ¼ to ⅓ of the width in its height. The color is stark white to creamy, sometimes developing yellow or ochre as the edges dry out. This species is very soft, easily torn or broken and has a distinctively fluffy, hairy, or stringy looking cap (compare image to weather worn Hericium). On the underside, thin teeth, usually < 1 cm in length, hang which are usually similar in length to one another and closely packed. The context, or inner flesh, is also very fibrous or stringy.

Inedible

Genus *Steccherinum*

Description:

This moderate sized genus contains fruitbodies of various forms, many of which are crusts or effused-reflexed. The genus *Steccherinum* (stech-er-in-um) is included as a look-alike for Hericium due to the propensity for many species to be toothed (hydnoid) and due to the novice to confusing most anything toothed for *Hericium*.

Ecology:

Growing on the sides or undersides of dead-wood, especially that wood which still has bark (not decorticated). Fruiting like many other crusts in the cooler months but found year-round.

Fruitbody:

The species most likely to be confused with *Hericium* is *S. ochraceum*, known as the ochre spreading tooth fungus. The fruitbody is effused-reflexed with a

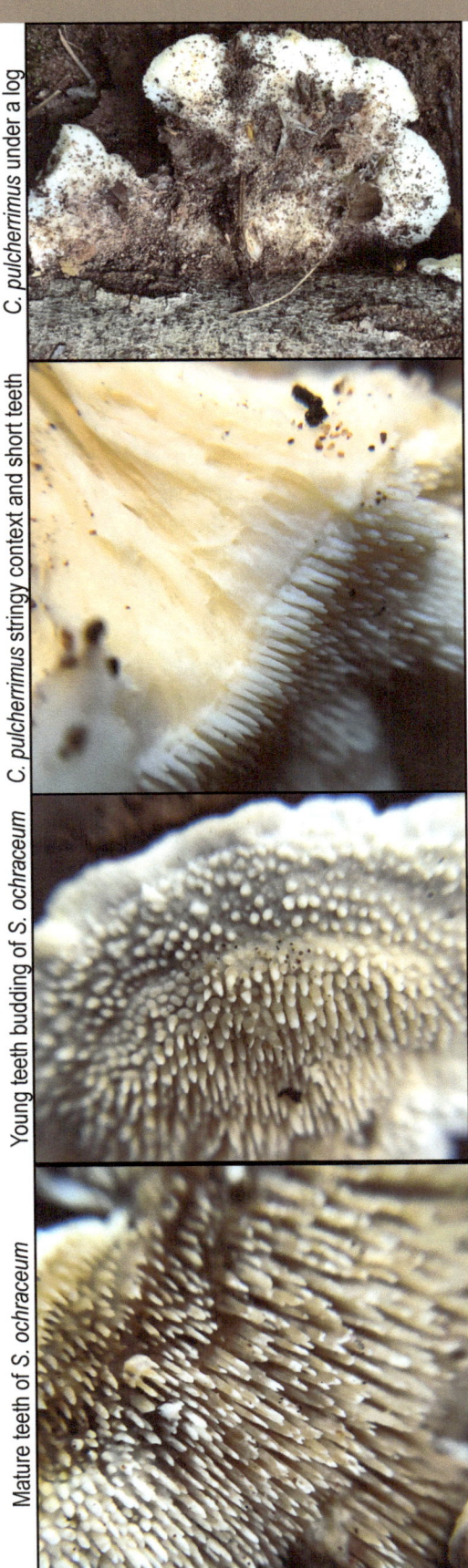

C. pulcherrimus under a log

C. pulcherrimus stringy context and short teeth

Young teeth budding of S. ochraceum

Mature teeth of S. ochraceum

single connection point per 'patch'. That is, the unconnected leather-like portion of the fruitbody can be bent away from the substrate up until said connection point – but is otherwise very tightly pressed against the substrate. When developing, the fruitbody is white and produces white nubs along the bottom which slowly lengthen to become fairly robust teeth. In maturity, the teeth and most of the hymenial surface will become a reddish ocher in color, hence the species name *ochraceum*.

Genus *Postia*

Inedible

Description:

A polypore which may resemble *Hericium* from the top or side due to its white somewhat rounded and fuzzy appearance. The pores on the bottom and odd coloration should dissuade the forager from further considering it a possible *Hericium*. Sometimes called the Blue Cheese Polypore.

Ecology:

Growing on coniferous wood (primarily) in the cooler months. The species in Eastern North America are likely to include *P. livens, simulans, caesiosimulans*, and *populi* but not *P. caesia* since this is a European species (Miettinen et al. 2018).

Fruitbody:

Pictured is *P. livens* which is a soft bodied to spongy fruitbody which usually takes on a half-circle to shell-like shape. They are white to off-white with ochre undertones, developing steely-blue colors when bruised or damaged along all parts of the fruitbody. The cap is especially fuzzy to wooly, closer to *Donkia pulcherrimus* than *Hericium erinaceus*. The hymenial surface is poroid and not hydnoid (toothed) with irregular shaped pores.

Genus *Irpex*

Inedible

Description:

Another genus of crust fungi which often produces poroid or hydnoid (toothed) crusts which may be confused for the early growth of *Hericium*.

Ecology:

This genus grows along the sides or undersides of decaying wood in the cool or wet months. Species *Irpex lacteus* and *latemarginatus* may be found in

Unadhered portion of *S. ochraceum*

Shape, color, and texture of *Postia livens* cap

Postia livens hymenium

Irpex latemarginatus under a log

Hericium look-alikes

Eastern North America and produce toothed crusts.

Fruitbody:

The genus *Irpex* is really a polypore which begins as a white to off-white crust which may become effused-reflexed with shell-like, often fused portions. The fruitbody is amorphous in shape and ranges dramatically in its size based on the dimensions of the fruiting media/substrate. The underside will have irregular pores which elongate with age and become tooth-like structures. These broken pore 'teeth' are thus connected to one another forming jagged, uneven, and intermittent stalactites which are often oblong.

Inedible

Radulomyces copelandii

Description:

A species which has made its home in Northeastern America but may have been spread from Asia. This species is unlikely to be confused by the experienced forager for *Hericium* but due to the pendulous teeth, may be confused by the novice.

Ecology:

You are unlikely to run into this species in the Gulf states, but it is being reported further and further South and may eventually make an appearance in the Gulf states. Fruiting from the sides or undersides of hardwoods (especially oak) Spring through Fall. Often growing as either a small individual patch, gregarious patches, or as massive, fused groups.

Fruitbody:

The fruitbody of *Radulomyces* are crust-like with *R. copelandii* forming especially long and pendulous teeth. The fruitbody ranges from white to ochers depending on age and environmental exposures. While the crust-portion of the fruit is leathery, the teeth are surprisingly soft, yet durable. These teeth are closely packed together and can dangle well over 1 cm in length and may be split or fimbriate (finger-like) at the edge.

Varied colors and pendulous teeth of *R. copelandii*

Young *I. latemarginatus* pores

Mature broken pores of *I. latemarginatus*

Fimbriate tips and ochre color of mature *R. copelandii*

Young off-white *R. copelandii*

Hericium look-alikes

Morchella
Morels

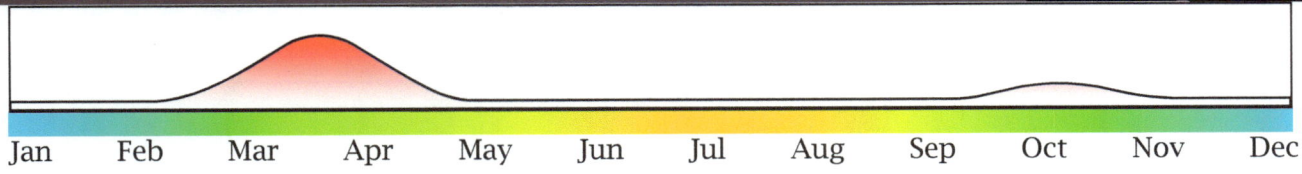

| Jan | Feb | Mar | Apr | May | Jun | Jul | Aug | Sep | Oct | Nov | Dec |

Typical Color Palette

Shape

deeply grooved/pitted cylinders

Hemenium:

smooth, entire cap

Typical size range

M. diminutiva

M. septentrionalis

M.'s americana/ulmarius

20cm

Growth

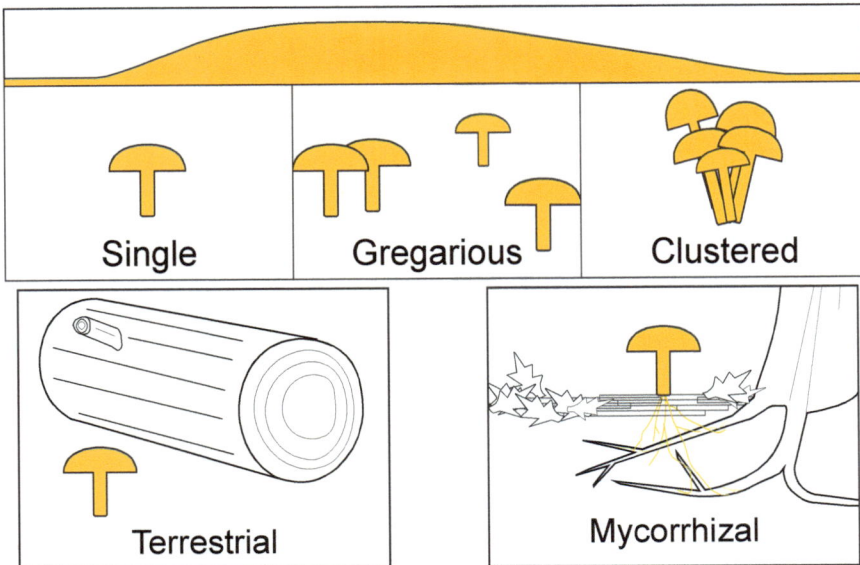

Single   Gregarious   Clustered

Terrestrial   Mycorrhizal

Morchella are mostly obligate mycorrhizal and associate with oak, elm, ash, and especially privet. Eastern species are not found in burn regions like their Western cousins.

Morchella

General description

Description:

The ever-popular morels can indeed be found in the Gulf states, though they will become less scarce the further away from the Gulf you get. These mushrooms have won the hearts of many by being both unique enough to positively identify with very little exposure and packed with enough earthy-umami flavor to add to many dishes. Work from the 2010s has greatly expanded our taxonomical understanding of this genus but this book will focus primarily on those species which are most commonly found in Alabama and neighboring states.

Species of the genus *Morchella* are divided into clade/section then species and those which may be found in Eastern North America (but not necessarily in the Southeast) are Section Distantes (black morels/Elata clade; those with ridges that darken with maturity) which include *M.*'s *angusticeps, exima, exuberans, importuna, laurentiana, norvegiensis, punctipes,* and *septentrionalis*; Section Morchella (yellow morels/Esculenta clade) which include *M.*'s *americana, diminutiva, prava, sceptriformis,* and *ulmaria*; Section Rufobrunnea (blushing morels/clade Rufobrunnea) include *M. rufobrunnea* (Baroni et al. 2018; Voitk et al. 2016; Richard et al. 2015).

Those species which you are likely to actually encounter in Alabama include *M.*'s *americana/ulmarius* (basically indistinguishable), *angusticeps, sceptriformis* (previously *virginiana*), and *diminutiva* (the smaller, more common/widespread version of sceptriformis). Besides the taxonomy, these species share common morphology with some small differences expanded upon below.

For the record the genus *Morchella* (and several related Families/Genera in the Order *Pezizales* contain hydrazine toxins, which fortunately are heat labile and can be destroyed by heat. That means the vast majority of poisonings which occur from consumptions of *Pezizales* is due to insufficient cooking. So please make sure you and anyone you may sell/gift *Morchella* to knows that they must be cooked thoroughly. Other oddities surrounding *Morchella* include a supposed GI reaction when consumed with alcohol, a myth which is largely refuted by authorities in the field. However, those associated with old apple orchards (or drupe

Morchella americana 'ball-on-a-stick' shape, grey, with irregular pits

M. americana with a taller, cone-shaped cap, grey in color with irregular pits.

orchards [pitted fruits]) may be of potential health concern as those locations often accumulate years of pesticide deposit which is further bioaccumulated by the fungi and are concentrated in the fruitbody of many mushrooms, especially *Morchella*. The same health concern comes with any *Morchella* gathered in any heavily polluted areas.

Fire morels (pyrophilic) are those which grow in great abundance at the site of previous fires, especially large-scale forest fires. These species (ex. *M. exima* and *exuberans*) are found on several continents but seem to be restricted to the Western side of North America – so there is little hope of aid finding *Morchella* from burned regions in the East. [The introductory image is of pyrophilic Morchella from Arizona].

Ecology:

The majority of species are considered obligate mycorrhizal, but there are two major species which thrive in mulch and similar terroir which are collectively referred to as "landscape morels" (*Morchella importuna* [black morel, Elata clade] and *rufobrunnea* [reddening morel, clade Rufobrunnea]). Even these non-mycorrhizal species are notoriously difficult to cultivate and require specially designed environments which the hobbyist is unlikely to achieve.

Morchella, like many groups in the Order *Pezizales*, fruit almost exclusively in the early Spring but may on rare occasions be found in the Fall (especially the pyrophilic species). They begin to emerge as their mycorrhizal partners move sugars from their roots to their leaves so look for leaves which are just unfurling to know when the time is best to seek them. Those mycorrhizal species form relationships with oak, ash, elm, tulip trees, fruit trees, and especially privet in the Gulf states, but may be found to associate with other tree species as well. All species of *Morchella* seem to be stimulated to fruit in locations with disturbed soil such as walking trails, near last-year's fallen tree, flood-zones, or similarly agitated regions.

Fruitbody:

A reason for the popularity of morels is that they really have very few look-alikes. *Morchella* are ascomycota, meaning that they release their spores from asci (sacs) which are held superficially along the entire non-stemmed portion of the fruitbody. As such, they lack the distinction between pileus and hymenium. The hymenial surface is typically a cone-shaped structure with deep pits or holes which are usually

Morchella

M. diminutiva with vertically arranged long pits and a light-colored cap.

A rougher stipe, discolored with age

Somewhat dried fruitbody

elongated and overlapping to form an irregular maze of deep grooves. Sometimes they are compared to a sponge in their visual texture. The elongation and ratio of height to width of these pits are helpful for identification, as are the general height and width of the fruitbody as a whole. Regardless of species, all *Morchella* have the same edibility and may be eaten (after cooking!) without discrimination.

A major distinction between *Morchella* and a sister genus, *Verpa*, is that the top – sponge-like portion of the fruitbody is connected to the stipe/stalk at the base of the 'cap' or with a very short inward gap. Furthermore the fruitbody will be hollow (great for stuffing).

The color range of the top portion of the fruit-body ranges from steely-greys to brown-ish charcoal black, through a range of browns and eventually yellowish tan and may include red undertones as in *M. rufobrunnea*. These earthy colors often deepen or darken as the fruitbody matures. For example, when young and small, both *M. diminutiva* and *septentrionalis* are indistinguishable, straw yellow. Over time, *M. septentrionalis* will darken slightly (though not really blacken) and grow a bit taller and a bit wider than *M. diminutiva*. *M.*'s *americana/ulmarius* will begin as light-grey and usually darken at maturity (though many prime specimens will be found with the steel-grey or washed tan color).

M. diminutiva grows to be 2 cm to 5 cm and will have a yellow-ish tan cap which is thin, more cylindrical, and has long vertically oriented pits and grooves. *M. septentrionalis* may reach 3 cm to 8 cm in height, have a slightly rounder cap, but will also have long vertically oriented pits and grooves. *M.*'s *americana/ulmarius* are indistinguishable and take on a wider morphology including long cone shapes to shorter 'ball-on-a-stick' shapes with much more irregular, overlapping pits and grooves. They range in size from 3 cm to well over 20 cm. *M. angusticeps* is the darkest of the bunch as a 'black morel' and has a much more consistent over-inflated cone shape with vertically oriented pits and grooves and ranges in size from 3 cm to 15 cm. *M. punctipes*, which have been reported from Northern montane Alabama have a short, rounded cone-shapes cap (1 cm to 5 cm) sitting atop a very long (proportionally) stipe, and sitting in total between 7 cm and 17 cm.

All *Morchella* take on a similar texture which is unique to the Order *Pezizales*. This texture is semi-bendable but can become crumbly very quick-

Morchella, young and ready for harvest

The telltale sign of a previous picker, the calamari-ring

Connection of stipe and 'cap'

The deep pits of *Morchella*

ly. The bottom of a basket carrying *Morchella* will often be covered with morel crumbs where the more delicate parts of the ridges were torn off due to movement. This is a good reason to avoid using a flimsy bag/basket as the morels will likely be ground up as you make your way back home.

Stipe:

The stalk of *Morchella* is typically shorter than the cap-portion, but seem to become elongated in maturity, sometimes becoming exaggeratedly long and misshapen. The color ranges from perfectly white to cream to yellow tans (though some species not native to our region have black stipes!). The stipe will be hollow and is mostly equal in width until a possible bulbosity at the bottom which itself is usually ridged or corrugated. The width of the stipe varies greatly and seems to expand dramatically with age, but is usually thinner than the cap. The visual texture is bald/glabrous but often has a buildup of mealy crumbles.

Internal structure of *Morchella*, hollow with no fuzz

Verpa

Choice

Edible and Good

Description:

Called the "thimble morel" or "early morel", this genus is actually separate from Morchella, but very closely related. All species in this genus are considered equally edible to Morchella, but alas, are not approved for sales in Alabama. Oh well, more for you! There are two species which occur in Eastern North America, but seem uncommon in Southern latitudes, Verpa conica and bohemica. These are described as less tasty to equally as tasty as morels.

The genus name Verpa directly translates from Latin as "prick" or sometimes, "little prick" as a direct reference to their phallic shape. Though as far as adult-themed names for mushrooms go, this is a relatively tame one.

Ecology:

Mycorrhizal with hardwoods and often fruiting a week or three prior to other Morchella, hence the name "early morel". Growing singly to gregariously in very early Spring. Verpa conica seems to lean towards a more Northern latitude distribution and may be absent in Alabama – but poor documentation of our fungi in the Gulf states may play a significant role in that assessment.

Fruitbody:

Looking remarkably like Morchella, Verpa have an elongated stipe with a smaller cap/head which is connected to the stalk at the very top (unlike Morchella which connects at the base [or midway for M. punctipes]). As such, they are well described as a thimble sitting atop a stipe. Sizes range from 5 cm to 15 cm, with most height being taken up by the stalk. V. bohemica has a cap which is brown/tan/yellow and pitted/corrugated similar to Morchella. V. conica shares the same color palette but has a smooth cap or one which is grooved and brain-like (more similar to Gyromitra). The overall texture of both species is similar to Morchella, but often described as being more delicate or more easily broken.

The stipe is white to cream to beige, mostly

Several *Verpa*

Verpa conica with relatively smooth cap

equal, and stuffed with a cottony material (another good way to discriminate these from Morchella).

Gyromitra

Edible and Good	Requires special Prep or *Not as good as* SPAM	Potentially Deadly

Description:

This genus is commonly referred to as the 'false morels' (specifically *Gyromitra esculenta*), though this author finds that to be a silly name when *Gyromitra* (ji-row-meet-ra or ji-row-mi-tra) is so easy to remember. *Gyro* is roughly translated to mean 'convoluted' while *mitra* is Latin for 'headdress'. Together the name *Gyromitra* means convoluted headdress, a reference to the shape of the cap. This genus is also housed in the Order *Pezizales*, though in the Family *Discinaceae*. Genus *Gyromitra* has several species, most of which are tasty edibles compared often compared with *Morchella* for taste and texture, assuming they have also been cooked thoroughly. However, there are some species which are patently toxic and require extensive detoxifying to become edible (this book does not endorse their consumption without developing experience and being very confident in the detoxification process). Regardless of the species, no *Gyromitra* are sellable in Alabama.

Ecology:

Species of *Gyromitra* which may be present in Alabama include *G.*'s *brunnea, caroliniana, esculenta,* and *korfii* – though the lack of appropriate documentation leaves some room for error. *G. caroliniana* seems to be the most abundant and may be restricted to Northern or montane Alabama. Based on online reporting, *Morchella* are far more commonly found than *Gyromitra* and all of which may be highly restricted in range given Alabama's warm winters.

This genus is unlike *Morchella* and *Verpa* in that they are considered saprobes but may form associations with some flora such as hardwoods and some conifers (especially *G. esculenta*). Regardless, they fruit in approximately the same season and may persist in fruiting throughout the Spring.

G. esculenta, multi-lobed, gentle convolutions

G. esculenta, split stipe, gentle convolutions

G. caroliniana with wide stipe

Fruitbody:

Genus *Gyromitra* has a wider range of morphologies than *Morchella* or *Verpa*, but most share the convoluted, brain-like sulci and gyri (the inward and outward folds, respectively) as the primary texture of their cap. Some species, such as *G. caroliniana* can form massive fruitbodies weighing many pounds each, while others such as *G. korfii* are typically smaller and more restricted in their size range. Like many other *Pezizales*, the hymenium is the smooth surface which is predominantly outward facing. The texture is remarkably similar to *Morchella* or the cup fungi *Peziza*, or the elfen saddles *Helvella*, semi-flexible but otherwise crumbly.

The cap of most species do not have a clear pileal/hymenial distinction as the entire (or at least most of) outward facing portion¬¬ is covered in microscopic asci (sacs) which can forcibly discharge the spores. The exact convolutions of the cap (perhaps apothecium is a better description?) vary between species and can help narrow down those possible identifications. *G. caroliniana* has a wine-red or burgundy color with a wide stipe and a (usually) rounded top that is irregularly and sharply convoluted. *G. esculenta* may also have red or burgundy colorations but is usually more brown, darker, and may have dark purple undertones. *G. esculenta* has a thinner stipe which may branch and a more multi-lobed appearance of the cap, which while irregularly convoluted, tends to produce shallower and gentler (generally rounder) inward folds. *G. brunnea* is unique in that it has (typically) three irregular and convoluted 'plates' which bend inwards and meet one another at the edges. *G. brunnea* has a medium width white stipe and cap/plate colors which range in the red-brown spectrum. *G. korfii* is far more irregular in shape than the rest with a single apothecial cap with convolutions that are deep, yet more gentle that *G. caroliniana* providing far more space between the folds.

Phallus

Inedible

Description:

A genus in the Family *Phallaceae*, the stinkhorns, which look particularly... phallic, hence the name. There are a variety of stinkhorns in this family with just as wide a range of morphologies ranging from squid-like foamy tentacles to elaborate cages to simple conical shapes. Even within the genus *Phallus*, there are a range of morphologies between species, but only one morphological type is relevant as a lookalike for *Morchella*, that of *Phallus hadriani* or *impudicus* (though there are some other species too).

Ecology:

Phallus are saprobes which can often be found in landscaped regions or mulch, sometimes in great numbers. They also appear in woody or leafy debris in or around wooded areas. They may fruit throughout the non-frozen year but seem to grow most prolifically in the late Spring and early Fall especially following the wet season.

Fruitbody:

Phallus, like most of the Family *Phallaceae* develop first as round eggs which will be completely or

Phallus hadriani with lilac egg and highly textured cap

Phallus ravenelii with reduced texture

partially buried. The eggs have a thin and soft fabric or leather-like shell with a dense gelatinous interior which forms several layers. Upon fruiting, the interior expands as the mycelium pumps water into the egg, eventually rupturing the outer membrane or shell. The fruitbody emerges and is often full grown within hours as the compact structure is expanded into a semi-dense foam like structure with a distinctive cap.

The stipe or stalk is usually pure white but may have some cream or off-white portions, textured as a foam with many air pockets, emerging from the ruptured egg. Perched upon the top is a green or grey (sometimes a putrid green-brown color) cap which does not expand to nearly the same amount as the stalk. This cap is covered in a liquid known as gleba, in which the spores are suspended. The gleba creates a foul odor which ranges from spermatic to fecal to rotting meat in order to attract insects to spread its spores. As the gleba is slowly liquefies it may drip down the sides of the fruitbody, furthermore the texture of the cap becomes enhanced. This upper texture is very much like *Morchella*, full of pits and ridges – but these are far more superficial than for *Morchella*.

Representative cap textures

| Morchella | Verpa | Gyromitra | Phallus |

Trametes versicolor
Turkey tail

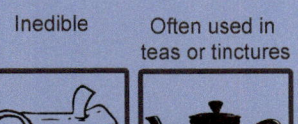

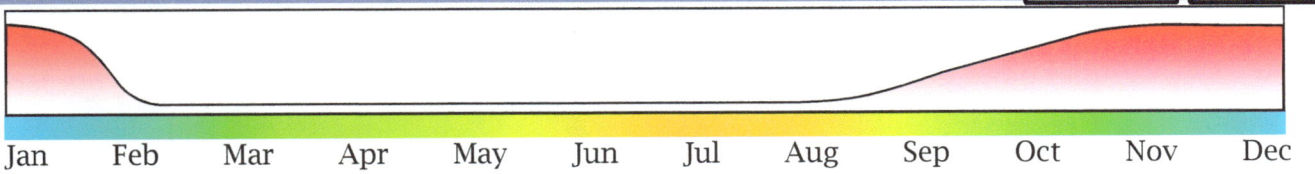

| Jan | Feb | Mar | Apr | May | Jun | Jul | Aug | Sep | Oct | Nov | Dec |

Typical Color Palette

20cm

Typical frond width/length range

T. versicolor group

Shape
A thin shelf or rosette

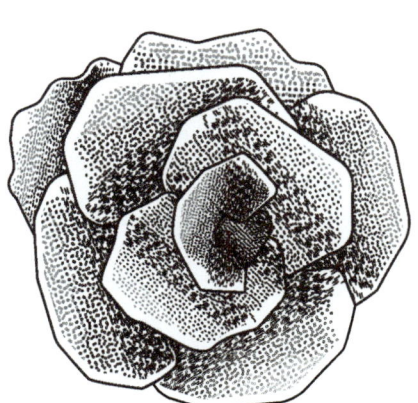

Hemenium:
Small Pores

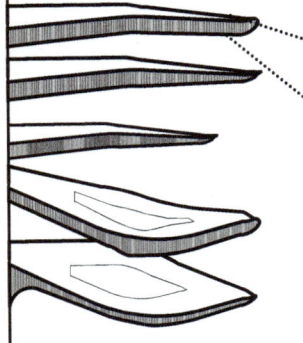

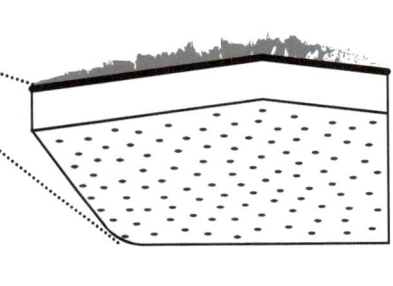

Growth

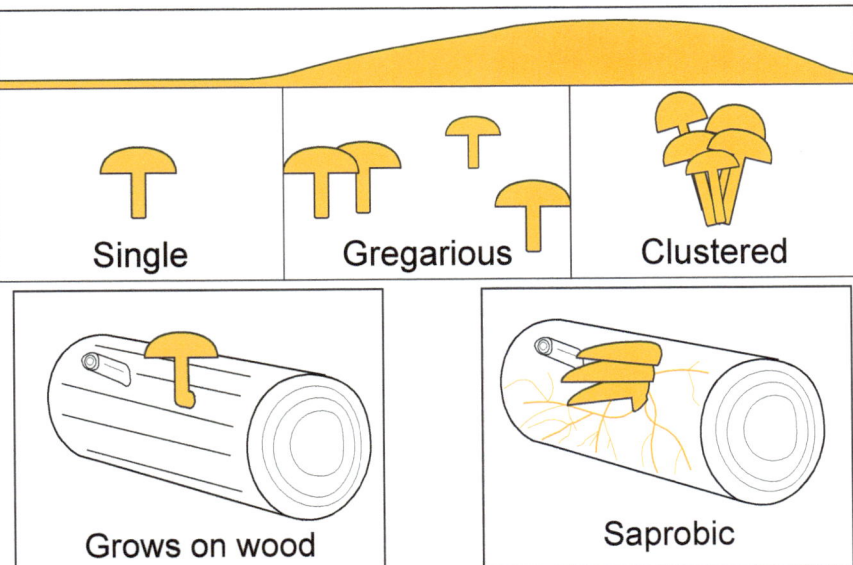

Single   Gregarious   Clustered

Grows on wood   Saprobic

Trametes is a fierce decomposer of wood, and is generally not picky about which ones. While the woody fruitbodies last ball year, they fruit most abundantly in the cool to cold months on wood with bark.

Trametes versicolor

General description

Description:

    Known as the turkey tail due to the felted striations which resemble the plumage of a male turkey. The latinized 'versicolor' is a direct reference to the many colors and color combinations which are common to this species. This species is part of the extremely common genus *Trametes* in the Family *Polyporaceae*. Perhaps a reason for the frequent discovery of this genus and most of its species is that they are both voracious saprobes on dead wood, and the fruitbody is tough enough to last for some time.
The "turkey tail" mushroom is a frequently sought after, but extremely common fruitbody which is, in the strictest sense – not edible. However, *T. versicolor* is one of the mushrooms which is commonly used as a tea or sometimes a tincture (an alcohol-based tea). Scientific studies with this fruitbody have been ongoing for decades with contradictory information abound. A recent meta-analysis (where all studies are ranked, weighted, and pitted against each other to come to greater conclusions) demonstrated net positive health effects - which were marginal at best (Zhong, Yan, Lam, Yao, & Bian, 2019). Regardless, this fungus is used as a supplement and is acceptable for commercial sales in Alabama. As a warning to those who intend to sell this wild foraged fungus, you may not provide medical guidance or claim that this fungus treats any disease as stated by the Food and Drug Administration (FDA) (Barber, 2020; Pace, 2020).

Ecology:

    T. versicolor forms a white rot on deciduous stumps and dead wood throughout most of the world and is extremely commonplace. While fruitbodies of *T. versicolor* can be found throughout the year, they tend to produce most of their growth in the cooler months and are less likely to be found degraded or environmentally damaged Fall through Spring. *T. versicolor* is often found growing on the same log as some of its look-alikes such as *Trichaptum biforme* and *Stereum* species (see look-alike section for descriptions), where these fruitbodies may grow adjacent to one another, but will not overlap (as the underlying organisms claim their portion of the log).

Fruitbody:

    The fruitbody takes the form of a flat (almost

Some of the brighter colors in *T. versicolor's* repertoire

Browns and steely-greys on the fuzzy (tomentum) pileus of *T. versicolor*

Trametes versicolor

never more than ½ cm thick), fan-like shape which ranges from ¼ of a circle to spiraling rosettes depending on the portion of the log the fruitbody is emerging from. Typically, the fruits begin as individual bodies which often grow into one another to form complex shelf-like structures. Individual 'fans' range from > 1 cm to 5 cm from media to tip, but when fused can become very wide along the width of the log. Specifically, the fruitbody may erupt as either resupinate (as a flattened crust along the media with no 'top' [apileate – lacking a pileus]) or effused-reflexed (as the projecting fruit which has a distinctive top and bottom [partially pileate – being "L" shaped with hymenium on the side of the media and bottom of the projecting portion of the fruitbody]). When growing from the top of a log, the fruitbody very typically takes on a fused rosette form and is less likely to have individual fans as part of the fruitbody.

When fresh, the fruitbody of *T. versicolor* is flexible but very difficult to tear by hand. Often, pulling on the fruitbody will rip the entire effused-reflexed fruitbody from the media before the fruitbody itself tears. Eating *T. versicolor* would be very similar to chewing wood or shoe-leather.

T. versicolor, as denoted by the species name, comes in varied colors which often include reds, yellows, steely-blues, and various browns, ochres, tans, and greys. Importantly, these colors come in stripes which emanate from the growth media towards the outer edge. The zonation (stripes) is further highlighted by the two textures, smooth and densely hairy/fuzzy. These textures alternate in the same direction as the color striations.

Hymenium:

The spore-bearing surface of *T. versicolor* is poroid. The pores count 3-8 per square mm which forms a stark contrast from the smooth underside of *Stereum* species, or the much larger (or widely spaced) pores of other *Trametes* species. This surface is white to cream in color sometimes discoloring to a yellowed white, but not dark or brightly colored. In age, the pores may expand enough to begin to disintegrate, providing a jagged tooth-like structure but the hymenium is not 'toothed'.

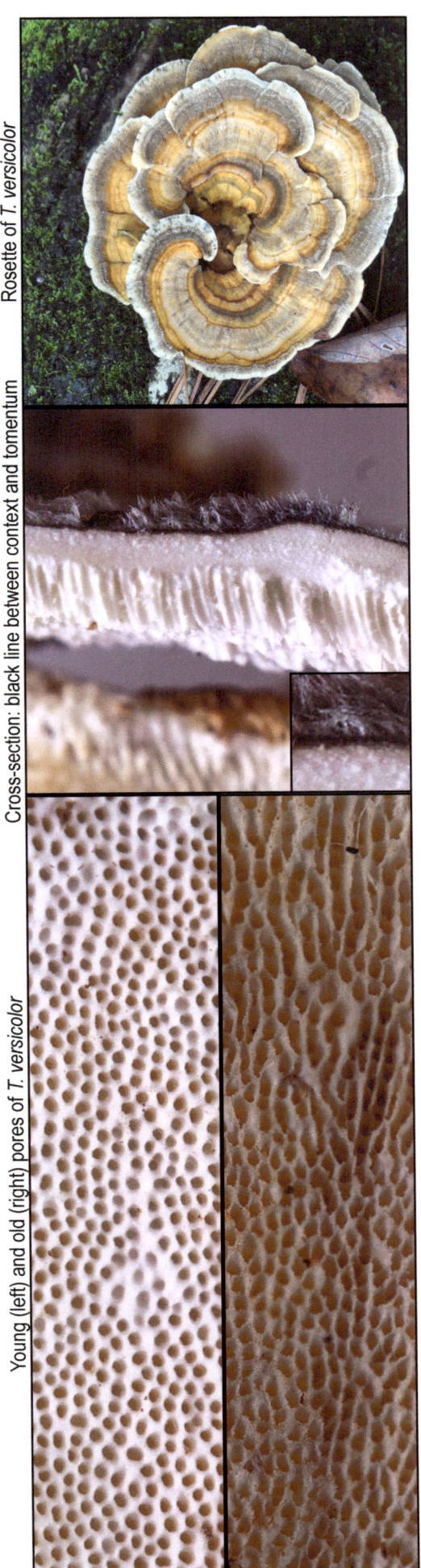

Rosette of *T. versicolor*

Cross-section: black line between context and tomentum

Young (left) and old (right) pores of *T. versicolor*

T. versicolor look-alikes

Other Trametes

Inedible

Description:

The genus *Tametes* is not large but contains several shelf-like or fan/fin-shaped fruitbody producing species. All of which are saprobes with different preferred hosts – though most are fairly promiscuous in their associations. With very little experience you will readily be able to discern *T. versicolor* from these relatives so this book will not go into great detail describing the individual species. Those most common species in the Southeastern United States include *T.s lactinea, hirsuta, conichifer, betulina, sanguineus,* and *aesculi* (also possibly, but unlikely *elegans*). There are others, but the descriptions of those mentioned species will be sufficient to help you confidently discriminate between them and *T. versicolor*.

As a final note, this book does not discriminate between *T. versicolor* and *T. ochracea*. For those with an interest in this discrimination *T. ochracea* is far less flexible and lacks the black line between the context and tomentum (hairy top; see image in *T. versicolor*).

Ecology:

All of the *Trametes* are saprotrophs on wood, creating a white rot and less likely to be found on well-decomposed wood. Most often these will grow from felled wood (usually hardwoods) with most growth occurring in the cooler months such as in Fall. Their tough, corky/woody texture allows most to be found year-round, though often not in prime condition.

Fruitbody:

Except for *T. conichifer*, all of the species here form a similar fruitbody shape which is a shelf or series of overlapping shelves growing effused-reflexed which are usually wider than they are deep from the growth medium. *T.s lactinea, hirsuta, sanguineus,* and *aesculi* range in thickness (top of fruitbody/pileus to bottom of pores) of 1 cm to over 3 cm, sometimes much thicker near the base which may include some resupinate portion. These species in particular are

T. hirsuta with color/texture zonation

T. lactinea with especially dark edge

T. betulina in situ

196   *Trametes versicolor look-alikes*

unlikely to form rosettes or similar structures and prefer horizontal growth. The thickness of these species as well as their larger size at maturity (widths of 5 cm to over 20 cm) should be a dead giveaway that they are not *T. versicolor*. Furthermore, *T. lactinea* and *aesculi* lack any fuzz or hair on their surface (they are bald/glabrous). *T. hirsuta*, *betulina*, and *sanguineus* all have some level of fuzz, but can be downright hairy for T. hirsuta and betulina. *T. sanguineus* is best known for being a wonderful cinnabar color (also see *T. cinnabarina*).

    T. betulina and *conichifer* are far thinner fruitbodies with especially thin context (*T. betulina* hymenium may be deep enough to call this claim into question). Both species will readily form rosettes or similar shapes when growing on the top of a substrate. In fact, *T. conichifer* almost always begins growth as small white bowls no larger than 1 cm in width and usually grows on thin branches or twigs. From here the fruitbody may develop a more fan/fin shaped projection.

    T.s lactinea and *hirsuta* are almost always zonate with a white/cream base color and tan/grey/charcoal colored growth bands, some of which seem to last from growth to growth

giving them a striped appearance. *T. sanguineus* is a bright red/orange/cinnabar while *T. aesculi* are either white/cream or sporting tan blotches on the pileus. Furthermore, *T. aesculi* often have a lumpy/bumpy pilues which is absent from the other species. *T. betulina* takes on a wide variety of colors and is zonate, often with tans, yellows, oranges, and white/cream colors – lacking those blues and greys present in T. versicolor. Finally, *T. conichifer* is almost always white/cream and usually has thin brown/tan rings.

Hymenium:

    Trametes is a genus known for having many species with modified pores. This means that while all are poroid, several have pores which take on unusual shapes. For example, *T.s lactinea*, *hirsuta*, and *sanguineus* have circular pores with a fair amount of distance between each hole whereas *T. aesculi* have pores which elongate to form wide, maze-like structures. On the far end of this spectrum is *T. betulina* which has pores so elongated that they appear as gills. Finally, *T. conichifer* starts with very shallow pores which elongate and become ragged/jagged with age.

Round pores of *T. lactinea*   Elongated, maze-like pores of *T. aesculi*   Expanded, jagged pores of *T. conichifer*   Modified gill-like "pores" of *T. betulina*

Stereum species

Description:

    Stereum is a genus of crust fungi, specifically those also called parchment fungi, which are extremely common and often confused with *T. versicolor* for the novice collector. While the genus has many species, we will only consider two groups those of the *Stereum ostrea* group and the orange *Stereum complicatum/hirsutum* group.

Ecology:

    Stereum are saprobes which grow on dead wood, most commonly on felled logs. They can be found year-round as their fruitbody is tough, yet flexible, and capable of withstanding environmental battering. Like many of the other fins/fans/parchment type fruitbodies, they seem to show their most prolific growth in the cooler seasons such as in mid to late Autumn.

Fruitbody:

    The fruitbody is very thin, parchment is a good description of the thickness of the fruitbodies for all of these *Stereum* species. They are tough, yet flexible when fresh and brittle when aged. The structure most encountered is the projecting fin or fan shape, sometimes half-circles, or conjoined individuals among usually dozens of others in minute overlapping shelves. Portions nearer to the base or underside of the affected wood may become effused-reflexed, in which a portion of the hymenium runs down, along the base of the wood itself, enveloping it in fused parchment-like hymenium. *Stereum ostrea* group specifically are much more likely to be individual fans which, while densely clustered, are more likely to not fuse with their neighboring fruit. This group have many striped zones which are predominantly reds (in the range of vermillion to burgundy) with yellow-tinted cream to bleached bone white zones. Many of the red portions will have very fine fuzz which can be washed off in a heavy rain. In large enough mass they can turn a log into a work of art.

    The other primary group of *Stereum* form fins which are wider than they are long and much more likely to have substantial portions of their media's underside covered in both effused-reflexed and resupinate parchment-like splotches. *S. hirsutum*, as the name implies (hirsute means hairy) have distinctive

S. ostrea group, especially red colored specimens

S. ostrea group, mostly white

S. hirsutum with fuzzy pileus

Trametes versicolor look-alikes

zonation between the pumpkin orange of most of the fruitbody, but also darker shades of orange-brown forming apparent growth rings on the surface. They fuse commonly, but most fruitbodies will be independent. *T. complicatum* is the extremist, often forming more resupinate structure than actual projections from the wood. These projections are wide and often fuse into continuous overlapping shelves on the wood, or as a single layer like a wee bedskirt around the felled branch. These too are pumpkin orange or close in color but are usually less zoned/striated.

Hymenium:

Importantly, while the general shape and growth habits of *Stereum* are similar to *T. versicolor*, the hymenium are not. While *T. versicolor* has small pores on the bottom, *Stereum* lack any structure available to the naked eye and are – smooth – like paper. This is true of all of the *Stereum*. The color of the hymenium is very similar to that of the pilus or ahymenial surface.

Inedible

Trichaptum biforme

Description:

Trichaptum is a genus with several species, but as far as typical *Trametes versicolor* 'look-alikes' this book will only cover two species, *Trichaptum* (Tri-kap-tum) *biforme* (bi-form) and *abietinum* (al-bi-et-ih-num). Both are extremely commonplace and along with the genus *Stereum*, make up the vast majority of persistent fungal fruitbodies on dead wood. In other words, this stuff is everywhere – so knowing how to identify it is a perfect place for beginners to start. This species is inedible due to its tough and undesirable fruitbody – but then again, this author would say the same about *T. versicolor*. Regardless, this genus is not toxic.

Ecology:

Saprobic on dead wood, *Trichaptum biforme* grows on hardwoods and *T. abietinum* on the wood of conifers. Otherwise, these species are more or less indistinguishable and can be treated the same outside of exacting taxonomy. *Trichaptum* grows prolifically and the tough fruitbodies keep for near a year before completely eroding away. While you may find a single fruitbody, you are much more likely to find large portions of dead wood completely covered in them,

S. complicatum growing from side of log.

Smooth, patchwork of parchment *S. complicatum*

Smooth hymenium of *S. ostrea* group

Lilac edged *T. biforme*

creating a textural spectacle alongside *Stereum* and *Trametes* species. The fruitbodies seem to grow in all but the coldest winter months but may produce much of their annual growth in the cooler late Fall months.

Fruitbody:

Trichaptum emerge from the crevices and splits in dead wood (especially that wood which still has bark and is not yet de-lignified by other fungi) as a corky amorphous blob from the bottom of media, or as distinctive fan-shaped shelves from the sides. New growth (especially during the fast-growing wet, cool season) is a remarkable shade of purple/lilac which is apparent on the edges of the individual fan-shaped shelves. That purple color is visible on the top and bottom of the shelves. On the pileus many growth rings are present between the newest growth and the base (connection to the media). The purple fades over a day or so into the creamy yellows, tans, and whites which are most commonly encountered.

Hymenium:

As the outermost region grows the underside develops small, irregularly shaped pores. These pores expand in width until irregular tooth-like structures are all that remain. These teeth often take on different shapes from cone-like to wider/oblong as the under-side dries and becomes pallid and eventually white, cream, or tan in color. This hymenial surface is typi-cally encountered as effused-reflexed (as the project-ing fruit which has a distinctive top and bottom) but may also be partially pileate (being "L" shaped with hymenium on the side of the media and bottom of the projecting portion of the fruitbody) or even forming a resupinate (as a flattened crust along the media with no 'top' [apileate – lacking a pileus]) portion along the bottom of the log.

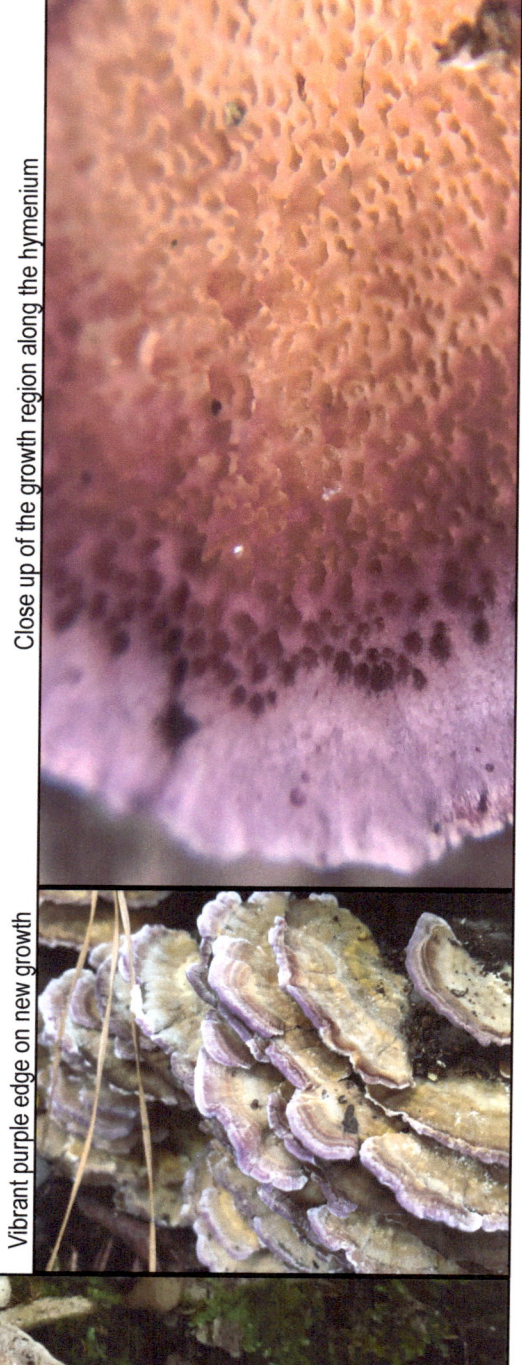

Close up of the growth region along the hymenium

Vibrant purple edge on new growth

Mature hymenium of *T. biforme*

Trametes versicolor look-alikes

Bjerkanda adusta/fumosa

Inedible

Description:

Less commonly occurring than *T. versicolor*, but often confused by the novice. These two species of *Bjerkanda* (jerk-and-era) are often lumped and referred to as the 'smoky polypore' in reference to the hymenial color. The genus name references Swedish naturalist Clas Bjerkander while the species name *adusta* is Latin for 'burnt' while *fumosa* means 'beautiful'.

Ecology:

Causing a white rot on dead or dying hardwoods, *B. adusta/formosa* fruit in the cooler months, especially the Fall. Both species are usually found in overlapping and semi-fused shelves, though individual shelves may be found.

Fruitbody:

The cap/pileus is usually scallop shaped, half circle, or even somewhat rectangular from above forming individual or multiple fused shelves. These may project > 5 cm from the substrate and fused specimens can become very wide. The height/depth of the specimens is < 1 cm, closer to 0.5 cm, substantially thicker than *T. versicolor*, but comparable to many other *Trametes* species. *B. adusta* may not be immediately identified from above as the scurfy to tomentose (very to slightly hairy) cap is usually white with tan/ochre bands, especially towards the growth tips. *B. formosa* has less to no fibrous hairs and takes on darker colors, usually zonate and ranging from white, tans, browns, and charcoals. An important distinction is that *B. formosa* may have an especially dark band at or just behind the active growth band at the edge/ margin. *B. formosa* is also reported to occasionally have an anise, or (in this authors opinion) a similar but more undefined 'herbal' odor.

Hymenium:

The critical and most obvious distinction between *T. versicolor* and *Bjerkanda* species is that pores of Bjerkanda are not white/cream, but rather smoky greys to charcoal. The pores, which are small and comparable in size to those of *T. versicolor*, begin with a hymenial layer which is lighter in color and darkens substantially closer to the substrate.

Young *Bjerkanda adusta* with little color

White growth region of mature specimens of *B. formosa*

Smoky-grey poroid hymenial surface

Ganoderma species
Reishi, Lingzhi

Jan | Feb | Mar | Apr | May | Jun | Jul | Aug | Sep | Oct | Nov | Dec

Typical Color Palette

Shape

A round, oblong, shell-shaped shelf with or without a stalk

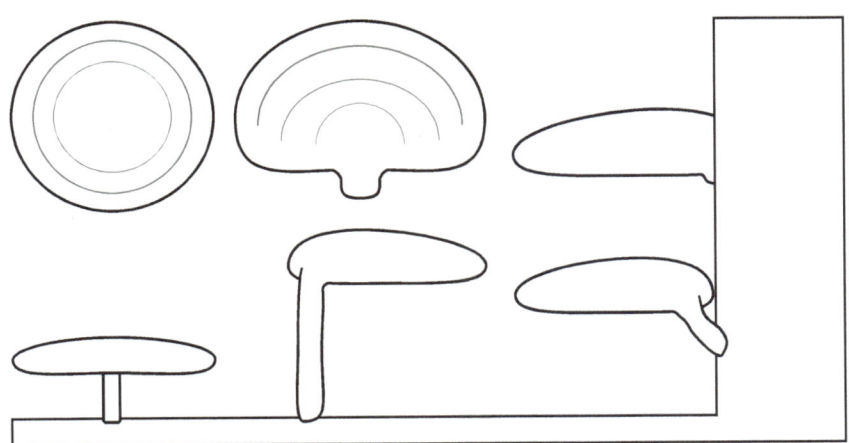

Hemenium: Pores

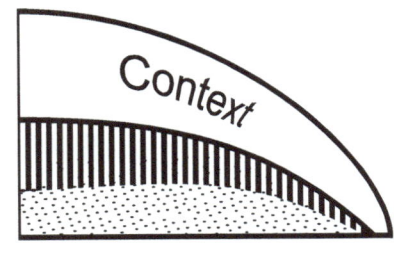

Pores/Tubes

Typical size range

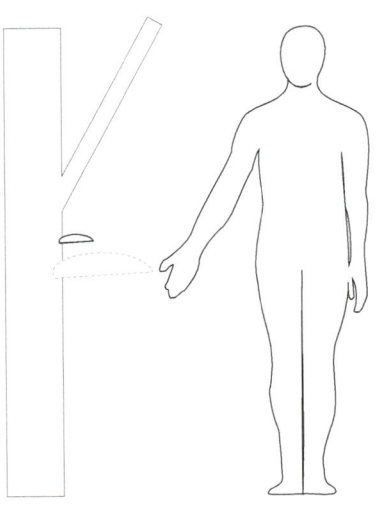

Growth

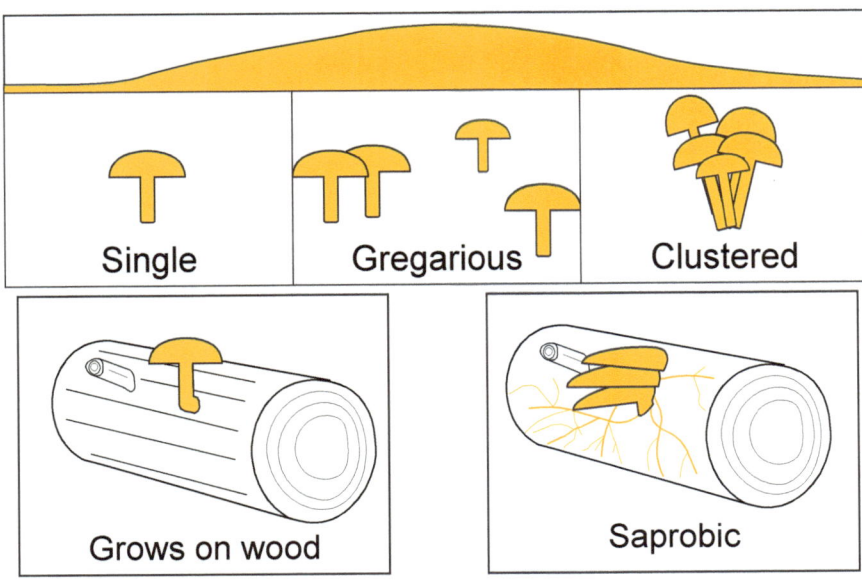

Ganoderma is a parasitic or saprobic decomposer of wood with species often delineated by host tree. They grow most during the early to mid Spring but dried specimens can be found year-round

Ganoderma

General description

Ganoderma is a genus of bracket or shelf mushrooms in the Family *Ganodermataceae*. The root *Gan* is Greek meaning "lustrous/shiny/bright" and *derm* for skin, together *Ganoderma* translates to "luster-skinned". This is an appropriate name since the genus is primarily defined by having a lustrous, shiny, or lacquered (lacate) appearance on the cap. Though several species do not have this feature. While all the species are woody/corky and not edible, they have a millennia-long history as the base of teas in Asia. Two species most common in the market for these teas *Ganoderma* 'lingzhi', known as reishi, and *G. lucidum* are considered a major part of traditional Chinese medicine. The popularity of *Ganoderma* being used in teas or as diet additives has expanded with the name reishi being used somewhat indiscriminately. Regardless of the misnomer, several species have been heavily researched in regard to the purported medical benefits. The current scientific consensus is that the potential medicinal value of *Ganoderma* or its extracts is very limited (Zhong et al. 2019; Jin et al. 2016; Klupp et al. 2015). This author's interpretation is that *Ganoderma* or its extracts may provide medicinal benefits on par with multivitamins and may be useful as a supplement or adjunct to first-line treatments and should be used medically following a discussion with the person's primary or specialty care provider. Luckily, no *Ganoderma* has been linked to any kind of fungal toxicity and is not listed as a contraindication to any medications at this time. Thus, they are considered safe for use as a supplement and are acceptable for commercial sales in Alabama. As a warning to those who intend to sell this wild foraged fungus, you may not provide medical guidance or claim that this fungus treats any disease as stated by the Food and Drug Administration (FDA) (Barber, 2020; Pace, 2020).

Ganoderma species *G. lingzhi* and *lucidum* senso stricto are found in Asia, however we have a host of closely related species here in the Southeastern United States which are considered equivalent in application for teas tinctures, or as use as supplements. Though certain species have been specifically highlighted for wild harvest sales in Alabama: *Ganoderma curtisii*, *G. tsugae*, and *G. sessile*. To discern these

Ganoderma curtsii with the classic shell/shelf shape and varnished pileus

Ganoderma pore body

An old Ganoderma with an intact lacquered shell

species from the many others, present in the Gulf states the greater morphological differences should be considered. Once divided into two groups based on cap luster, *Ganoderma* is now divided into six groups based on DNA sequences and morphological differences: *G. colossus, applanatum, tsugae, lucidum, meredithiae,* and *resinaceum* groups. Each group will be treated separately.

All *Ganoderma* will have a crust-like pileal surface with a spongy, corky internal context that is lightweight (especially when dried). These species are saprobic and form a white rot. All will drop a thick, predominantly brown/tan spore print, though the exact shade varies. All but the most tropical will grow year-round sans in freezing temperatures, especially following monsoon seasons.

Ganoderma/Tomophagus colossus

Description:
Recent DNA work has actually separated *G. colossus* into a separate genus, **Tomophagus**, where it was originally placed in 1905 (Hong and Jung 2004). Though this fungus is still very closely related to those other *Ganoderma* - and the morphology is strikingly similar.

Ecology:
Growing almost exclusively in tropical or subtropical regions, to include the Gulf Coast states, *T. colossus* is known to fruit predominantly on the wood of non-pine trees. This species will grow singly or gregariously.

Fruitbody:
As indicated by the species name, *T. colossus* can grow to immense size (> 30 cm) but like many *Ganoderma*, is lightweight. The cap is roughly convex taking on yellow, ochre, and brown colors and presenting the shiny, lustrous sheen on new growth, but is white and dull on the active growth region along the margin. The lustrous sheen may be dulled with environmental exposure and older portions may become dark brown. Like many *Ganoderma*, the pileus forms a crust over the spongier internal context. This crust is thin and easily dented emphasizing the especially soft texture compared to *Ganoderma*. The internal structure or context lacks resinous/melanoid bands.

The hymenium is white/cream with small an-

Context including resinous bands, pore cross-section on the left with pileal tissue on right

T. colossus in situ

MS+TT

Bisected *T. colossus*

MS

gular to round pores. This surface will darken to tans and dull browns with age.

Stipe:

No true stipe (sessile) but the fruitbody may be raised by a pseudostipe with pores on at least one side.

Ganoderma applanatum group

Description:

Also known as the artist's conk due to a peculiar feature in which resins in the pore-layer can be released by scratching the surface, which becomes permanently darker than the unscratched portions. This allows the artist to draw on the hymenial surface with any sharp object and for this drawing to become a permanent fixture as the fruitbody dries. The species name applanatum comes from the Latin *applanatus* meaning 'flattened', a reference to the shape of the fruitbody. Another in this group is G. *megaloma*, *loma* being Greek for 'border' and *mega* describing the large/wide border which separates this hoof-shaped species from the genus *Fomes*. Finally, *G.*'s *lobatum* and *lobatoideum* which are 'lobed', in that the fruitbody expands during growth sessions by growing on top or bottom of the previous fruitbody.

Ecology:

This species group is widespread and commonly encountered in the Gulf States growing on hardwood.

Fruitbody:

Growing from a single point, but not stipitate (stalked) forming a wide half-circle to shell-shaped shelf. Flattened to hoof-like with a much harder crust that is not easily pushed into with a fingernail. The pileal surface is not lustrous and ranges in color from near-white greys to darker greys in *G.*'s *applanatum*, and *megaloma* and various tans/ochers and some red/yellow banding for *G.*'s *lobatum* and *lobatoideum*. Typically, the margin or outer regions are lighter in color and may have a white band of active growth. The surface is often finely cracked.

The hymenial surface is white and poroid and may have tan/brown streaks where the fruitbody has been touched or damaged in the environment. The hymenial surface contains a resin which discolors the pores when released by even gentle touching. This feature is popular for artists and

Cracked, pale grey surface of G. applanatum

Fresh poroid hymenium of G. applanatum

G. lobatum with overlapping growth

Ganoderma   Images of *Morchella* scratched into *G. applanatum* foragers alike to draw on with any sharp object. Some of these drawings are stunning.

Ganoderma tsugae group

Description:

A group of especially lustrous capped *Ganoderma* which grow on directly on wood as parasitic saprobes. This group consists of *G.'s lucidum, sessile* and *tsugae. G. lucidum* will not be explicitly covered as it is not found in the Southeastern US ecoregions but may be found cultivated.

Ecology:

This group grows directly from wood. *G. sessile* is found on hardwoods while *G. tsugae*'s preferred host is hemlock but may be found on other coniferous woods.

Fruitbody:

This group is defined by their especially shiny, lacquered caps and growth directly from wood. Like the other *Ganoderma*, the shape is semi-circular to shell-like with gentle concentric ridges (sulci). The pileal surface is thin, varnished, and usually some red color with orange, yellow or burgundy undertones. There are some varieties of *G. tsugae* which are blue/purple. The margin where the active growth occurs may be white, cream, or yellowish. Fruitbodies range from 3 cm to well over 15 cm. Inner flesh is white to cream in color and lacks melanoid/resinous bands.

The hymenial surface is porous, white to creamy and becomes tan/brown with age and spore release.

Stipe:

The word sessile means "attached directly by the base with no stalk or peduncle", which is an apt description of *G. sessile* since it lacks a stalk, except for when it doesn't. When stipate (stalked) the stalk is shorter than the cap. On the other hand, *G. tsugae* will have a short stalk which is colored to match the rest of the fruitbody.

G. tsugae growing stippate on hemlock

G. tsugae lacquered cap and colors

Hymenium of G. sessile, dried (L) and aged (R)

G. sessile highly wrinkled surface

Ganoderma meredithiae group

Description:

Containing the terrestrial growing and stipitate (stalked) lacquer-caps such as *Ganoderma curtsii* and *curtsii f.sp. meredithiae*. The '*f.sp.*' (*forma specialis*) is an indication that this is a difference in form and is thus acceptable for wild harvest sales in Alabama.

Ecology:

G. curtsii and *curtsii f.sp. meredithiae* are a species known to grow in Eastern North America as white rot inducing saprobes. The only substantial difference between them being that *G. curtsii* grows on the dead or dying wood of hardwoods while *G. curtsii f.sp. meredithiae* prefers coniferous wood. Both forms prefer to grow from decomposing buried wood or even wood chips, and thus, appear terrestrial.

Fruitbody:

Other than the wood preference, these forms will be treated the same. The *meredithiae* group have prominently lacquered or shiny caps which may dull with age. The color range of these species is particularly wide compared with the other *Ganoderma* and may include yellows, reds, and purples, often with most fruitbodies from a single organism being similar in color range. The cap is mostly rounded and convex to flat, often with rounded zones of height (sulci) which are related to the ebb and flow of active growth. The general shape is rounded to shell shaped. The context will be white to cream when fresh, dulling to a crumbly/spongy tan when aged. Both species contain resinous/melanoid bands inside of the context. The hymenial surface is white/cream and dulls to a tan/ochre with age and spore-drop.

Stipe:

This group sports distinctive non-centered stipes which are similar in composition to the cap such they have a lacquered crust and a lightweight corky interior. The stipe will be similarly colored to the pileus. The stalk may be shorter or longer than the diameter of the cap and often has many bent joints and ridges.

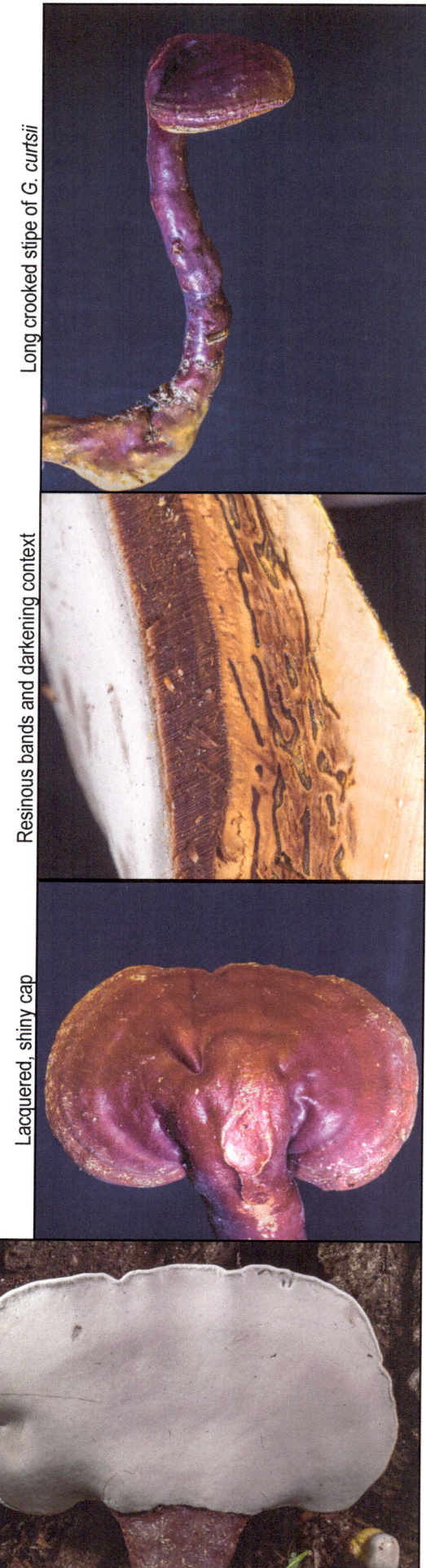

Long crooked stipe of *G. curtsii*

Resinous bands and darkening context

Lacquered, shiny cap

Fresh white pores

Ganoderma 'other' group

Description:

This group is the catch-all for other _Ganoderma_ which includes those without lacquered caps and with brown/tan/yellow context (inner flesh). Since the genetic and morphological descriptions of several _Ganoderma_ species are in taxonomic flux these others are included here with minimal description including _G._'s _martinicense, parvulum, tuberculosum, weberianum_, and _zonatum_. Due to the overlapping morphology and common need for microscopy (or very high-quality specimens) this book recommends checking _Ganoderma_ finds which do not match the previous groups with those species named here in external resources.

Ecology:

Growing from hardwoods at the level of root or trunk include _G. martinicense, parvulum_ (also fruit trees), and _weberianum. G. tuberculosum_ can be found on hardwoods or coniferous wood and _G. zonatum_ grows on palm trees.

Fruitbody:

G. martinicense takes on yellow to burgundy red colors with a white/cream growth region along the margin. Its shape is semicircular to amorphous blobs with a laccate pileus and either a lack of stipe (sessile) or with a dark laccate central stipe (stipate). The central location of the stipe is a good indication of this species or a close relative. This fruitbody sports radial ridges and some perpendicular wrinkles. _G. martinicense_ has resinous bands and darker brown flesh.

G. parvulum takes on predominantly burgundy colors with yellow-ish stretches near new growth and is well laccate. This species may be sessile or stipate and is generally smaller than the other _Ganoderma_ listed here. The pileus may be lobed or more likely, sprouting new smaller shelves at random intervals within or along the sides of the main fruitbody. The flesh/context may be multitoned consisting of yellows, browns, and greys. _G. weberianum_ looks very similar but has a white/cream context and is predominantly found in tropical regions such as Southern Florida.

G. tuberculosum is named for the Latin epithet _tuberculosum / tuber_ to mean a tumor, knot, or hump in description of the very knobby or tumor-like shape of the pileal fruitbody. While laccate along most of the surface, large bumps and newly developing growths form white poroid sections giving the entire fruitbody a gnarled look. The pileal surface is yellow-ish tan to burgundy, zonate and wrinkled and heavily cracked in age. When not gnarled, the fruitbody is semicircular/shell-shaped, sessile, and thin-shelled. The context is dark brown and these fruitbodies are found predominantly in subtropical regions.

G. zonatum is another named to describe it as _zonatum_ is Latin for "banded", a fine description of the obvious concentric zones of the pileal surface. While the growth of this species on palms (especially palmettos) is the best discriminating feature, the fruitbody can also be identified by the stark bands, dark brown context, wide growth, and sessile connection.

Old _G. martinicense_, especially wrinkled, creamy context

Ganoderma look-alikes

The woody polypores can be a challenge to identify due to the plethora of overlapping features, variable morphology, and their resistance to quick degradation like the fleshy mushrooms - leaving weather-worn shelves strewn about the woods. This means that older woody polypores can become nearly impossible to identify. Luckily, only those fresh *Ganoderma* specimens should be used for wild harvested mushroom sales giving the picker clear discriminating features to use for identification: a laccate (varnished, lacquered) pileal crust which is thin, a corky to spongy context, and fairly well-defined gross shape (circular to half-circle or shell-shaped).

However, many other woody polypores share some of these features and should be ruled out. This section will only cover two of the most convincing look-alikes, but also consider investigating the following groups. The genus *Fomes* has several species which can be confused with *G. applanatum* group. The genera *Fomitella* and *Fomitiporia* share color and shape profiles with many *Ganoderma*. *Foraminispora rugosa* can make a convincing look-alike for *G. meredithiae* group. *Fuscoporia gilva* shares a color profile with many *Ganoderma* as does *Heterobasidion irregulare*. *Inocutis texana* has a similar color profile but more yellow-pores and a different pileal texture to *Ganoderma*. *Microporellus dealbatus*, while significantly smaller and with a different growth media (host) bears a resemblance to the color and shape of *G. zonatum*. *Nigropous vinosus*, while darker and thinner than most *Ganoderma* bears a superficial resemblance. *Trullella polyporoides* appears as a very small, yellow-colored, shell-shaped, and pseudostalked polypore with a resemblance to *Ganoderma*.

The woody/corky polypores are almost all considered inedible with a few species being considered edible when very young and fleshy, but only one genus is considered toxic: *Haplopilus*. *H. croceus* and *rutilans* are both considered <u>potentially deadly toxic</u> but fortunately do not look remotely like *Ganoderma* as they are more brightly colored (*croceus* is yellow and *ritilans* is pink/tan/ochre) and velvety to minutely fuzzy on the soft pileal surface.

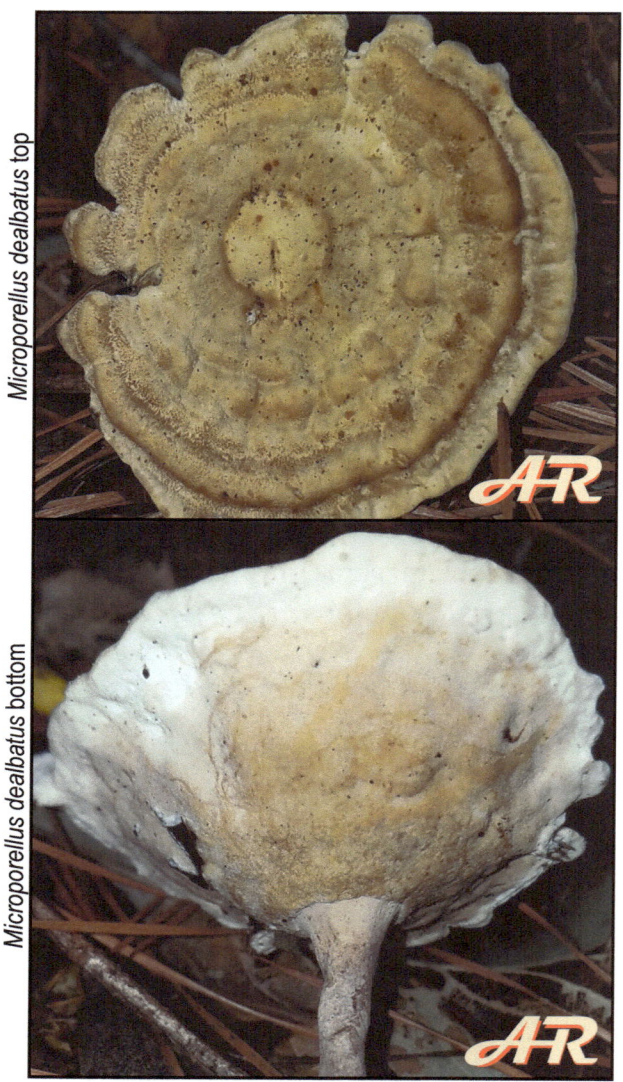

Microporellus dealbatus top

Microporellus dealbatus bottom

Ischinoderma resinosum Inedible

Description:
   This edible polypore can be con-

fused with *Ganoderma* due to the overlap in color and shape. Often the soft outer edge is removed for consumption, leaving any especially tough portions behind.

Ecology:

Growing on recently dead hardwood, especially near sources of constant moisture such as streams. I. resinosum grows in the early fall, but dried fruitbodies may persist for some time.

Fruitbody:

I. resinosum may most easily be separated from *Ganoderma* by its soft tissue which lacks any external crust or lacquer and is finely velvety when prime and effused-reflexed growth. While the colors of *I. resinosum* are similar to the warm earthy tones of *Ganoderma*, it will lack the bright yellows, oranges, or purple hues and the zonation of the fresh fruitbody are much more gradual. When fresh the pores bruise brown and may produce guttation. Aged specimens become hard and tough.

Fomitopsis pinicola group

Inedible

Description:

A group which includes the North American native *F. mounceae* and *schrenkii* which are colloquially called the "red belted polypore"

Ecology:

This group grows on soft or hardwoods and are regionally differentiated – but most typically grow in cooler climates or higher elevations. Specifically. *F. schrenkii* is the most likely to be found in Alabama or nearby states and is more likely to be found on coniferous wood.

Fruitbody:

F. pinicola group take a hoof, conk, or fan-shape which are reminiscent of young *Ganoderma*, especially since they may take on a lacquered red-yellow-mahogany region (a band) from which they derive their common name. The pores typically take on a cream to tanned color and individual pores are much wider (3-5/mm) than those of *Ganoderma*.

I. resinosum from above

I. resinosum from below

Fomitopsis from above

Fomitopsis from below, note large pores

Further Reading

This book was designed to be as comprehensive as possible for those primary edible and toxic species as related to the certification for wild mushroom sales in Alabama. However, it is in no way comprehensive regarding the vast array of other mushrooms which you may encounter in our region of the globe. If you are interested in further expanding your mushroom knowledge there are many commercially available books I highly recommend. Do be aware that at their time of publishing some fungal taxa may not have yet been established, refined, or otherwise modified to reflect the current phylogeny, yet the descriptions are likely to be stable.

Mushrooms Demystified
Mushrooms of the Gulf Coast
Mushrooms of the Georgia Peidmont & Southern Appalachians
Boletes of Eastern North America
Amanitas of North America
Fungi of Temperate Europe (vols 1 & 2)
Mushrooms of the Carolinas
Ascomycete Fungi of North America
Polypores and Similar Fungi of Eastern and North America
Milk Mushrooms of North America

If you are interested in taking your education further than these books, I recommend becoming familiar with the online resources available to the public from social media to nonprofit, academic, and government webpages to include the vast array of published scientific articles.

Citations:

Alvarado, P., Moreno, G., Vizzini, A., Consiglio, G., Manjón, J. L., & Setti, L. (2015). Atractosporocybe, Leucocybe and Rhizocybe: three new clitocyboid genera in the Tricholomatoid clade (Agaricales) with notes on Clitocybe and Lepista. Mycologia, 107(1), 123–136. doi: 10.3852/13-369

Barber, S. B. (2020). Half Hill Farm Inc - 609440 (Warning Letter No. MARCS-CMS 609440). Division of Human and Animal Food Operations East V.

Baroni, T. J., Beug, M. W., Cantrell, S. A., Clements, T. A., Iturriaga, T., Læssøe, T., ... O'Donnell, K. (2018). Four new species of Morchella from the Americas. Mycologia, 110(6), 1205–1221. doi: 10.1080/00275514.2018.1533772

Beug, M. W., Shaw, M., & Cochran, K. W. (2006). Thirty plus Years of Mushroom Poisoning: Summary of the Approximately 2,000 Reports in the NAMA Case Registry (pp. 47–68). McIlvainea. Retrieved from McIlvainea website: https://www.researchgate.net/publication/237708345_Thirty_plus_Years_of_Mushroom_Poisoning_Summary_of_the_Approximately_2000_Reports_in_the_NAMA_Case_Registry

Boa, E. (2004). Wild edible fungi : a global overview of their use and importance to people. Undefined.

Brundrett, M., Bougher, N., Dell, B., Grove, T., & Malajczuk, N. (1996). Working with Mycorrhizas in Forestry and Agriculture. Australian Centre for International Agricultural Research. doi: 10.13140/2.1.4880.5444

Cartwright, K. T. S. G. (1937). A reinvestigation into the cause of "brown oak", Fistulina hepatica (huds.) fr. Transactions of the British Mycological Society, 21(1–2), 68-IN7. doi: 10.1016/S0007-1536(37)80006-6

Characteristics of the russuloid fungi. (n.d.). Retrieved April 9, 2022, from Russulales News website: https://www2.muse.it/russulales-news/in_characteristics.asp

Hallock, R. (2015). A Mushroom Word Guide: Etymology, Pronunciation, and Meanings from Over 500 Mycology Words. CreateSpace Independent Publishing Platform.

Heilmann-Clausen, J., Verbeken, A., & Vesterholt, J. (1998). The Genus Lactarius. The Danish Mycological Society.

Hong, S. G., & Jung, H. S. (2004). Phylogenetic analysis of Ganoderma based on nearly complete mitochondrial small-subunit ribosomal DNA sequences. Mycologia, 96(4), 742–755. doi: 10.1080/15572536.2005.11832922

Jin, X., Ruiz Beguerie, J., Sze, D. M.-Y., & Chan, G. C. F. (2016). Ganoderma lucidum (Reishi mushroom) for cancer treatment. Cochrane Database of Systematic Reviews, 4, CD007731. doi: 10.1002/14651858.CD007731.pub3

Klupp, N. L., Chang, D., Hawke, F., Kiat, H., Cao, H., Grant, S. J., & Bensoussan, A. (2015). Ganoderma lucidum mushroom for the treatment of cardiovascular risk factors. Cochrane Database of Systematic Reviews, (2), CD007259. doi: 10.1002/14651858.CD007259.pub2

Looney, B. (2013). Systematics of the genus Auricularia with an emphasis on species from the southeastern United States. North American Fungi. doi: 10.2509/naf2013.008.006

Miettinen, O., Vlasák, J., Rivoire, B., & Spirin, V. (2018). Postia caesia complex (Polyporales, Basidiomycota) in temperate Northern Hemisphere. Fungal Systematics and Evolution, 1, 101–129. doi: 10.3114/fuse.2018.01.05

Pace, R. M. (2020). Mushroom Revival, Inc. - 610361 (Warning Letter No. MARCS-CMS 610361). Division of Human and Animal Food Operations East I.

Petersen, R. H., Borovička, J., Segovia, A. R., & Hughes, K. W. (2015). Transatlantic disjunction in fleshy fungi. II. The Sparassis spathulata – S. brevipes complex. Mycological Progress, 14(6), 30. doi: 10.1007/s11557-015-1049-8

Richard, F., Bellanger, J.-M., Clowez, P., Hansen, K., O'Donnell, K., Urban, A., ... Moreau, P.-A. (2015). True morels (Morchella, Pezizales) of Europe and North America: evolutionary relationships inferred from multilocus data and a unified taxonomy. Mycologia, 107(2), 359–382. doi: 10.3852/14-166

Singer, R., Hesler, L. R., & Smith, A. H. (1980). North American Species of Lactarius. Mycologia, 72(3), 649. doi: 10.2307/3759547

Voitk, A., Beug, M. W., O'Donnell, K., & Burzynski, M. (2016). Two new species of true morels from Newfoundland and Labrador: cosmopolitan Morchella eohespera and parochial M. laurentiana. Mycologia, 108(1), 31–37. doi: 10.3852/15-149

Zhong, L., Yan, P., Lam, W. C., Yao, L., & Bian, Z. (2019). Coriolus Versicolor and Ganoderma Lucidum Related Natural Products as an Adjunct Therapy for Cancers: A Systematic Review and Meta-Analysis of Randomized Controlled Trials. Frontiers in Pharmacology, 10, 703. doi: 10.3389/fphar.2019.00703

Photographs:

The following individuals graciously made their photographs available for the creation of this book. I would like to thank them for providing not only works of art, but figures which can provide education and spark enthusiasm for the study of mushrooms and fungi. The following individuals will have their photographs marked with their initials.

Kelcie Brown (KB)

Tim Pfitzer (TP)

Alan Rockefeller (AR)

Alisha Millican (AM)

Ron Pastorino (RP)

Jan Newton (JN)

Geoff Balm (GB)

Malachi Mooneyham (MM)

Matt Schink (MS)

Tony Tomasen (TT)

Sarah Prentice (SP)

Joan Knapp (JK)

Becca Mahoney (BM)

Alder Burns

Other Contributions

I would like to thank Anna McHugh for the edibility icons which have been modified here, but kept true to the spirit of simplicity, general design, and good humor.

I would like to thank Logan Borosch for his help in fact-checking this book.

I would also like to thank the hundreds of individuals in the mycological community who have aided me in my own journey and pointed me in the direction of high-quality information – without this vast community, I would not have been able to pass on such knowledge.